T0245660

WILLIAM HENRY JACKSON'S LENS

HOW YELLOWSTONE'S FAMOUS PHOTOGRAPHER CAPTURED THE AMERICAN WEST

TIM McNEESE

TWODOT®

ESSEX, CONNECTICUT
HELENA, MONTANA

A · T W O D O T® · B O O K
An imprint of Globe Pequot, the trade division of
The Rowman & Littlefield Publishing Group, Inc.
4501 Forbes Blvd., Ste. 200
Lanham, MD 20706
www.rowman.com

Distributed by NATIONAL BOOK NETWORK

British Library Cataloguing in Publication Information available

Library of Congress Cataloging-in-Publication Data
Names: McNeese, Tim, author.
Title: William Henry Jackson's lens : how Yellowstone's famous photographer captured the American West / Tim McNeese.
Description: Essex, Connecticut : TwoDot, [2023] | Includes bibliographical references. | Summary: "William Henry Jackson was an explorer, photographer, and artist. He is also one of those most often overlooked figures of the American West. His larger claim to fame involves his repeated forays into the western lands of nineteenth-century America as a photographer. Jackson's life spanned multiple incarnations of the American West. Jackson's story was long and his life full, as he lived to the enviable age of 99. This biography presents the good, bad, and ugly of Jackson's life, both personal and professional, through the use primary source materials, including Jackson's autobiographies, letters, and government reports on the Hayden Surveys."—Provided by publisher.
Identifiers: LCCN 2022048492 (print) | LCCN 2022048493 (ebook) | ISBN 9781493064731 (cloth) | ISBN 9781493064748 (epub)
Subjects: LCSH: Jackson, William Henry, 1843–1942. | Photographers—United States—Biography. | Geological and Geographical Survey of the Territories (U.S.) | West (U.S.)—Biography.
Classification: LCC TR140.J27 M39 2023 (print) | LCC TR140.J27 (ebook) | DDC 770—dc23/eng/20221021
LC record available at https://lccn.loc.gov/2022048492
LC ebook record available at https://lccn.loc.gov/2022048493

∞™ The paper used in this publication meets the minimum requirements of American National Standard for Information Sciences—Permanence of Paper for Printed Library Materials, ANSI/NISO Z39.48-1992.

To my seven grandchildren—
Ethan, Adri, Finn, Beckett, Cora, Atticus, and Will.
May all your explorations lead to great destinations.

Contents

Acknowledgments

*M*uch of this book was produced through the process of sitting in my university office for many hours reading, researching, and writing. But it also required travel, and many thanks to my faithful traveling companion, my wife, Beverly, the retired English professor. Wherever I went, she was there at my side. Our time spent in Yellowstone was nostalgic, as we revisited geysers and mudpots and hot springs from previous visits together when we led students from York University on a pair of study trips exploring the Lewis and Clark Expedition. Other experiences the two of us shared on the road included a return to Colorado that helped me get in touch with Jackson and his nineteenth-century travels. For all the miles, I am grateful, and for our fifty years together, I cannot thank her enough.

Thanks also to York University administrators who have always been so supportive of my research and writing. Thanks especially to President Dr. Sam Smith, who was as excited to see this project through as myself. Thanks also to Dr. Shane Mountjoy, YU provost, for his support.

To write a book such as this required me to stand on the shoulders of several other professional individuals, all of whom lent specific contributions to make this book the best it could be. Hopefully, my list of those who assisted is complete and includes the following:

Thanks to Sarah Parke, acquisitions editor at TwoDot, who accepted my proposal for a book on Jackson and saw me through the entire process. Although she has since left TwoDot, her assistance at every level of production was crucial to the formation of the final manuscript. Thanks to Lauren Younker, Sarah's replacement at TwoDot during the final stages of production, as well as Andrew Yoder, production editor at TwoDot.

Thanks to Jori Johnson, Collections Access Coordinator at the Stephen H. Hart Research Center at History Colorado (Denver) for supplying photographs and Bethany Williams, Collections Access Coordinator, Stephen H. Hart Research Center at History Colorado, for assistance in accessing materials at the research library.

Thanks to Meredith Mann, librarian at the Brooke Russell Astor Reading Room for Rare Books and Manuscripts Archives at the New York Public Library for providing hundreds of pages of Jackson's Civil War diaries and letters to his wife Emilie Painter Jackson, none of which are digitalized.

Thanks to Sarah Marino, research librarian at the Yellowstone Heritage & Research Center in Gardiner, MT for providing one-of-a-kind materials on Jackson.

Thanks to John R. Waggener, archivist at the American Heritage Center at the University of Wyoming for providing me access to materials including photographs and the Fritiof Fryxell Papers. Thanks also to Nora Plant for accessing a single, much needed photograph which required an extra element of digging through the university's archives. The book conclusion would have been different without this piece of the puzzle.

Thanks to Park Ranger Eric Grunwald at the Scotts Bluff National Monument for accessing photographs of Jackson.

Thanks to Morgan Jaouen at the Jackson Hole Society and Museum in Jackson, Wyoming, for assistance in accessing Jackson materials.

Thanks to the good folks at the Library of Congress including Ryan Brubacher, reference librarian in the LOC's Prints and Photographs Division, for guidance in locating photographs, as well as Frederick L. Plummer, senior laboratory technician at the LOC, plus Tomeka Myers in the library's duplication services department. Ryan was a great help in locating photographs for my previous book on John "Black Jack" Pershing, and his assistance on this book is equally appreciated.

Introduction

"Know Thyself," October 6, 1861

$\mathcal{O}$n April 12, 1861, Confederate forces bombarded Fort Sumter, a federal military installation located in Charleston Harbor, an attack that opened the Civil War. Eighteen-year-old William Henry Jackson had an important decision to make: whether or not to enlist. His parents discouraged him from signing up, and his friends offered the same advice. Perhaps the war would be short-lived, they said, and the need for hundreds of thousands of young volunteers would prove unnecessary. Jackson was torn between a youthful sense of self-preservation and a nagging patriotic duty. Ultimately, he erred on the side of caution. As Jackson later wrote in his autobiography nearly eighty years later, it appeared to him that "there were enough soldiers."[1]

Jackson was, after all, an upwardly mobile professional man in Rutland, Vermont. In 1858 he began working in a local photographic studio, learning the finer points of a technology barely older than himself. Jackson was hardly a directionless young man in search of himself. He had found a place, an interest to pursue, and enlisting in war would only interfere with that pursuit. So he remained out of the national fray and left the enlisting and the fighting to others with less to lose. In his words, "Why give up a promising career[?]" With the encouragement of family and friends, Jackson was satisfied the army life was not for him, even though "my country's need may have been great."[2]

Then, in October 1861, Jackson received further encouragement from a total stranger. A doctor was visiting his small town whose reputation preceded him. Orson Squire Fowler, fifty-something with a long gray beard, arrived to read the bumps on the heads of the local residents. Jackson was among the many in his community to attend Fowler's sessions, who then tolerated the doctor's fingers running over their skulls. O. S. Fowler was one of America's leading phrenologists.

Jackson has already taken on the western style in this self-portrait, ca. 1867. Collection of the Jackson Hole Historical Society and Museum, Jackson, WY. Accession #1958.2725.001. Used with permission.

The study of phrenology was the brainchild—pardon me—of an idiosyncratic Viennese physician named Franz Joseph Gall, who believed the brain, as the organ of the mind, influenced the shape of one's skull. This provided a means for assessing a subject's specific mental and physical aptitudes. Since the human mind is composed of several distinct, innate faculties, each had its place in the brain. Thus, an expert could "read" the distinct bumps on one's head and, with an understanding of the map of the skull, uncover hidden truths that might reveal the subject's true potential.

Phrenology emerged on the American scene in 1832 with the arrival of Johann Kaspar Spurzheim, a fifty-five-year-old German physician and adherent of the controversial new scientific study. As a student of Gall's—who had died in 1828—he had already popularized phrenology in Europe and was ready to plant it on fertile American soil. But he had little time to convince Americans to take phrenology seriously. He soon died of typhoid in Boston, which dramatically cut short his planned American tour. As for Spurzheim's skull, it was removed, along with his brain and heart, and preserved in jars of alcohol as if they were holy relics.

In the aftermath of Spurzheim's death, a pair of brothers, Orson Squire and Lorenzo Niles Fowler, picked up the mantle of phrenology proselytizing. They hit the road as itinerant phrenologists, traveling throughout New England, speaking in support of phrenology, and reading heads, for a fee. Early converts included such influential Americans as Walt Whitman, John Greenleaf Whittier, and Clara Barton. The American minister Reverend Henry Ward Beecher—brother to Harriet Beecher Stowe, the diminutive author of *Uncle Tom's Cabin*—was an adherent. (He had been a college classmate of Orson Fowler's.) The Fowlers created the popular three-dimensional, white porcelain bust that included a veritable personality map of the brain for easy reference. The brothers soon developed a cottage industry based on spreading the influence of phrenology, what with speaking engagements, busts for sale, a popular journal, and the opening of a phrenological museum and library in New York City by 1834. Their business slogan was straightforward and pithy: "Know Thyself," a tagline that suggested clients could encourage the development of their best selves once they were in the know. All that was required was a few uncomfortable minutes of a stranger's fingers running over one's head.

All this appealed to Jackson. During the autumnal week of Fowler's visit, he "was one of his most devoted sitters."[3] Fowler did an examination and then wrote out in flowing longhand his analysis of the bumps on Jackson's head. As for Jackson, he was intrigued, as Fowler's analysis rang like music to his ears, beginning with the good doctor's opening: "You, Sir, have a noble head throughout."[4]

Fowler dedicated more than one thousand words to analyzing Jackson's bumps, which he wrote out in his swirling, left-tilting hand. His analysis ran from the obvious to the sublime. Following are some of the highlights:

> You have a fine body, and a good head, have a powerful constitution, have physical stamina enough to sustain your head, and yet you have been brought up a great deal too delicately. You require to rough it more than you have done. . . .
>
> Should knock about outdoors, skate, slide downhill, tear around, anything for exercise, and remember unless you do take good care of your bodily powers, they will not be adequate to the development of your head, so that your splendid talents will wane. . . .
>
> Your love of home is large, so is friendship . . . in fact all your social affections are hearty, and hence you will be much prized by those who know you. . . .
>
> You might want to be pitched right in, head-long into the river of business of life. . . . Are too cautious, and procrastinating, will hesitate too long about pursuing your business, and then pursue it too tamely. . . .
>
> You need roughening up, for you were too delicately born, and educated. . . .
>
> Your mother lacked expectation, so that you were born with two [sic] little spirit of adventure. . . .
>
> Your love of the beautiful and perfect is large, have really a fine imagination, are stylish and elevated in sentiment and conduct. You are noted for the classical throughout your character in manners, in sentiment, in expression in everything. . . .
>
> Would excel as a newspaper editor or writer. Are a good judge of human nature. . . .
>
> Your mechanical genius is far above mediocrity, and will enable you to draw, make, copy, anything you like, and give you excellence as a painter . . . for you are really a genius, and no mistake. . . .
>
> Your life is to be decidedly a success, just in proportion as you preserve your health, so make that paramount. Nature has done splendidly by you, and your natural place is a mechanical, or artistical, or both united.

Jackson took every word of Fowler's phrenological examination of his head to heart. He was pleased to discover he was, according to the good doctor, a genius. This convinced him even more that his life should not be wasted as a possible casualty of war. He was destined for greater things in life, if he just played his personal cards right. There was so much that Jackson thought insightful on Fowler's part. He did have "a fine body" and "a good head." As his ninety-nine years of life would one day attest, he had "a powerful constitution," considering the privations he put himself through in the name of his photography.

That Jackson had not led an extremely exertive life to date was clear to the young man himself. He could not then even begin to imagine just how rugged his life would become. Fowler's admonitions that the young Vermonter might "need roughening up, for you were too delicately born" do not begin to describe the exertions Jackson would experience through his repeated travels, many taking him across parts of the American West not yet fully explored. Fowler expressed concern that Jackson's softer side might stifle his manliness. To the doctor, Jackson was "too delicately born" and "born with too little spirit." He referred to Jackson as "timid," "delicate," "cautious," and "tame." Jackson was informed he had aptitudes both mechanical and artistic. In fact, he honed these various attributes—the skills of the artist and the photographer—throughout his life into a single way of life. He brought together his love of photography and painting with his love of travel and adventure to create a personal legacy of accomplishment that lives on even today.

Within five years of Fowler's phrenological report, the "delicate" Jackson embarked on a series of adventures that would, over the next twenty years, include crossing the Great Plains as a bull whacker driving ox-drawn wagons along the Oregon Trail; herding mustangs from California to Nebraska as a neophyte vaquero; traveling along the nation's first transcontinental railroad documenting the technological wonder with his camera; and traipsing across the West through eight grueling summers from Wyoming to Colorado to New Mexico and back again, risking his life climbing mountains, all for the sake of the best camera shot. His work required him to lug heavy equipment over difficult landscapes, using large-framed cameras that produced wet plates that required quick processing under difficult conditions. Yet he produced hundreds, even thousands, of photographic masterpieces that are still considered some of the best, most iconic black-and-white photos produced of the West during the nineteenth century.

He experienced cold, hunger, grizzlies, heat exhaustion, and a host of other privations and dangers unknown to most contemporary Americans. And as he traveled, he wrote, sketched, and took photographs of many of the nation's unknown wonders. The litany of his personal firsts as a photographer is astounding, including the first photographs of Yellowstone's geological wonders, the Tetons, the Garden of the Gods, Mesa Verde's ancient Anasazi ruins, Chaco Canyon's Pueblo Bonito, the Mount of the Holy Cross, and mountain ranges from Wyoming's Wind River to New Mexico's Sangre de Cristos.

The story of William Henry Jackson's life would one day transcend the presumptions and educated guesses of Dr. O. S. Fowler. He would rise far above mediocrity and make himself into a pioneer of sorts. He carried photography into the American West. In doing so, he was a pioneering explorer.

William Henry Jackson represented a different sort of American pioneering explorer. While others, including explorers from Meriwether Lewis and William Clark to John C. Fremont to John Wesley Powell, encouraged the opening of the American West through their discoveries, Jackson helped document the West and revealed the great expanse of its plains, mountains, and deserts to the less intrepid. Jackson's photographs actually showed a West others simply talked and wrote about. He removed the degree of separation between those who took risks and those who did not. His pictures revealed a world sometimes indescribable. They were his way of saying to the uninformed and the curious, "See, here it is. This is the West I've seen. Wouldn't you like to see it for yourself?" Just as mountain men and miners and cowboys opened up the great reaches of the West, so did Jackson. What others accomplished with traps and guns and pickaxes and lassoes, Jackson did with his cameras. His story is a unique one worth telling.

In August 1862, despite Fowler's report of Jacksonian genius, William Henry did enlist in the Union army; during his entire service, he never fired a shot in anger. He survived the great national upheaval to then do service to his country a second time as one of the first of his kind to advertise the West and encourage the advancement of the American republic into places previously unknown. His photographs became collodion calling cards, enticing others to follow him.

Fowler did get some things right, though. He pronounced a verdict on the life Jackson had not yet lived, one that promised success. Indeed, William Henry Jackson's life was just that—a success. He managed to meld together the "mechanical" and the "artistical" in ways no one had ever done before and likely would never do again.

William Henry Jackson's story was long and his life full. He became an explorer, photographer, and artist and provided pictures designed to dispel various geological myths and stereotypes while serving as enticements to draw commerce, investment, scientists, and even tourists into the western regions of the United States, which in the opening years of the century were little understood and unmapped—mysterious lands that required a camera and a cameraman to reveal their secrets.

His work helped to advertise the necessity of creating Yellowstone National Park to preserve the West for future generations. His photographs were the first ever taken of the exotic wonders of Yellowstone, dispelling all doubts regarding the existence of great geysers, boiling mud pots, grand waterfalls, and a scenery most sublime.

Ultimately, Jackson's life spanned multiple incarnations of the American West. In a sense, he played a singular role in revealing the West to eastern Americans. This book represents a compelling story, one that begins with a young man born in the East who makes his way west and leaves his ultimate mark, not as a sodbuster or a cowboy or a miner or a fur trapper, but as an explorer who, armed with a camera, became one of the foremost chroniclers of the American West.

An Easterner by Birth, 1843–1860

*H*e was born in the East, a real live nephew of his Uncle Sam. But the West would one day claim him as its own.

His birthplace was Keeseville, New York, and the date was April 4, 1843. William Henry Jackson was the first of seven children born to George Hallock Jackson and Harriet Maria Allen. His father's people came from Ireland, having immigrated to America at the opening of the eighteenth century; they were stern Quakers who settled in New Hampshire. A century later, Will Jackson's great-grandfather removed his family to a farmstead near Keeseville, where Will's father was born in 1820.

His mother's family, the Allens, were of English extraction and had landed in Troy, New York, around 1795. His mother, born in 1821, received more formal education than was common during the early nineteenth century in America, having attended the Troy Female Academy, which was later renamed the Emma Willard School. In Jackson's autobiography, *Time Exposure*, he describes his mother as a "city girl," while his father grew up on a farm.

His father received a formal education of sorts beyond the farm, attending a country school for several years, plus a couple of years at a private academy. George's teen years saw him tied down to farm work until he turned twenty, when he left home to seek his future. Young George traveled around the young United States, as far as the Mississippi River. Jackson was never clear about exactly what his father did during these years, but in time George returned to New York State with money enough to open up a blacksmith shop and an accompanying carriage-building operation. At twenty-one he met his future bride, and they married on June 15, 1842. Will arrived ten months later.

When William was a year or so old, the family moved to Columbus, Georgia—the year was 1844—and remained there for nearly four years. In 1846 the United States was at war with Mexico, and one of his mother's brothers was serving. The Mexican War drew Edward Allen farther west than any other family member at that time, and Jackson retained memories of his uncle's return from the conflict as "a lean and sunburned soldier" who came to his family's house early in 1848. William had no specific recollections of his uncle's service, but he "understood that Uncle Edward had been away fighting against a wicked man. To me General Santa Anna—whose name I did not know—was the same scoundrel King George III must have been to a small boy seventy years before."[1]

Another Jackson relative involved in war became legendary, one whose story connected to the murky origins of America's Uncle Sam. Jackson wrote of an uncle named Sam Wilson who was born in Arlington, Massachusetts, in 1766. In Jackson's version, Sam and a brother moved to Troy, New York, in 1789, the year the town was incorporated, and established a brick yard that thrived into the early nineteenth century, providing the capital for a second business, a slaughterhouse large enough to "kill, cut and pack 150 head of cattle per day."[2] Come the War of 1812, New York troops stationed in and around Albany received beef and pork in barrels provided through a supplier named Elbert Anderson, but according to Jackson, the animals were slaughtered in his uncle's facility. Barrels labeled "U.S E.A." made reference to Anderson's arrangements with the US government. Questions raised by curious soldiers allegedly elicited a response from those in the know: "What! Don't you know Uncle Sam Wilson? Uncle Sam's a great patriot, and he's feeding up the army to lick the British." Thus, according to Jackson family lore, their "Uncle Sam" was destined to become the young nation's most enduring caricature.

In later years, Jackson could recall little about the family's southern transplantation until his father removed them again, returning to upstate New York. William's most vivid memory was of the family's departure down the Chattahoochee River on a river steamboat. Plattsburgh, New York, where his father had attended a local academy for a year or two, was soon home once again. George purchased a two-hundred-acre farm between Plattsburgh and Keeseville, Will's birthplace. This placed the family in Peru Township in a Dutch colonial house, set back from the main road, the drive flanked by rows of poplars. Another child had joined the family by this time, Jackson's brother Edward, who was eighteen months younger. A sister, Mary Elizabeth, arrived in 1849. Another brother, Fred, came along in 1851.

Jackson's earlier autobiography includes vignettes of memories both warm and common to rural American farm life. He recalled the family kitchen—a large room measuring forty feet long, where his mother stood at a wood stove, cooking, baking, and putting up jelly—laden with large loaves of bread, molasses cookies, gingerbread, and "thick apple pies." Clothes were washed in the same room. A great fieldstone fireplace dominated the room. Pantries and cupboards stored the family plates and crockery. A "wide-planked table, of pine or maple" witnessed countless family meals. It was there Will and brother Ed played while a hired girl rocked infant Mary Elizabeth's cradle. Food hung from the great room's beams, including drying apples and newly shucked corn.[3] Fruit came from the family's trees or grew wild along the perimeters of local meadows, including apples, pears, plums, cherries, quinces, and a variety of wild berries. Oranges were a Christmas treat, while pineapples and bananas were too exotic to make the family table. But it was a table heavy with food from the farm: milk, butter, eggs, and fresh beef, lamb, and chickens in abundance. Vegetables ran in seasons, including fresh varieties through the summer and dried sorts in winter. As a young boy, Jackson could remember his first taste of white sugar: "It was a great day when my father came home with a snowy five-pound loaf."[4]

The far end of the house's culinary center was the family's sitting room, which featured a tall secretary, several rocking chairs, and a horsehair sofa. Evenings included his mother reading to the children by the light of a turpentine-fueled reading lamp. Jackson found destiny in his parentage. The dominant skill sets he honed for most of his adult life focused on two related talents: his ability as an artist, a painter of both oils and watercolors, and his extraordinary, natural propensity as a photographer who entered the field while in its near infancy. His successful father had enough money to afford some of the latest gadgets of the age, including a camera. Several years before Jackson's birth, George purchased a camera and was experimenting with the new daguerreotype process. He did not turn his interest into another business—carriage building satisfied him—but the novelty of it intrigued the young Jackson. He writes in his autobiography how his first camera "came into my hands as a toy when I was a very small boy. I hadn't any real idea what the lens-box was intended for; but I got the feel of a camera almost before I could walk. It may sound foolish, yet I can't help believing that this childhood experience helped to direct my life."[5]

Those days of professional photography for Jackson lay far in the future. As a farm boy, there were constant chores, the list extending longer with each passing year of maturity. He fetched kindling for the fire, brought in the eggs, herded cows for milking, and hefted water from the well. His father occasionally rewarded young Jackson's contributions with a silver three-cent piece. He recalled a local barn raising and playing follow-the-leader with other boys as the fathers labored. One day the boys, a dozen or so, climbed over the new barn's rafters and pegged beams and took a sip or two from an available cider jug. Will could remember becoming tipsy and his brother Ed being so far gone he had to be carried home.

When Jackson was eight years old, his family again removed to the South. George received a commission to open up a factory of some sort—Will could not recall its exact nature—in Petersburg, Virginia. Like their Georgia sojourn, their time in Virginia was short. His most vivid memory outside his family circle was of the African Americans he saw at every turn, "who were my constant playmates. I remember, too, the great tobacco plantations, with hundreds of Negroes at work in the fields. I was too young to understand that they were slaves; but when the War of the Secession began to brew I thought of those black men and women again." Jackson would one day take up arms in that war as a Union soldier.[6]

After a year or so in the South, George moved his family again, this time to Philadelphia. Again, the stay there was short. Low wages worked against the family being able to make ends meet, so Jackson's parents opened up a tobacco and candy shop in the front room of their home to supplement the family income. Such moves from one community to another postponed William's formal schooling (the family may have needed his labor at home), but he recalled one life's lesson—his first cigar, "a ferocious black stogie we had purloined from the little tobacco-and-candy shop which my father conducted on the side." The experience proved negative. Throughout his adult life, Jackson occasionally puffed on everything from cigarettes to a hookah, but he admitted in his later years, "I still don't care for smoking."[7] In 1853 a fifth child entered the family, Frank, and soon the expanding circle posed, dressed in their Sunday best, at a downtown studio while a local photographer took their daguerreotype.

Young Jackson's early schooling was typical of the Jacksonian era, when public schools were largely still in their first generation of offering democratically accessible free education provided by the state. But by the time he was ten, his parents gave his education a new priority. They felt Jackson's "schooling was in a sorry state" and made the decision to move from Philadelphia to upstate New York and the bustling town of Troy.[8] It was arranged for William to make the move ahead of his parents and live with his mother's older brother, George Wilson Allen. William was measured for a new suit of school and Sunday clothes, which set the family back an astronomical $8. All he called his own was fit into a new packing trunk measuring thirty by fifteen inches, trimmed in brass, with a padlock attached to secure his worldly goods. He hid away the trunk's key in the pocket of his new clothes.

His solo trip to Troy proved a youthful adventure, the day opening with the entire family of seven riding in a hired carriage to the railway station, where his father handed him a ticket and placed him in the appropriate car, along with his brass-framed trunk. His mother gave him a brown-paper package of sandwiches for his journey to the distant lands of New York. As the train pulled out of the station, William wasted no time devouring his sack lunch, as he sat back and looked spellbound at the scenery. The train trip was the first unaccompanied journey of his life, in which "even the car I rode in was a thing to excite me."[9] From Philadelphia to New York, ten-year-old William was master of himself for the first time. The trip involved more than just trains. At that time, Philadelphia and New York City were not connected directly by rail and would not be for more than half a century. Jackson's train ran through New Jersey to the coast, where the passengers then took a lengthy ferry boat trip across the harbor to Manhattan. New York City was already home to more than one million residents, but it was a much smaller version of its future self. As Jackson later remembered it, there were "no great liners coming up through the Narrows, no Statue of Liberty on Bedloe's Island, and not a single skyscraper."[10] The steeple of the Old Trinity Church dominated the skyline of the lower end of Manhattan Island at the corner of Wall Street and Broadway, not only New York City's tallest building but also the tallest in the entire country, its construction completed only seven years earlier. From the ferry, William carried his trunk to a Hudson River side-wheeler steamboat bound for Albany, its fore dominated by a pair of "perilously tall smokestacks" that "threw out immense clouds of black smoke."[11] Will ate the last of his food and slept in his berth until morning.

William's boat trip was followed by a stagecoach ride from Albany to Troy, a short excursion of only six miles, his trunk firmly tied down atop the coach. By noon he was in the waiting arms of his Uncle George and Aunt Ellen. George was a successful retailer, and Will remembered each evening his uncle bringing home the day's receipts and handing them to his nephew to tally to the penny, which was more difficult than it might appear "since at that time specie was still rare, and a large proportion of the coinage in circulation was foreign. Spanish pesetas, French francs, English shillings, and Mexican dollars were as familiar as American silver and equally acceptable as currency."[12]

In time young Jackson's education outside the home became a priority. The school building—Troy's Fourth Ward School—represented more than the standard rural one-room, clapboard variety so common in mid-nineteenth-century America. Jackson's school was a substantial, three-story brick model, well-appointed with modern accoutrements, including easel blackboards. (Wall blackboards were not common yet.) Steel engravings and lithographs—the products of a new method of mass-produced printing—adorned the classrooms, including patriotic images of George Washington. In one, Jackson recalled, GW was crossing the Delaware, while in another he was wintering at Valley Forge. The nation's first president shared space with the fourteenth, the newly elected Franklin Pierce, as well as with dark-eyed images of Daniel Webster, who had only recently died.

The three Rs dominated Jackson's days in the Troy Fourth Ward School. His best subject was arithmetic, a skill he honed by practical experience, including counting his uncle's money. Decades after his schoolboy experiences, he could not recall whether he had been exposed to studies in geography, though he was destined to travel the world one day. History lessons centered on emotional civic morality tales marking the advancement of the American republic. Writing was emphasized through the development of a steady and fluid penmanship, a skill assumed requisite for the man of success. Paper was expensive enough for young students to make do with practicing their letters on slate tablets, with final—"exhibition pieces"—versions penned in ink on paper. (Jackson's handwriting was never enviable.) Still, his penmanship served him well during his long life of diary and journal keeping. As for reading, Jackson seems to have been a voracious natural, as he notes in his autobiography: "The Art of reading . . . was never a difficult one for me. I always had enough curiosity about things in general to dig for myself."

One of Jackson's least favorite subjects was public speaking. Schoolboy declamations were popular during his boyhood—at least among teachers—but Jackson had a youthful aversion to them. "As a boy," he wrote years later, "my most dreadful experience was that long, solitary walk down the aisle on Speech Day to deliver the words some great man had spoken or written down before me."[13] Jackson's youth was set in the midst of one of America's great ages of oratory, and schoolboys were often required to perform their best versions of speeches by the venerable Webster or go-to poets such as William Cullen Bryant, John Greenleaf Whittier, and Henry Wadsworth Longfellow. Despite his boyhood dislike of speaking, he would deliver many speeches throughout his adult life, noting, "I never particularly minded getting up before my audience when I had something I wanted to say."[14]

All work and no play might have made Jackson a dull boy, but while delineated playgrounds at school were a future innovation, William and his school chums had opportunities to engage one another outside the school building. A vacant lot adjacent to the school provided the venue for after-school activities, as Jackson recalled: "The game I best remember was the still-popular one-o'-cat, two-o'-cat, a kind of scrub baseball."[15] Wintertime delivered other popular activities—"There's snow on Jacob Street Hill!"—including ice skating; sledding; and shinny, a form of early hockey, sans any protective gear, with heated stick play sometimes resulting in serious cuts and bruises.[16] In time William's family joined him in Troy, and his time under Uncle George's roof came to an end. Despite his propensity to enjoy outdoor games and sports with his fellow youths, Jackson was already showing a strong interest in art, especially drawing. In his first autobiography, *The Pioneer Photographer*, published in 1929, he admits, "It was not studying books . . . which interested me most. I much preferred to draw pictures for the amusement of my classmates." Perhaps this relative detachment explains why he did not remain in school past the eighth grade.[17]

His mother—she was an artist by hobby—took note of his artistic interests and soon purchased a copy of a popular art primer, J. G. Chapman's *American Drawing Book*. This gift from his mother changed the ultimate trajectory of Jackson's world, as he observed: "No single thing in my life, before or since that day, has ever been so important to me." He stated that he had been drawing up to that time with "a burning zeal," while producing drawings with little technical aptitude. His "houses were flat," "horses stood on stilts," and "rivers ran up hill." With the help of Chapman's text and tips, William gained much-needed artistic insights, revealing the "mysteries of perspective, the rules of composition and design, the laws of color values, and how to model."[18]

The land was a central pivot for Chapman, who emphasized the mythology of beauty and perfection founded in Greek and Roman models, while transplanting such ideals into scenes of American mountains, rivers, and forests primeval. In Chapman's words, the land represented the truest of republican inspirations: "Of all the application of art to the purpose of the amateur, landscape occupies a deservedly high place."[19] Chapman extolled the importance of Americans creating an art of their own. Just as the likes of Washington Irving, Nathaniel Hawthorne, James Fenimore Cooper, Herman Melville, and other eastern voices were busy forming an American literature reflective of America's growth and expanding nationalist pride, so Chapman believed American painters, especially landscape artists, should respond to his clarion call for artistic expression grounded in republicanism.

Much of this emphasis in support of the founding and development of an American art form in the mid-nineteenth century likely flew high over Jackson's head as a hopeful, teenage artist in training. He was more concerned with how to accurately sketch the human form as he practiced "copying and recopying the heads of Apollo and George Washington."[20] But in the end some of Chapman's emphases likely rubbed off on him. Jackson would one day utilize both his artistic and photographic skills in capturing the American landscape even as the boundaries of the United States progressed farther and farther west. That portion of the country, the Trans-Mississippi West and beyond toward the setting sun, would serve as his muse, as he filled canvases and wet plates with images of a New World as exotic as any known to the Greeks or Romans.

Jackson's parents were as supportive of his artistic inclinations as their middle-class ideals could manage. Their home on North Fourth Street was situated on a deep lot that included a small two-story outbuilding that provided space for the family's tools and other outdoor items, plus storage and a woodshed. The second floor featured a clean, expansive space made available to young Jackson as an artistic workspace, a studio of sorts. There the budding artist set up shop, taking lessons from his Chapman manual. His mother provided a professional eye, and "her judgment of my work was the detached appraisal of an artist, not the foolish praise of an admiring parent."[21] Jackson remained jealous of his mother's time, although she had five children to care for, not one.

Such was Jackson's commitment to his art at an early age. Painting proved a necessity to him, and he recalled decades later how he "drew or painted every day," largely landscapes, both "real and imaginary,"[22] as well as portraits of his family. He worked in both oils and watercolors, although he sometimes found it difficult to keep himself supplied in materials and paints. At age twelve he took a job to support his artistic habit, working in the office of a local judge, a friend of his father. It was summer work and included "running errands, carrying mail to and from the post office, finding reports, and copying outgoing correspondence with a letter press." The $2 a week he earned kept him in paints and brushes. The following summer he landed another job working with a cousin who was a printer.[23]

Then came a moment of realization for young Jackson as he discovered he could receive money to engage in his artistic passion. A local druggist named Johnson—his son, Ira, would one day work for Jackson in his photographic studio in Omaha, Nebraska—needed professional-looking signs for his store displays, and he hired William to paint these display cards with neatly styled letters of blue, red, and gold. The job didn't last long, but Jackson managed to earn a few dollars, and the work incentivized him to seek out other employment as a painter. He found work painting screen doors. This was a popular practice during the 1850s. Screens were utilized not only to keep the flies outdoors, but also to show off the world to the provincials of Troy, New York. Screens were painted with scenes of distant landscapes. as Jackson later described in his autobiography: "Here were Mr. Jones's parlor windows parading the virtues of home life among the Romans; there was Mrs. Smith's testifying to her travels through the Black Forest and an idyllic honeymoon on Lake Lucerne; just beyond, Dr. Robinson's eloquently bespoke his love of grazing cows, old mills, and waterfalls. It was a wonderful world—and a live market for a boy who could create it."[24]

Soon Jackson was as busy as his brushes would allow, painting screens for fifteen cents each. (He later became confident enough to ask for two bits.) Given the cost of materials, he made little actual money, but he was gaining experience and a small-framed reputation. Word spread, and orders nearly poured in for window cards for storefronts, signs for church socials, and political posters. His breakthrough opportunity—"my first 'big' commission"—came when a local theater impresario hired Jackson to paint a row of large jars as a backdrop for a production of *Ali Baba and the Forty Thieves*. For his work he received a dollar and a "hearty slap on the back from the stage manager."[25]

Young Jackson's early artistic itch had been scratched, thanks to support from his parents and local Troy residents. But in 1858 he began working for a local businessman, C. C. Schoonmaker, taking a job that combined his love of art with an early flirtation with photography. Schoonmaker's River Street studio was one of many first-generation photographic studios in the United States.

A studio such as Schoonmaker's was constantly busy due to the popularity of wet plates, which involved a chemical process that produced pictures on glass using chemicals. But Jackson was not hired as a teenage photographer (the term at that time was "operator"). He was employed to put his artistic skills to technical use. Photographs of that era were often less than sharp, and retouching was its own art form. Jackson sharpened photos and "warmed them up" through colorization, utilizing watercolors.

Jackson was still a young man, and he was now learning new skills on the fly. Even though he was initially a colorist and retouch man, he "was in a position to learn a lot about photography," knowledge that would ultimately dramatically alter the direction of his life.[26] The camera technology was simple enough that a teenage boy, with proper instruction, could wield the typical camera of the era. Studio portraits were usually taken with a single large box camera designed to accommodate the glass plates on which the image was to be fixed. Unlike most cameras from the late nineteenth century until the advent of digital, cell phone technology—although phone photos are usually taken with an accompanying "click" for reasons of nostalgia, it would seem—the boxy cameras did not utilize shutters that opened and closed. Instead, photos were taken by exposing light through a lens by simply uncapping the lens for a proscribed number of minutes. Subjects were required to hold as still as possible throughout those minutes, a task difficult for many, especially children, prompting photographers to utilize a support rod and clamp behind a subject's head to keep it in place. Otherwise, blurry photographs were all too common. Subjects were even encouraged to hold their breath during the exposure time frame for as long as possible. In most cases, the size of the glass plate determined the size of the resulting photograph. Enlargements were possible using a "solar camera," which featured a condensing lens. Such cameras were often set up on rooftops where the natural light could be maximized. This is the world of cameras young Jackson entered during the 1850s.

By the time Jackson entered his teen years, he was working and learning more about the world outside of Troy, New York. The old Whig political party had collapsed early in the 1850s—William was likely named for Whig president William Henry Harrison, who had died in office a few years before Jackson's birth—and a new party, the Republicans, had emerged from its ashes by 1856. As a thirteen-year-old boy he heard the name John C. Fremont, the Republican candidate for president. But Jackson had first heard of Fremont as a great western explorer, who had made several forays into the Far West as a young man and gained national attention for mapping some of the more mysterious corners of the region for the federal government. Jackson could not have known as a youth that he, too, would one day explore in the name of the US government and document what he saw with cameras.

Jackson knew of the Mexican War and his Uncle Edward's role and of new lands added to the United States, including Nevada, Arizona, New Mexico, and California. The war raised new concerns over the expansion of slavery into the West—opposition to such expansion was the primary political position of the Republican Party—and Will proved staunchly opposed to the peculiar institution. He participated in several antislavery marches down Troy's Main Street and attended a mass rally against the southern practice. For that rally, he likely had painted some of the political placards on display. He also carved several pumpkins into jack-o'-lanterns as window decorations for the rally. Fremont lost, but Jackson's interest in Republican politics endured. He closely followed the 1858 senatorial race between Illinois Senator Stephen Douglas and Abraham Lincoln and was disappointed when "the Illinois legislature re-elected the Little Giant to the United States Senate."[27]

International news sparked young Jackson's imagination as he read about the laying of the transatlantic cable linking the US and British telegraphic systems. Overland mail routes across the West similarly connected St. Louis with San Francisco, allowing the delivery of a letter in fewer than four weeks. Now, as Jackson later wrote, "the Eastern seaboard was scarcely a single month removed from the West Coast."[28] The year 1859 brought stories of John Brown's ill-conceived raid at Harper's Ferry, Virginia, and of the derring-do of a French tightrope aerialist who walked a 150-foot-high wire stretched across the Niagara River just below the massive falls. In the midst of his dizzying feat, Monsieur Blondin dropped a line to the Niagara steamer *Maid of the Mist*, a wine bottle was attached to it, the line was drawn up, and the aerialist drank the contents, tossing the empty bottle into the river as twelve thousand anxious spectators watched in safety. But newspapers in these final years of the 1850s were filled with stories of an increasingly divisive sectionalism engulfing the country as opponents and supporters clashed politically over the expansion of slavery into the West. Jackson sat in the audience at a local Troy theater, where he took in a performance of *Uncle Tom's Cabin*, a production he later recalled as "a real thriller."[29]

Jackson left home at the age of sixteen. During his upbringing, his family had remained bound to the East. The 1840s and 1850s were years of great movement for millions of restless Americans as the West opened up more and more far-flung territory. States were being added to the Union. The 1840s witnessed the great migration of hundreds of thousands of Americans, first to the Oregon Country and, by the decade's end, to California in search of gold. It was a demographic shift that continued well into the 1880s, this migratory tendency for whole families to pull up eastern stakes and seek their fortunes in the West.

These various movements resulted in the relative depopulating of the East. During the 1870s, following the Civil War, several eastern states—including Maine, New Hampshire, Vermont, and New York—lost population, while such western destinations as Kansas, Colorado, and California increased their populations several times over. New York State, Jackson's adolescent home, only increased in population by one thousand souls between 1860 and 1870, despite European immigration into the state during that same decade. The township in which the Jackson family lived during William's youth—Peru Township—declined in population by 35 percent during the 1860s. But the Jacksons stayed put. It likely did not occur to young Jackson that the West would ever prove as enticing a destination for him as it one day would. For the moment, the West remained a region unclearly formed in the minds of many Americans, including William Henry Jackson. The nation was on the verge of splitting North and South, war was on the horizon, and its coming would soon alter the direction of millions of Americans' lives, including that of the young man from Troy.

2

Gone Soldiering, 1860–1866

The politics of 1860 continued to excite Jackson, but change was taking place in his immediate world as well. After two years of retouching and other finishing work on photographs for Schoonmaker, his boss spoke highly of Jackson to another photographer, Frank Mowry, in neighboring Rutland, Vermont, during a visit by Mowry to Schoonmaker's studio. Mowry ultimately hired William away from Schoonmaker to do his hand tinting and other photographic work. It meant a move and a pay increase, as Jackson began earning $6 a week. His room and board—including having his laundry done—factored out to $3.50 a week, but Jackson still felt he was moving up in the world, even though he "was still not a photographer."[1] Mowry took on Jackson as an artist, a "brush-and-pencil" man.

Work in the Mowry studio was similar to the work he had been doing for Schoonmaker, with one important difference. At that time, Mowry was shifting away from daguerreotype photography to tintypes and a new form of visiting card called cartes de visite. These were larger than visiting cards and quite popular. From these, Mowry was making enlargements for wall portraits, and Jackson did the oil painting to colorize these works. These were "whole-plate" portraits that cost customers between $2.50 and $5 each based on glass plates measuring 6½ by 8½ inches. In addition to the colorization options, the client could select from a number of specialized backdrops—Niagara Falls, the Pyramids of Giza, architectural ruins of Athens—plus flanking columns or draperies to give the photograph more of a third dimension. While enlargements proved popular and a real moneymaker, most glass plate shots were printed at quarter and half sizes by the dozen.

Through all this studio work, Jackson was learning more and more about actual photography and cameras and how to process plates and printing. At the same time, he was becoming accustomed to working with clients and the other moving parts of running a photographic studio. Work could extend throughout the entire week for photographers. The regular workweek at that time, for those living in towns, stretched from Monday through noon on Saturday. This meant photographers were busiest on Saturday afternoons. Sunday afternoons were also a natural time for photographic portraits, since subjects were already dressed in their Sunday best. These experiences provided him the knowledge to one day open his own studio.

Rutland proved a good move for Jackson's career and his social reach despite the extended workweek. His $6 weekly wage was "enough to live on decently." He made friends among other young men in the community. He and his pals shared "many delightful times" in Rutland and outside the town, taking rural excursions into the Green Mountains for picnics, fishing forays, and mountain climbing. But Jackson's favorite social activity was a buggy ride with a young girl at his side. His "social director" was the middle-aged daughter of the elderly couple, the Fishers, from whom Jackson rented a room on Center Street. "Miss Fisher saw to it that I met young people," Jackson later wrote, "and my life, even on a tiny salary, was thoroughly happy."[2] He had to live frugally, and some expenditures were completely out of the question. He limited his expenses by not smoking—which he did not enjoy anyway—and rarely consumed alcohol. He took in a few entertainments, including plays. But he did spring from time to time for the cost of renting a buggy to share with a young miss on a Sunday drive, including dinner at a roadside restaurant. Other courting options included hayrides, picnic lunches, small parties, and holiday dances, all "under the sternest chaperonage."[3] Such evening activities usually wound up by 9:45, as many girls were required to be safely home by ten. But these youthful days of work and play "were broken into all too soon."[4]

The election of Abraham Lincoln as the nation's first Republican president only managed to accelerate the confrontational regional politics over slavery. Just as he had for John C. Fremont in 1856, young Jackson campaigned for Lincoln. Jackson remembered the political doings in Troy on Election Day eve. Evening delivered a great political parade featuring a band tootling "Yankee Doodle," "John Brown's Body," and "The Star-Spangled Banner." Black-coated Republican leaders marched behind the musicians, and the parade gained thousands of adherents as it made its way across town to University Hill and the community's Rensselaer Polytechnic. (The following year, the school was renamed as the Rensselaer Polytechnic Institute, the name it retains today.) With the mob scattered across the campus grounds, organizers set off Roman candles that lit up the night sky.

Come Election Day, Jackson was at work in the Schoonmaker studio—Mowry did not lure Jackson from Schoonmaker's until a month or so later—since lots of potential clients would be in town to vote. William, despite his campaigning activities, was still too young to cast a ballot himself. But that evening, after he left the shop, he was downtown in the midst of a crowd anxious for telegraphic information regarding the election's returns. As dispatches arrived, a citizen armed with a megaphone shouted out what he knew. Since Troy was a Republican stronghold, each vote tally for Lincoln elicited shouts of excitement. By 2:00 a.m. the results seemed clear: Lincoln and his running mate, Hannibal Hamlin, from neighboring Maine, were surely elected. The next morning, an overly anxious Jackson pondered what might have happened if the South's best candidate had actually won the election. He made himself physically ill thinking about it, considering that "life under the tyranny of a slaveholder . . . would be unendurable." A trip to the newspaper office confirmed his best hopes: "Lincoln was safely in."[5]

The following spring, the divide between North and South widened into a great gulf. Just weeks following Lincoln's election in November, southern states, starting with South Carolina, began taking overt steps to sever their ties with the United States. Lincoln was perceived as an abolitionist, a wide-eyed radical ready to destroy slavery with the wave of his hand. It did not help the southern perspective to realize that the man from Illinois had been elected virtually without a single southern vote, which seemed to render the views and political notions of the South immaterial. Separation seemed preferable to northern dominance, so state after state began to slip out from under federal allegiance. Lincoln's Inaugural Address on March 4 sought a conciliatory tone—"We are not enemies but friends"—but the South would have none of it, and the drumbeat for war was heard from Virginia to Texas. April delivered civil war as southern forces in Charleston, South Carolina, opened up shore batteries and pounded Fort Sumter, a federal outpost that was more symbolic than threatening. With the shelling of the island outpost, the animosity between the North and South shifted from "a clash of ideas" to a clash of men and arms.[6]

Jackson may have been too young to vote, but he was old enough to enlist in the Union army. He did not join as a knee-jerk reaction to Fort Sumter as so many others did that spring and summer. Many of his neighbors and fellow residents in Rutland thought the conflict would be brief, so short that there would be no time for them to join and participate in the fight before the smoke of war dissipated. Lincoln called for seventy-five thousand volunteers, and Jackson later expressed his belief at the time that, "If our fine army wasn't big enough, those 75,000 new soldiers could handle the situation in South Carolina—and any other places where the flag was not respected."[7]

But as the months following Fort Sumter unfolded, the new war proved deadly and much larger than the discontented of South Carolina. In July, following the Union defeat at Bull Run in Virginia, eighteen-year-old Jackson "began to weigh the thought of enlistment." His parents hoped he would stay out a bit longer, and Mowry agreed. Through the first year of the war Jackson did, in fact, hold off enlisting. With each passing month it appeared the conflict might drag on longer than many had anticipated. Jackson continued to absorb war news. The report of the phrenologist Professor Orson Squire Fowler convinced Jackson for a short while that perhaps he was too valuable to be wasted in war: "Your mechanical genius is far above mediocrity, and will enable you to draw, make, copy, anything you like, and give you excellence as a painter, perhaps even sculpture, for you are really a genius, and no mistake."[8]

But the successful campaigns of General Robert E. Lee during the long summer of 1862, including the Seven Days and Second Bull Run finally broke Jackson's resolve and that of many of Rutland's young men. Lincoln, in the face of a protracted war, called for three hundred thousand enlistees, a call reinforced with the threat of a Union draft. A group called the Light Guard already existed in Rutland, but until that summer it was more like a social club than part of the state's militia. On August 18, 1862, Jackson joined the Rutland Light Guard, reporting to Captain Levi G. Kingsley. His notebook entry for that date includes the following: "I had previously made up my mind to enlist. God knows that the country needs men, and I regard it as the duty of every able-bodied man, who can possibly do so to enlist at once, the sooner the better and it is better by far to enlist voluntarily than to be dragged into the army as a conscript. Nothing to me would appear more degrading."[9] On August 19 he officially became a member of the Light Guard and two days later traveled to Troy to inform his parents of his decision, with whom he had discussed the possibility of enlistment in his letters; now he had actually pulled the trigger.

Jackson's service only began as a member of the Light Guard. Soon he and his fellow Vermonters were mustered into the regular US Army as Company K of the Twelfth Vermont Volunteers. Along with other regiments of Vermonters, the Twelfth formed a portion of the Second Vermont Brigade. For nearly six weeks Jackson and his comrades experienced the rigors of marching and drilling. His brother, Ed, arrived at his encampment on September 5, a surprise to Jackson, "as he was entirely unexpected." Since several enlistees had already been dismissed from the company's ranks, Ed found a place in his brother's unit. The Vermont boys experienced several equipment shortages at first—government-issued blankets appear to have been in short supply for a while—but in time the company received everything it needed.

On the afternoon of October 4, Major Austin of the regular army mustered Company K into official US Army service. Two days later Jackson and his comrades received their $100 enlistment bounty and back pay of $10.70.

Will then forwarded $40 to Miss Fisher for room and board and $70 home to his parents. His diary entry for the next day, Tuesday, October 7, simply reads: "Started today for Dixie."[10]

By noon that day the Second Vermont Brigade marched to the train station in Brattleboro, bound for Washington, D.C. Jackson had gained 10 pounds since enlisting, placing his weight at 160 pounds spread over his five-foot-nine body. Flags flew everywhere amid patriotic bunting, and many citizens cheered as the boys clambered into boxcars to start their rail journey. The following morning their train rolled into New Haven, Connecticut, where they waited most of the day until they sailed out on the steamer *Continental*. They docked at Perth Amboy in New York City (Jackson spent many of his later years living in New York) and again found themselves waiting. Jackson recalled standing in line to receive food from an army cook who, when a young man complained he had received no meat in his stew, "plunged his bare arm into the kettle, brought up a great hunk of beef and splashed it square into the disgruntled soldier's tin plate."[11]

Hours later the Vermont men were on their way to Philadelphia, still in boxcars. They ate dinner in the City of Brotherly Love and were then on their way to Baltimore. Passing through the city took hours, since an outdated ordinance prohibited trains passing through town under their own power, necessitating the use of teams of horses to pull the cars to the edge of town. Once under steam, the Vermonters' train arrived in Washington, D.C., at 8:00 p.m. on October 10. With his arrival in the nation's capital, a city surrounded by dozens of army encampments to provide the federal government some military protection, "the war that I had heard so much about became real," wrote Jackson. "So far it had been a war of distant armies identified by the names of their generals. Now it was a war of soldiers—who ate and drank and smoked and swore and slept on floors, like me."[12]

Through October, Jackson and his company remained a part of the Washington, D.C., defense perimeter one mile east of the Capitol. This provided him the opportunity to explore the nation's capital. At that time, the Capitol dome was covered with a framework of wooden scaffolding, part of the conversion from its older iron dome into a fully stone edifice. He visited the Capitol and studied "the rather primitive art then on display there." He also toured the Smithsonian Institution. Jackson thought such an opportunity represented "a wonderful chance for a boy from the country to see something of the great world outside."[13]

By the end of October the Vermont troops were ordered to strike their tents and pack up for a new assignment location. On October 29 they marched along Pennsylvania Avenue, then crossed a brick bridge spanning the Potomac onto Virginia soil. Eight miles from the capital, they pitched their tents anew. As Jackson observed, "It was a peaceful-seeming country. All was quiet. Yet we stood now on the soil of the Confederacy."[14]

Over the next six weeks—November 2 through December 12—the Second Vermont Brigade remained on picket duty, still within sight of the Union capital. Winter came quickly, with a four-inch snowfall during the first week. Jackson's encampment was in the midst of thick woods that provided some protection from the wintry winds. Tents were augmented with three-foot-high log walls, their cracks daubed with mud, the tents now serving as roofs. Some shelters featured makeshift brick stoves—the bricks purloined from local farms—and "we lived a warm life and a dry one for the first time in many weeks."[15]

The Vermont boys saw no action during these cold weeks spent guarding the Virginia side of the Potomac River. (During the first week stationed on the west side of the river, Jackson barely avoided detection by the sergeant of the guard for sleeping on guard duty.) The men were kept busy through daily drill and pick-and-shovel work on their earthen fortifications, but days still blended uneventfully into each other. The weather often kept the men in their tents, but warm days allowed for foraging in the local countryside. The recurring, sometimes lengthy stretches of quiet provided Private Jackson with the opportunity to return to his art. He even sketched small pictures to accompany the letters he wrote to friends and family. Many of these sketches he drew on three-by-five-inch cards, which later led some to claim Will Jackson was the inventor of the picture postcard, a claim he denied. His talent having been revealed to his comrades, many asked him to sketch their portraits. Several of the boys had their tintype photos taken while in Washington, but out in the encampments, there were no cameras.

Jackson was popular among his fellow Vermonters. He was often in the company of his brother Ed and others from back home. One of his friends, Ruel Rounds, became his traveling companion following the war when Jackson decided to take his first trip into the Far West. The boys received monthly pay of $13 but had little opportunity to spend much, except at camp sutler stores, which charged high rates for everything from writing paper to alcohol. When they played cards, including poker and seven-up, players usually had little money to wager.

As 1862 drew down to its final weeks, the Vermont men remained in camp, failing to see action. But the weather and circumstance proved to be the enemy instead. On December 6 Jackson wrote in his notebook, "Some what windy at night—froze hard. Seven soldiers in the Convalescent camp died this night—ice froze inch and a half thick."[16] Less than a week later, the Second Vermont Brigade received orders to pack up and move, this time to Fairfax Court House, Virginia, where they remained for several additional weeks, outside of town in a piney woods. Jackson did not like the change of scenery, penning, "The country through which we traveled is the most desolate God forsaken place I've seen yet. . . . Fairfax Court House is a dirty nasty hole, the houses are old dilapidated rickety and dirty concerns."[17] During the two weeks at Fairfax, the men continued to see no action, although several dozen of them were assigned a reburial detail near the Chantilly Battlefield, as many of the Union dead had been first interred in shallow graves. Christmas came and went without much celebration.

Then, on December 28, action seemed imminent. Jackson's diary notes: "We lay in breathless silence expecting at any moment to see the enemy come dashing over the hill. We were ready for them, our guns pointed to the spot where they were expected to appear. The moments passed away however and nothing more was heard of them."[18]

Jackson did not see action that day. In fact, throughout his time in uniform during the war, he saw virtually no combat firsthand. "We never got into the thickest of the fray," he later wrote. "My soldier days were not particularly exciting."[19] There were close moments, when the enemy came within killing range, but little came of it.

By late January the Vermonters were on the move again, this time to Wolf Run Shoals, where they settled once again into days spent with no action and long hours of drill. Pay came periodically to the men, and on January 29 Jackson received three months' wages at once, prompting him to take a trip to Alexandria, Virginia, to buy a new pair of boots. With little activity involving the enemy, Jackson continued to have time to sketch, including portraits of comrades. Between these, he drew landscapes and field fortifications, which ultimately attracted the attention of one of his superiors, a New Hampshire officer, Captain Charles Edward Blunt.[20] On February 20 Jackson was given the official assignment "to sketch and draw."[21] Blunt gave few specific instructions, which allowed Jackson to sketch anything and everything he chose, creating permanent images of camp life. One of the more important subjects of his drawings was the occasional map he drew of the field layout, trench and encampment positions, and breastworks. After a week of doing sketches, he showed his work to Captain Blunt, who was extremely pleased. He even dispatched Jackson to Washington the following day to retrieve a new supply of paper.

From late winter until early spring, Jackson was busy sketching. The enemy remained out of sight but was rarely far away. Will later recalled one vivid event in mid-March when Confederate cavalry, under the command of Colonel John Singleton Mosby, rode into Fairfax Court House, where General Edward Henry S. Stoughton was headquartered in a fine requisitioned house. That night Mosby and a handful of his raiders entered the house, found

Stoughton in his bedroom, and whisked him away, to the humiliation of his fellow Vermonters. Stoughton was later exchanged and set free, but it marked the end of his days as a Union commander.

Jackson's sketching sometimes placed him in the wrong place and time. In early April, "zeal led me into one of the few dangerous situations I encountered during my service."[22] He had been working on a map of Bull Run Creek. One lengthy stretch of embankment was shrouded in overgrowth, so he located a log raft and boarded it to float downriver. Slipping along the river, sketching its curves and noting copses of willow and oak trees, the sound of cocking muskets suddenly startled him. From the river's edge, he heard a voice: "Who goes there?" He was quick to respond: "Friend." As he headed to the river's edge, several Union picketers came into sight. They took him into their custody and delivered Jackson to their squad sergeant. Jackson showed him his pass. This explained his presence so far downriver, but the sergeant dressed him down "for my careless behavior in openly riding down a stream that had already been the scene of two fierce battles."

Throughout April, the biggest excitement came with a twelve-inch spring snowfall. Jackson turned twenty that month. Stoughton's replacement, General George J. Stannard, arrived on April 22. Early May brought another move for the brigade, this time to Catlett's Station. In all the confusion of packing and pulling up stakes, Jackson experienced a personal tragedy—he lost his sketchbook and never recovered it. Some members of the brigade, including Jackson, engaged in several raids that month, if only at the expense of a local farmer named Quisenberry, who owned a sprawling farmstead. Vermont boys raided his barn on three occasions that month and managed to steal two sacks of bacon, two calves, and a pig.

Some of the Vermont men did finally see action in late May. On May 22 a small unit of Confederate cavalry attacked a Union-held rail line and burned a train near the federals' encampment outside Catlett's Station, prompting the train's twenty-two guards to hightail it into some local woods. Jackson later wrote: "[Union] cavalry pursued them. [The enemy] posted their cannon in a narrow defile in the road and twice repulsed the 5th [New York]. Co. H of the Vt Cavalry charged and took the piece. We lost in all four killed."[23] But Jackson had once again avoided the fight.

At this time a portion of the Vermont men was transferred to Union Mills, including William. It was another slow month without any enemy in sight. Jackson continued his sketching—assumedly in a new sketchbook—and even found time for occasional swims in the local river. He even managed to go courting a few times among "a number of vivacious young ladies living in the vicinity of Union Mills."[24] On June 7 he received exciting news from home informing him he had a new baby brother named Allen.

But soon the bucolic days of the Second Vermont Brigade shifted abruptly to tense weeks of enemy troop movement and sightings. General Robert E. Lee was taking his army into the North, to Pennsylvania specifically, raising various alarms among Union commanders. Virginia, Maryland, and Pennsylvania began to swirl with activity, as indicated in the pages of Jackson's diary for 1863:

> Tuesday 9th [June]   Rumors of big cavalry fight at Culpeper Court House
> . . .
>
> Wednesday 10th   Firing heard off in the direction of Rappahannock Station. Large detail at work felling trees into the Bull Run
>
> Sunday 14th   Advance guard of 11th corps came in . . .
>
> Monday 15th   Early in the morning the 11th corps came in and pitched tents and about noon the 1st corps . . . we came across detachments of the 2d, 6th and 12th corps All morning this way. The whole army seems to be in motion . . .
>
> Tuesday 16th   The army still moves on. Hear rumors of the rebs being in Penn.
>   At Chambersburgh [*sic*], nearly took Milroy [Union commander] at Winchester—this evening the 6th corps baggage train is bivouacked here. Woods all afire on the opposite side of the Bull Run . . .
>
> Wednesday 17th   The army baggage still continues to pass through this place, bound northward . . . Canonading [*sic*] heard in the distance.[25]

What Jackson and the men of the Second Vermont Brigade could not have known with certainty during these tense weeks of June 1863 was that, indeed, many Union forces were on the move, searching for Robert E. Lee and his Army of Northern Virginia.

During the final two weeks of the month, both armies shifted positions and moved hundreds of thousands of men, including the Second Vermont. Everything seemed fluid. Lee was constantly in motion, while on the Union side, General Joseph Hooker, who had lost a large-scale battle in early May to Lee at Chancellorsville, was replaced by another commander, General George G. Meade. No one knew where the armies might cross paths until June 30, when advance units of federals and rebels spotted one another in the streets of the small Pennsylvania town of Gettysburg. Over the next three days, the largest battle of the Civil War played out, and the Second Vermont Brigade played a role. Yet as monumental—and bloody—as Gettysburg proved,

William Henry Jackson still saw no action himself. His regiment was detailed to guard twenty-three hundred prisoners being moved to Baltimore.

On Saturday, July 5, the Second Vermont Brigade was on its way by train to deliver those Confederate captives to Baltimore. Not all the Second had managed to remain out of these days of intense fighting at Gettysburg. Prior to the real fighting, the brigade was divided, with three of the regiments sent to the front to help occupy Cemetery Ridge, the fortified backbone of a long Union line of entrenchments that became the centerpiece of the Gettysburg battle. A second element of Vermonters was assigned picket duty, while Jackson's unit was detailed to guard baggage trains. This meant Jackson did not see any of the fighting at Gettysburg, even though members of his brigade did, and their efforts proved significant.

This was the nature of Civil War battles. For every frontline soldier who fired his gun in the heat of a conflict, there were many others who carried out additional auxiliary duties, responsibilities less deadly but just as crucial. Virtually all armies throughout history have been reliant not just on frontline fighters but also on rear personnel, those who provide the troops who actually fight with the materials and support they need to perform their duties. For every soldier at the front there are several others who remain at the rear or are removed from the action, including cooks, supply coordinators, stevedores, and a host of other roles. Jackson's unit may not have been directly engaging Confederates on the field at Gettysburg, along flash points from Culp's Hill to Cemetery Ridge to Little Round Top. But they still carried out their duties during those early days in July, including guarding baggage cars and wagons, relaying information, and ultimately guarding thousands of prisoners. These duties do not represent service less than that carried out at the front. That Jackson was in uniform for more than a year and never found himself in heated action should not take away from his commitment to the Union cause. After all, when he signed up for military duty, he did not know where it would place him, whether in battle or at the rear. He still made the commitment and performed his duties according to his orders.

The train carrying twenty-three hundred Confederate prisoners, living casualties of the Battle of Gettysburg, rolled into Baltimore on Sunday, July 5, and Jackson's Twelfth Regiment set up their protective cordon. The prisoners were delivered to Fort McHenry, the site of a British naval bombardment during the War of 1812, from which emerged the grand American symbol, the "Star-Spangled Banner." With the Gettysburg victory behind them, the regiment was granted a thirty-six-hour leave. Jackson took time to explore the city as he had Washington the previous year, including watching a performance at the Holliday Street Theater and staying in a room at the Calvert House hotel, where he slept in a bed for the first time in months.

The leave marked the end of service for Jackson's regiment. Their enlistments up, they were delivered north to Brattleboro, again in boxcars, this time so crowded that some soldiers had to ride on top of the cars. Excitement marked their journey. They were heading home, having completed their service, and some had even seen battle, fighting that delivered a much-needed Union victory on a grand scale. Word soon spread of another federal success, this one out West at Vicksburg, Mississippi. General Ulysses Grant had brought the city to its knees through a lengthy siege. The rail route back to Vermont "brought enthusiastic crowds to the stations to look at part of the army that had at last won a real victory." As his service ended, Jackson, now a young man of twenty, "considered with some amusement the fact that many of us had spent the best part of a year at the front without once firing our guns at the enemy."[26]

The Vermont men arrived back in Brattleboro early on July 9, before word had reached many Vermonters of their young heroes' return. The applause they received was from strangers lining rail station platforms. For Jackson, it mattered little. He was home, had seen more of the country than previously, had performed his patriotic duties, and was grateful for the experience. He was now more concerned "with plans for the future to pay much attention to what people might think of something that was past."[27] Before the boys of his regiment scattered, the governor held a public review of the troops, after which Jackson set out for Rutland.

Upon Jackson's and Edward's return home, their parents could not have been prouder. Their sons were heroes. Jackson took a week following his return to reconnect to his family and generally do nothing if he did not have to. His parents were more than happy to oblige. Soon he was intent on getting his life back in Rutland. He had a bit of money from his bounty payment and final pay, but most of that went to buy new civilian clothes. Army life had filled him out a bit, and his old clothing no longer fit. Mowry was happy to have Will back in his studio, but their business relationship needed adjusting. So many of the young men in uniform wanted military photographs, there was plenty of work. Will was soon busy once more putting his unique talents to work hand tinting enlargements and straight oil portraits, and soon he renegotiated with Mowry to pay him by the photograph or portrait rather than a weekly salary. Not only did Mowry agree, he also rented a large room in his studio to the young veteran for minimal rent.

Jackson was soon busy both day and night. Orders for hand-tinted photographs were constant, including portraits of Lincoln, Grant, and other Union generals. Young George Armstrong Custer was a favorite. He had made brigadier general by the age of twenty-three and was considered a dashing hero. As Jackson wrote later, "The children loved him, the ladies adored him, and all men envied him."[28] For a retoucher like Jackson, Custer's portrait offered a color fest, including his golden hair, his gold-braided green-gray velveteen uniform, and his buff, wide-brimmed cavalier hat. Jackson's constant work brought him more money than he had ever made before, with his income typically between $10 and $12 a week. (His military service had paid that amount, but monthly.) Jackson was making a middle-class place for himself in the Rutland community. He could be seen about town, wearing his new clothing and eating in restaurants. He further supplemented his income by offering art lessons to the young women of Rutland.

Jackson's interest soon landed on one young lady. "I had a sweetheart," he later wrote. "She was the belle of the town." After several months of courting, Jackson and Miss Caroline Eastman felt they had an "understanding" that their futures were going to be spent together. A June 1866 wedding date was set. She was attractive and vivacious (Jackson's word), and it did not hurt that her stepfather, a Mr. McDaniel, was one of the more substantial men of Rutland. Jackson also made time for male companionship, and he and his young comrades formed a small club known only by its initials, SSC, which stood for the Social Sardine Club. This circle of companions met to share meals and various entertainments, including having their photograph taken together. As Jackson later wrote, "I was, in the words of a song that had not yet been written, sitting on top of the world."[29]

But Jackson's world was soon introduced to even better opportunities. Close to Christmas of 1864, a successful photographer from Burlington, Mr. F. Styles, approached Jackson to come and work for him. When Jackson seemed hesitant, Styles assured him, "I've already had quite a talk with him [Mowry], and he told me he wouldn't stand in your way. Now I need a man who can do the kind of work you handle here. What's more, I'll make it worth your while."[30] Styles then offered Jackson $25 per week. It was a princely sum to William, ten times his recent army pay. At the time, an enviable salary might come in at $1,000 a year. Here was a complete stranger willing to offer $300 above that amount. Jackson could not believe his luck.

Still, he did not immediately jump from Mowry to Styles. During his service to Mowry, the Rutland photographer had treated him well, paid a decent wage, and given him various opportunities. "I had a long talk with Mowry," wrote Jackson years later. "He told me that Styles was an enterprising man and that Burlington was a good town. He added that the salary promised me was more than I could expect to earn in Rutland."[31] Jackson had other concerns on his mind. He was already engaged to Caroline Eastman, and plans for marriage were underway. In the end, Jackson took Mowry's advice and accepted the new position in Burlington.

Burlington proved a good move for young Jackson. Soon after Jackson began his new job, the Civil War ended with Lee surrendering to Grant at Appomattox Court House, Virginia. His brother Ed was there to witness the culmination of the divisive, four-year conflict. Church bells rang across the North heralding the Union victory. Within a week, the bells were again ringing, this time to mourn the death of President Lincoln. In time, a train carried his body from Washington, D.C., back to his home in Springfield, Illinois. Jackson recalled later, "Burlington was far from the route of the train that carried Lincoln . . . but the town took full part in the national mourning. I recall one clear detail . . . when Mr. Styles came in for the day's work, he paused for a moment before the Lincoln portrait, then draped it with a heavy black band that was not to be removed during my time."[32]

Jackson's new job proved a positive change both professionally and personally. He was making more money than ever, which allowed him to buy new clothes, including "rich ties and brocaded waistcoats" and to eat in restaurants and even afford various entertainments. Styles rented him a spacious room above the studio "practically free of rent." He intended to save part of his money but somehow didn't manage to put any more aside than when he had made much less. He spent money on musical instruments for which he had no talent and became obsessed with physical fitness, purchasing "weights, pulleys, dumbbells, and Indian clubs."[33]

He was also spending money on his sweetheart, taking weekly sojourns to Rutland on Sunday, leaving early enough to arrive, visit, and leave all before day's end. From Monday through Saturday he worked and still managed to find time for social activities, including picnics, dancing, and attending a literary society, a common social activity for young, middle-class men and women during that era.

Jackson's post–Civil War world had slipped into a comfortable, satisfying groove that included a well-paying job, a sweetheart on the string, an active social life, and a promising future. But soon his "rosy happiness and the promise of prosperity . . . were suddenly dispelled."[34] Just days following his twenty-third birthday, he spent that weekend on his weekly jaunt to Rutland to visit his fiancée, Caddie. Then something went wrong, something Jackson could never fully explain to himself:

> I had, as usual, gone to Rutland to spend the day with Miss Eastman and her family. Some time during the afternoon we had a difference, a difference so slight that I haven't the remotest idea now [writing decades later] of its origin. She had spirit, I was bull-headed, and the quarrel grew. When I started for the depot after supper Miss Caddie said coldly, "Good night, Mr. Jackson." With equal formality I responded, "Good night, Miss Eastman," and bowed from the hips. All the next week I was upset. I arranged to take

Saturday off, and late Friday afternoon I went to Rutland, hoping that I could mend the breach. If I had possessed the wit of a squirrel, I would have acknowledged my fault—whatever it was—and been forgiven.[35]

But Jackson could not repair the damage. How intently he tried is unclear, and even the direct cause of the original argument was never fully explained. The break seemed, to him, irreparable. "I failed miserably," he wrote. "I was, so to speak, discharged." The relationship and the wedding were off, and Jackson was soon making serious decisions that would alter his life even more. Not only did he leave Caddie behind, but also his job, Burlington, and even his adopted state. (Jackson did retain a daguerreotype of Caddie, which he kept for the remainder of his life.)

Circumstances led him "to pull up stakes and drift away from Vermont for a long, long while." Will could not have known at that difficult moment of disappointment and disillusionment "that this misfortune was to send me to such far-away paths of adventure." He would soon make his way into the West.[36]

3

First Foray West, 1866

*J*ackson wasted little time putting both emotional and actual distance between himself and Caddie. He forwarded a packet of letters she had written to him. "Within twenty-four hours I was on my way," he later wrote. "Direction New York City, destination unknown." He was intent on leaving everything behind, including home, work, friends, and old familiar places. Once he left Rutland, he never saw Caddie again. Even though the train stopped at Troy, he did not depart to announce his intentions to his family. "I was running away," Jackson wrote.[1] He left Vermont on a Saturday and reached New York City the following day. But his departure from Caddie Eastman was not entirely complete even as he readied to leave Vermont. At the Troy station, he "took from the pocket over my heart a small picture of Caddie and enjoyed a few moments of exquisite sadness."[2]

Once the train had pulled into New York's Chambers Street Station, Jackson began to wander. He thought he knew where City Hall Park was located, so he picked up his bag and headed in that direction. After so much walking, he realized he had entered the city by a different rail depot than he recollected, one several blocks farther from the park. By the time he reached his hotel, he had walked three miles.

Monday delivered a strong dose of reality to Jackson. He had left Vermont with no real plans other than escape. He had no idea where he was going next, and he had little cash in his pockets—maybe $30—with which to get there. But the day also delivered a surprise. As luck would have it, as he strolled south to Manhattan's Battery, which he had seen as a soldier, he chanced upon an old comrade—Ruel Rounds, whom Jackson called "Rock" because he was a marble cutter by trade—who had served alongside his fellow Vermonter in Company K. Jackson's immediate impulse was to dodge his old

27

friend, given his circumstances. But Rounds spotted him at the same moment, and a reunion was soon in the making.

Soon they were sharing a meal, during which Jackson discovered his friend to be as directionless as himself. Will shared the details of his recent breakup, and the two young men began to consider their next step, one they thought they might take in tandem. Rock was unemployed and penniless, and New York City did not offer any immediate answers for either young man. But Rock had more of a plan than Jackson, even if it was unclear how the two could accomplish it logistically. "Why not," proposed his friend, "try for a berth with one of the silver-mining companies in Montana Territory?" The western mines needed young men, and mining represented the possibility of work and a salary even if the boys were clueless just how grueling such work could be. Maybe the pair of Vermonters could even strike it rich on their own. But the plan met with obstacles immediately. Jackson and Rounds attempted to sign up at the local offices of several western mining interests but were summarily turned down. The pair was not immediately deterred. They thought they might head west on their own hook. They were soon joined by a third youth, a friend of Rounds named Billy Crowl. He had a job already, clerking with a New York firm, H. B. Chalfin's, but "because he led a rather wild life, was losing the confidence of his employers." Crowl decided to peremptorily leave his job and join his comrades on an adventure that was still uncertain in its details. The trio planned to leave the city the following Saturday, after Crowl drew his final pay.[3]

Money was the immediate impediment. Rock had none and neither did Jackson, whom a pickpocket had robbed. Will soon sold his pocket watch and gold chain for a fraction of their worth. With Jackson's $66 and Crowl's small payday, the young men had enough funds to make their way by rail to Detroit, several thousand miles short of western Montana. Crowl assured his comrades that money lay at their Detroit destination, where he had a sister who would loan them the necessary $150 ticket fare to reach the Far West.

The boys left New York City as planned, purchasing second-class tickets. The train stopped over at Niagara Falls, where the three friends enjoyed the sights, including a tour through the Cave of the Winds. They continued their journey on the Great Western Line, experiencing true "second class" accommodations, riding in boxcars labeled "immigrant cars." These were "common box cars fitted with hard benches," wrote Jackson. "It brought back the troop trains of the war—except that these cars were filled with the blended stench of garlic, bad whisky, and bodies that had never been bathed."[4]

Once in Detroit, the promised infusion of funds from Crowl's sister did not materialize. Billy still claimed to have hope, telling his comrades his father would likely come through with the needed funds. Over the next several days, as Jackson and Rock remained in Detroit, Crowl traveled to see family, but he did not return with any money. Things became desperate—Jackson's lack of a plan was starting to bear bitter fruit—as the young men moved to cheaper hotels and restaurants. Their money finally petered out completely. The destitute Vermonters even pawned some of their clothing. Jackson and Rounds were reduced to panhandling. As he later wrote, "On a snowy night we walked the streets for some time without a penny to pay for lodgings, until finally we interviewed a policeman. He advised us to go to the police station, where the men not only provided cots for the night, but also contributed a little money for our supper."

An immediate reprieve followed this low point. The very next morning Billy Crowl, who had been away for several days, caught up with his comrades with $20 he had finagled from his brother-in-law, plus a rail ticket to Chicago. The excited trio now enjoyed a decent meal, redeemed their clothing at the pawnbroker's, and then, for perhaps the first time, "sat down to plan for the journey ahead of us."[5]

It quickly became clear they still did not have enough money to proceed together to Chicago, their next planned destination. It was soon agreed that since Jackson had ponied up the most money to date, he should take the train to Chicago while the other two comrades would wait for other funds Rock was expecting from back home.

Once in Chicago, Jackson found immediate work as a sign painter for a Mr. Swift, whom Will described later as "not only the slowest of mortals but an old sourpuss besides. Yet I was happy to stick with him until something better should turn up." In the meantime, Jackson had reconnected with a local academic painter named Rawson, who had visited the Mowry studio during Will's employment, and who now provided him with a room to stay in without charge. More than a week later Rounds and Crowl showed up, looking bedraggled, after having ridden the rails to reach Chicago. They came without any funds, as Rock's hoped-for monies had not materialized. For the time being, the trio decided to remain in Chicago—what other choice did they have?—where Jackson continued his work as a sign painter while the other two went to work cutting marble outside the city.[6]

Things began looking up for the three comrades. Paychecks were coming with regularity and money was set aside. Jackson took on a second job teaching a new acquaintance—a young, prosperous man called St. Clair—how to paint, work that extended for three weeks, as the two regularly hit the road in search of landscapes. Jackson soon had funds to buy a train ticket to St. Joseph, Missouri. By then his comrades had purchased their tickets. The three agreed to meet at Quincy, Illinois.

But Will Jackson had finally realized his professional relationship with St. Clair had not proven tenable. He received payment from his client and promptly overspent $8 on a set of two dozen Winsor and Newton watercolors, plus another $3 on a flageolet (a woodwind instrument similar to a modern-day recorder) and an instruction book. (He kept these items for many years.) St. Clair seems to have strung Jackson along, encouraging him to accompany him cross country, perhaps with the intention of opening up an art studio somewhere. Jackson's diary entries seem distracted during these days. He experienced an epiphany on June 6, as he wrote, "Upon this day I was to have been married. Pleasant to think of! An outcast and runaway. Hiding the very fact of my existence from those who hold me dearest."[7] The two men began to quarrel. Jackson even became homesick, writing letters back home. He began painting a color portrait of Caddie based on her daguerreotype. By mid-June, the two men had reached an impasse. St. Clair paid the last he owed to Jackson, then took off with all the paintings he and Jackson had produced. Having managed to free himself from St. Clair, Jackson struck out to rendezvous with his two friends with little money to show for his involvement with the mysterious St. Clair.

William took a steam packet downriver and soon met his comrades, who were waiting for him. The old gang was back together, but money was still a problem. After purchasing their tickets, they pooled their funds, which totaled $3.50. Prior to their departure from Quincy, the boys slept on the station's benches and took food as they could find it. It was a relief when they finally boarded the train, one pulled by a small, wood-burning engine, and were on their way to St. Joseph. At that time, the western Missouri town marked the farthest advance of the railroad.

Jackson would ultimately create a grand and full-length career based on two specific talents—his ability with a camera and his aesthetic skill with a paintbrush. Yet he was also capable of expressing himself through the written word. His mind always remained acute and capable of recalling great detail. His words also reveal one who was greatly influenced by minute images produced by light flashes and an instinctive awareness of the subtleties of light and dark. Jackson proved talented in all three arenas, including the canvas, the camera, and the cadence of words.

Nearly two months had passed since Jackson had made his momentous decision to abandon Vermont, and they had proven difficult months, indeed. He had impulsively left home and friends—"a large circle and the best I ever knew"—without plans and no sense of direction except to point himself toward the West. He had faced poverty and hunger and difficulties previously unknown to him. It would have been less than surprising if he had at some point during those weeks reconsidered his decision to leave Vermont, but such thoughts gained little real traction. On June 5 he wrote the following in his diary: "I am inclined to think sometimes that it would have been much better had I remained a few months at home so as to have paid off debts & accumulated a little store to travel with. Then again I think, and with reason, that I have taken the best course possible. I should have led a most miserable life in Vermont. Other folks could not but help see what the trouble [was], and the exultation of many with the I told you so & sneers of others would have used me up pretty thoroughly." Instead, Jackson was looking toward a new life in the West. He could not have delineated his future in any detail during those early June days, but the past was passed, and he saw a world of promise in front of him. "It comes hard to leave all the friends I have made in Vermont. . . . They think strangely of my actions I know. I shall never return to that country, unless I can return quite rich or famous. As plain, ordinary Will Jackson, I shall remain out of the sight of all that knew me as the young man that was going to marry C.E. [Caddie Eastman]."[8]

Jackson, Rounds, and Crowl now walked the dusty streets of St. Joseph in search of their opportunity in the West. They found it in a want ad in a local newspaper headlined with the words: "100 TEAMSTERS WANTED."[9] The trio of easterners was not even certain exactly for what the advertisement was trying to solicit. Checking things out, they discovered the "teamsters" sought were bullwhackers, the western equivalent of oxen drivers. The three easterners knew next to nothing about driving oxen, but the advertisement appealed to them. The company drove oxen from Nebraska City—less than one hundred miles north of St. Joseph—to Montana, the very place in the West Jackson, Rounds, and Crowl were intent on reaching. The pay was adequate at $20 a month.

But getting hired was not as simple as it seemed. When the three friends applied at a local employment agency, the hiring agent sized them up as easterners lacking the adequate grit for the job. Jackson wrote later in his diary, "Our tall hats & paper collars went against us very much I know. Our appearance for teamsters was not very favorable."[10] He hired them anyway, as recruitment was going slowly. He informed them they would have to pay the agency's fee of $1.50 each for lining up their employment. This presented an immediate impediment. Between them, the three friends could barely scrape a dollar together. They had spent everything just reaching St. Joseph. They had only three days to come up with the money, as a boat bound for Nebraska City was scheduled to leave at that time.

It seemed unlikely all the tumblers would line up for the trio to find employment as western teamsters. The following day, Jackson, Rounds, and Crowl split up in search of jobs to raise the needed funds. Nothing panned out. The local photographic studios were not hiring, and Rounds could not begin to find stonecutter work out on the treeless Great Plains. Then the unlikely happened. After looking for work, Rounds and Crowl hung around the river docks talking to the locals about their situation. One of the men, a complete stranger to Jackson's pals, pulled them aside and pressed a five dollar note into their hands. Jackson later described this gift as "an act of spontaneous generosity that has been equaled only once in my experience." An hour later the same Good Samaritan—Jackson remembered his name as Smith—gave them a second fiver to buy the necessary provisions and food.[11]

The following day, the three compatriots boarded the Missouri River steamer *Denver*, which they shared with several hundred Mormon emigrants bound for Salt Lake City. Other young recruits anxious to take on the challenges of becoming teamsters were onboard as well, numbering a dozen or so, all assigned to the boat's upper deck so as to remain out of the regular cabins occupied by the large number of Mormons. Nebraska was a sweltering two days upriver. Upon arrival, the bullwhacker recruits met up with an agent who accompanied them to a local hotel, the Cincinnati House, for breakfast. Company men soon distributed the necessary gear to Jackson and the others. "I got a pair of blankets, raincoat, shoes, a Colt's revolver, cartridges, and some other things," wrote Jackson, "amounting in all to about forty dollars, which was charged against my wage account."[12] With a monthly pay of $20, this meant Jackson and his friends would work two months just to break even.

The three comrades had signed up with a wagon outfit operated by a Matt Ryan of Nebraska City consisting of twenty-five Jackson wagons, each requiring six yoke of oxen or a dozen per wagon. This was the standard number of wagons for a "bull outfit," plus a mess wagon. Such a train could represent a significant investment, amounting to between $18,000 and $20,000. A wagon boss might receive the princely sum of $75 to lead such a mass of wagons, oxen, and men. Teamsters, or bullwhackers, were paid in the ballpark of $20 to $25. In addition, the bullwhackers were provided daily rations at a cost to the company of fifty cents daily per man.

The freight wagon train was bound for Virginia City, Montana, with each wagon loaded with up to eight thousand pounds of foodstuffs and alcohol. The young recruits were informed they would drive the oxen along the Oregon Trail, perhaps to Salt Lake City, in case the Powder River route proved too dangerous due to hostile Indians. Each wagon would move under the direction of a single teamster, who would be responsible for driving the oxen; maintaining them and the vehicle; and making certain their wagon and teams made progress, crossed rivers safely, and saw their cargoes finally to their appointed destinations.

Ryan was the owner, but the freight wagon boss was Ed Owens. Before leaving Nebraska, Jackson sketched a portrait of Owens, who bears a vague resemblance to an early version of Buffalo Bill, complete with long wavy hair, a full goatee, and a broad-brimmed hat similar to a sombrero. The pencil sketch features clean lines, and Owens's piercing eyes seem to scan a distant horizon for trouble. Jackson found him to be one of the most patient of men, one who even avoided profanity.

The wagon master provided the expertise needed for the trail and the leadership hub necessary for a successful westbound wagon train whose purpose was to deliver necessary freight to distant outposts by driving cantankerous, mealy nosed oxen. Owens rode at the head of the caravan either on a horse or a mule. He was a figure everyone relied on and few challenged.

The wagons were prepared to leave Nebraska City the following day, and Jackson and his fellow greenhorns were soon learning their job in real time. These young men were becoming what their trail names implied. To men on the western plains in the mid-nineteenth century, an ox, which is a castrated bull, still retained the name "bull." Thus, those who drove oxen were referred to as bullwhackers. Jackson's fellow bullwhackers represented a cross-section of men of previous experiences. Many were former Union soldiers, young for the most part, although their ranks also included four or five older, seasoned veterans of the trail, who had taken up the hard life on the Plains years earlier. For them, this was not their first wagon train going west. Most of the men had never even seen an ox-drawn wagon, much less driven one. They came from back East, hailing from Pennsylvania, Ohio, Indiana, Illinois, and obviously Vermont. Some had spent years working in offices; some had worked in the river trade along the Missouri or Mississippi Rivers. One of their number was a French Canadian. In Jackson's words, "We were a Foreign Legion in miniature."[13]

Every man had his wagon and oxen to tend to by day. Days began early, the dawn just winking its own eyes open, with a loud cry, "Roll out! Roll out! The bulls are coming!" Soon the men understood the day was crashing upon them, as the entire encampment came to life. Within minutes the bulls—more than three hundred in number—were driven into the interior of circled wagons and the yoking began. Each teamster came to know his own dozen bulls and brought them together two by two, with yokes and chains firmly in place. In time, it became commonplace for this entire process to take less than an hour to complete. On the first morning, for Jackson and his fellow neophytes of the trail, the process of wrangling, yoking, and linking to the wagons took eight hours.

Each passing day provided its own lessons. Not only were the men green, but so were their animals. Jackson wrote of these early days, "What with contrary and unbroken steers, who gee when they should haw, and disregard entirely the whoa, jamming right ahead and getting mixed up with other teams to the exasperation of other drivers, one begins to think he is earning more than twenty dollars a month and his grub."[14] Jackson struggled to learn the ropes. Everything was unknown, and it was all unfolding in a new place, a West he barely understood. "I was completely discouraged two or three times," he wrote of his first days on the trail, "& would have given up entirely had there been any such thing, but there was not & the only way was to go ahead." On July 2, his heart led him to "scratch off a hasty note to C. [Caddie]." Even after putting a thousand miles between himself and his former fiancée, Jackson still seemingly had hopes of some sort of reconciliation. It was a letter for which he never received a reply other than silence.[15] He admitted in his diary entry that day, "I have made a fool of myself by not going back or at least by going farther West."[16]

Initially the wagon train made only one drive across the plains a day, given the lag time during the morning just to get rigged up and underway. But in time they managed two drives a day—with a meal between—covering an average of fifteen miles total. If the train was on the road early enough, the entire outfit might stop around 10:00 a.m., with the oxen unyoked and a meal taken, often the first of the day. (The men could sometimes scrounge a bit of cold bread and bacon from the cook wagon early in the morning, but that was a matter of catch-as-catch-could.) The teamsters were divided into four messes, with each bullwhacker rotating various duties. Cooks might bake loaves of bread in large Dutch ovens, prepare several gallons of coffee—the requisite trail drink—and slice up long, thick slabs of bacon. A cook shouted "Grub pile!" and the anxious, hungry young men lined up with tin cups and plates. Each then looked for any available shade where he might eat and engage in a half hour of restive meditation.

Then the oxen were once again yoked and chained to the wagons, and the whole outfit creaked forward for the afternoon run. This half of the day often did not end until close to or even after darkness had fallen. Evening fires were a must. Wood was often scarce, and then buffalo chips became the fuel. Plains bison herds squeezed out these round piles almost everywhere and, in dried form—the modern-day equivalent of dried grass beneath one's lawn mower—they made good fires, hot enough to cook food. Bullwhackers anticipating the need for buffalo chips often hung gunnysacks on the sides of their wagons and collected them as they found them.

Bullwhackers such as Jackson faced trials each day, but at least the Nebraska roads they crossed were not an impediment. Jackson noted that "the roads in eastern Nebraska were excellent," adding that he "never saw finer ones, broad, level, and smooth, and yet entirely unimproved." Onward they drove their wagons along the Great Medicine Road. After two weeks they reached the Platte River Valley and Fort Kearny, on July 11.

As the wagon train moved farther west, the specter of Indians on the trail raised its head. These young men were not only inexperienced bullwhackers, they knew next to nothing about Native Americans, other than what they might have read in books or newspapers. Before arriving at Fort Kearny, the party had its first encounter with a band of Otoe, which devolved into a confrontation between Billy and one warrior over tobacco. While some of the boys saw the event as humorous, wagon master Owens would have none of it. He called his men together and gave them the lesson many had failed to realize. Again, in Jackson's words, "Owens looked at us for a long moment before he spoke. 'Indians don't drop by in this country for a cup of tea, gentlemen. That's one reason why we've got a stand of carbines with us. Never forget it, never forget it!'"[17]

He explained to his men how, while Crowl and the Otoe had tussled over tobacco, a second Otoe warrior had been encircling the camp on his horse, taking a count of the men.

By the time the wagon train passed Fort Kearny, Jackson considered himself a veteran of the western trail and a "full-fledged bullwhacker." He knew his twelve bulls and had broken them to the point of near docility. His biggest challenge was just keeping pace with the other two dozen wagons in the train. Climbing hills taxed the oxen, and Jackson made liberal use of his whip, the "whacking" part of bullwhacking. The whips were large, extending out twenty feet, "with a strip of buckskin as a popper at the end of the lash, and with a stock, or handle, some twenty-five or thirty inches in length." Learning how to sling the whip to create a popping sound "like the report of a pistol" became the pride of every new bullwhacker, including Jackson. Putting the whip to good use, especially on a bull that seemed reluctant to pull his weight, as a motivation tool usually did the trick, making "him hump up and almost go through his yoke."[18] Jackson also used his voice to encourage the bulls, leading him and many of the other bullwhackers to become hoarse early on the trail.

West of Fort Kearny, the road took on a new challenge. In the summer of 1866 rumors flew within the fort grounds of hostile Indians ahead. This led the fort's commander to issue a regulation requiring all freight wagon trains passing along the Platte Valley to include no fewer than thirty wagons, and every man was required to be well-armed. Jackson notes in his autobiography, "I had a Colt's revolver and also a Spencer carbine and was therefore 'well heeled.'" Owens's train was supplemented with ten additional wagons in need of an escort.[19]

The augmented wagon train crossed the South Platte River about three miles north of Julesburg, Nebraska, on July 24. Crossing a river could entail significant preparation, given the dangers and difficulties of oxen wading through the unstable bottoms consisting of "shifty quicksand." Wagon teams were sometimes doubled up to eighteen yoke each. During such crossings "the cattle were excited and reluctant to enter the water," wrote Jackson, "and when we got them in, it was difficult to make them string out and pull, as they should."[20] The South Platte crossing took two days to complete given the required recrossings to fetch each remaining wagon. In the midst of the crossing, approximately fifty Cheyenne Indians showed up, "big braves on little horses, squaws leading the pack ponies, dogs and papooses perched on top, and other juveniles paddling along in nature's garb only."[21] Jackson describes a crowded scene involving bullwhackers, hundreds of animals, soldiers, and Indians. At the end of the first day of crossings, Jackson was dressed only in a wet shirt, with the rest of his clothes on the opposite bank in a wagon. He and others managed to make a fire from the remains of a broken ox yoke and prepared a meal, with a thunderstorm threatening in the wings. He had just laid himself down beneath a buffalo robe inside a wagon when the storm unleashed with pounding hail, followed by incessant thunder and lightning that crackled straight overhead.

The rain came and went, and the caravan continued on with no significant mishaps, although such perishable commodities as sugar and flour were shifted to the top of wagon loads to avoid water exposure. They followed the North Platte to the northwest, as small bands of Indians passed them heading east. All along the way, Jackson found time to take up his pencils and pens and sketch the scenes unfolding before him. Notable mile markers along the trail—Courthouse Rock, Chimney Rock, Scotts Bluff—drew his attention. "We were now in a new and exciting country," Jackson observed. "The rolling plains and rounded ridges had given way to high bluffs and sharply chiseled buttes. The yellows were turning into reds and saffron, while the blues were becoming deep purples. And the air was so clear that the highlands to the west seemed almost within grasp. What deception!"[22]

Jackson was responding to his new western environment with the eyes of an easterner. He had not yet discovered the true sweep of the land that stretched widely out before him in every direction. Back east, vistas were largely limited, shrouded by great forests that stunted landscapes. Out in western Nebraska and eastern Wyoming, everything turned panoramic, environs where distance lost its limits. Rock formations spotted in the distance might still be days away for a slow moving, ox-drawn caravan. But Jackson still tried to capture some of the West's beauty and wonder and limitless horizons. He utilized his art as he did his words. He was passing through a world new to him, but so wild and exciting, he did not want to forget what he saw. His sketches provided a means of remembrance, his diaries another. He drew the land as the land drew him in. And each passing mile altered his view. Writing of the wagon train's approach toward Scotts Bluff in western Nebraska—situated just miles from the eastern Wyoming border—he saw something new every day. His imagination led him to see distant bluffs as "some fabulous city out of the *Arabian Nights*."[23]

Once beyond the bluffs, Jackson faced a near-death experience. Following the narrow road on the downslope toward Fort Mitchell, his bulls began to gallop too fast, causing the back portion of his wagon—the "back action"—to begin to slide off, threatening the wagon and the animals, as well as Will, who was trapped between the wagon and the rim of the canyon. Frantically, he swung and snapped his whip as never before. Somehow the animals grunted forward and pulled the wagon back to safety.

The caravan reached Scotts Bluff on August 3. The following day they encamped near a ranch along Horseshoe Creek, where they saw a large encampment of Indian tepees. Three days after passing through Scotts Bluff, the wagon train party reached Cooley's Ranch, where the wagon train was met by one of its owners, a man named Everhardy, who inspected the wagons, animals, and men. He culled out approximately one hundred of the most worn-out oxen and replaced them with new stock he had just driven up from Texas. This was designed to help the herd continue to make good progress on the trail, but "the immediate result was almost a repetition of our first days out of Nebraska City." The young men were now seasoned bullwhackers, who once again were wrangling frisky, unbroken animals.[24]

On August 7 the wagon train rolled into Fort Laramie, one of the most important way stations on that leg of the Oregon Trail. Earlier wagon trains of emigrants marked the fort's location as one-third of the distance from St. Joseph to Oregon or California. Jackson writes little about the fort in his autobiographies. He came to the outpost excited, knowing letters from home might be waiting for him. Jackson found several, postmarked from Troy, Rutland, and Burlington. He "became so absorbed in them—my first mail since leaving the Middle West—that I hardly noticed the fort."[25] One disappointment was the absence of a letter from Caddie. Jackson did take note of a Mormon immigrant train encamped near the fort of three or four hundred pioneers including English, Danes, and Norwegians. "Each little family group had its own fire," wrote Jackson, "making a lively and interesting scene, particularly at night, when their corral resembles a military bivouac."[26]

Reaching Fort Laramie placed Jackson's wagon caravan within a few days of the spot where the Powder River Road turned north toward Montana. The great draw to the region was gold. Already Montana miners had panned and mined $16 million worth of gold in and around Helena. With the increase in its non-Indian population, Montana was admitted as a US territory in May

1864. The original capital was Bannack, but the capital was soon moved to Virginia City. Helena became the capital in 1875.

Just beyond Fort Laramie, the Owens caravan caught up with another wagon train of bullwhackers that had originated out of St. Joseph. It was one Jackson and his two comrades had applied to join but had been rejected. Local patches of berries, including currants and cherries, soon diverted many of the bullwhackers. Jackson, while taking his turn as cook, made a berry shortcake, which did not turn out exactly as he had hoped. In a portion of one of his diaries (the 1923 version), he wrote, "it was not 'short' at all, in fact the crust resembled a hard baked loaf of bread. Its redeeming merit was in the sweetness of the berries. Rock made a raid on the sugar bags in his wagon and got two or three pounds of fine white sugar which enabled me to give the boys a real treat."[27]

The wagons approached the heart of Lakota country. For years the Lakota had chaffed under the expansion of Anglo-American settlement and exploitation across the lands they claimed as their own. In 1864 the Lakota had assumed control of a portion of the Oregon Trail. They cut telegraphic wires, burned outposts, including stagecoach stations, and spread fear throughout the region. As Jackson's caravan passed along the trail, they witnessed many derelict sod homes and cabins burned out by Lakota warriors.

Despite the Bozeman Trail representing the shortest and easiest route into Montana, the wagon caravan did not veer onto it. Stories of Indian movement and threatening actions rendered the Powder River Road unsafe for a wagon train so small. Only trains consisting of up to three hundred wagons—a rarity on the trail—were considered defensible from Lakota attack. Owens made the decision to remain on the Oregon Trail, a good move considering the Bozeman witnessed a swirl of violent activity just days later as the Lakota chief Red Cloud led an attack on Fort Reno, then under construction. Over the remaining months of August, the trail became known as the "Bloody Bozeman."

Jackson had his own opinions concerning the decision to remain on the Oregon Trail and bypass the shorter but more treacherous Bozeman Trail. He understood why Owens might be inclined to choose the longer path, but Will had reached a point where his judgment was shifting precariously between realities. Out in the distant reaches of frontier Wyoming, he was on the bubble, torn between continuing westward toward an uncertain future or back to the East, where his future was still just as elusive. Events over the following days helped him finally make up his mind.

On August 18 the caravan reached the Platte River Bridge, the only one located on that neck of the Platte. It was a substantial structure, based on nearly three dozen heavy log piers and stretching nearly a quarter mile across the river. The bridge was operated as a toll crossing, and Owens had to shell out $5 per wagon to use it. West of the bridge, the rugged landscape continued as the wagons passed along the high country east of the Continental Divide. Information passed between wagon trains, including stories of Indian attacks, and each night the wagons were circled and guards placed around the perimeter. Along this leg, the trail was good. Reaching the Sweetwater River, the men found abundant grazing ground and a plethora of buffalo chips to light their campfires. This was fortunate, as the region was nearly devoid of trees, featuring "nothing but sagebrush and willows, except far up in the hills, where there were a few pines beyond reach."[28] Each night brought the lonely, distant cries of wolves and coyotes. There was plenty of game to hunt including antelope, sage hens, and rabbits. The caravan was also running in tandem with a large Mormon wagon train.

Jackson and his fellow bullwhackers began to suffer physically at this point on the trail. Part of their problem was likely their diet, plus the region's arid atmosphere. Will had developed sores in his mouth and on his lips, which he attributed to "the alkali water & the quantity of soda the boys put in their bread." He was suffering from indigestion, unable to eat anything or keep it down. He and a comrade made some flapjacks, which several of the boys enjoyed. Then nine of them agreed to take one hundred pounds of sugar from the wagon freight and hope they would not have to pay for it later. It was a necessary move, Jackson thought, writing, "But I feel as though I must have something of the kind. Just bread & bacon & coffee is rather dry without something to sweeten it."[29]

The decision to raid the sugar supply would prove a mistake. Little happened without Ed Owens knowing about it, and he soon detected the theft of the sugar. The wagon boss informed them they would have to make good on the missing sugar, since all of it was consigned for. Rock became the focus of Owens's wrath. With one hundred pounds pilfered, at a market value on the trail of 75 cents per pound, restoration was beyond Rock's ability to pay. Soon he and another bullwhacker were implicated in the theft. An argument broke out between Owens and the two men. Rock shouted that they would not pay and "that Owens could like it or be damned."[30] The accused bullwhackers then made a fateful decision, which Jackson describes: "The upshot of the matter was that Rock and Gray packed up their goods & left the train. Ed tried to retain their outfit but did not succeed." The wagon train had lost a couple of bullwhackers, and Jackson had lost his best friend in the West. "So departed the first of the Three Musketeers," Jackson penned wistfully in his diary.[31]

At that same time, another problem was developing for the bullwhackers, one that challenged their odds of successfully delivering their wagons to their appointed destinations. Some of the oxen were dying from sheer exhaustion. They were also disappearing due to theft. On Wednesday, August 22, the caravan began the day with between sixty and seventy head of oxen missing. Local ranchers were sometimes the culprits, although catching anyone in the act was difficult. The following day, Jackson entered in his diary, "Oxen still dying. Some of the boys are coming down to 5 yoke & they will come to less before we get through. One ox missing & supposed to have been stolen."[32] That same day the caravan passed near the shadow of Independence Rock, one of the important mile markers on the Oregon Trail. Also, one teamster was struck by lightning and killed that day.

The actual crossing of the Continental Divide almost went unnoticed. The land did not present any obvious change indicating a pass in the Rockies, but rather a wide divide that went on for miles between peaks, "with two solitary buttes to the south, and the Wind River Mountains to the north, whose snow-clad summits were first seen from a point on the Sweetwater sixty miles distant."[33] The first sighting of the Rocky Mountains was on August 27. Since this was high country, the men of the caravan could feel a decided chill in the air. As Jackson recorded in his diary that day, "Their summits were covered with snow & if it were not for that we should not have noticed them."[34]

The shift in the weather proved demonstrable and even permanent. As Jackson observed, "We seemed in the regions of the clouds. As we gained the highest point & came in sight of the snow clad Rockies, a cold westerly wind struck us that seemed more Nov. like than August. The wind blew very hard and we shivered muchly until we arrived at the corral. Taking us so unprepared it seemed very cold indeed."[35] Jackson became concerned over his lack of appropriate clothing. He had nothing to wear but a "thin pair [of] pants, shoes without socks, thin shirt & light coat. May suffer a good deal before I get through."[36] A lack of adequate clothing would create significant problems for Jackson down the road.

Having crossed the Continental Divide, the wagon caravan ascended gradually. But the weather continued to be problematic. As Jackson wrote, "In this . . . land we were experiencing, even in August, a wide swing of the thermometer. From mid-morning until close to sunset we sweated almost as we had on the plains in July; but after dusk and all through the night and early morning the air was biting cold."[37] On August 30 the weather included a heavy sleet storm and sharp air. Fortunately the bullwhackers had picked up several pine logs when they passed St. Mary's Station, which were burned. "Bull chips at their best never sent up a blaze to compare with the fire we had that night," wrote Jackson.[38]

Reaching the Rockies not only shifted the rise and fall of the landscape; it also excited Jackson. He saw new colors and felt the cold air in his lungs. "The road was good and on the down grade now," he wrote. "The air at eight thousand feet was exhilarating. The Wind River Mountains blue-purple and topped with snow, were a splendid sight."[39] The bullwhackers had been in the company of another wagon train—a Mormon train—which put the young teamsters in the proximity of young ladies, whom Jackson described as "charming—at least the two who rode in my wagon were."[40] The presence of Mormon women created something of a problem at river crossings. It was customary for the bullwhackers to strip down to their long shirts by doffing their pants. During one such crossing on September 5 on the Green River, the boys did just that. In Jackson's diary for this date, he later penned the words "Naked legs & Mormon women."

The following day brought Jackson to a different kind of crossroads. Just a few days earlier, Ed Owens had announced to his teamsters that the train would not be going into Salt Lake City. The plan was to reach Fort Bridger and then leave the Oregon Trail. The question of whether the caravan would or would not go as far as the Mormon capital had never been made clear prior to that moment, and the decision disappointed Jackson deeply. It was then he acted as brashly as he had months earlier when he had chosen to leave Vermont, Caddie, and everything he knew. "In a flash," he wrote, "I decided to go to Salt Lake. Montana, goal of my dreams these many months, dissolved into thin air."[41]

Jackson was soon making new plans and involving others in his altered schemes. He managed to convince six or seven other young bullwhackers, including Billy Crowl, to leave the train with him. Why exactly Jackson and his comrades were so intent on continuing on to Salt Lake City is unclear. Jackson even seems uncertain himself, as he wrote, "It was one of those things that no sensible person could ever explain—but then none of us was an intellectual mastodon."[42]

But making a pact to leave the wagon caravan was not the same as informing Ed Owens of the young men's plan to depart at this juncture on the trail. The trail boss, usually calm in nature, did not take the news well. Jackson wrote, "I won an uncontested election as party spokesman, and on the morning of the seventh I stepped up to tell Ed we were leaving. At that our normally mild wagonmaster exploded in all directions. When he had goddamned us all to the deepest hell I waited for the other seven to take their places beside me, but I stood alone, except for Bill Maddern."[43] The others decided to stay with the train rather than face Owens's wrath, but Jackson and Maddern remained firm in their decision. The departure was almost immediate as the train pulled out, leaving the two bullwhackers behind. As with Rock, Jackson never saw Bill Crowl again. He did settle up with one of his comrades before leaving. Back in St. Joseph, a man named Smith—Jackson would refer to him in his diary as "Samaritan Smith"—had given the Three

Musketeers $10 to pay the fee to join the caravan. Now that he was leaving the train, Jackson paid Smith back for his kindness.

In short order, Jackson and Maddern reached a local stage station where they hired themselves out putting up hay for a dollar a day. Their new employer, named Collwell, promised to provide them the means to reach Salt Lake City. The two bullwhackers felt fortunate initially, but over the following three weeks, the work "was as tough as any I've ever done," wrote Jackson. In the end, the Mormon Collwell did not pay their wages but promised to pay them when he was next in Salt Lake City. The pair of rovers never saw the money. Instead, they signed up with another freight wagon train, this one including fourteen wagons, headed for the Mormon capital. Jackson enjoyed the next three weeks splendidly. His new boss, Ed Perry, "was an easy-going wagonmaster" in the mold of Ed Owens, plus the road was good and, as each mile brought them closer to Salt Lake, they ate better than they had in months, including fresh fruits and vegetables, milk, and eggs. The worst part of the trek was, again, the weather, as Jackson observed: "Mid-October suddenly became mid-winter."[44]

The trail alternated from frozen snowfield to ankle-deep mud. The animals and men struggled side by side, as wagons became stuck in the sticky clays of the West. The teamsters harnessed up twenty-four and even thirty-six oxen to single wagons—which included lighter Studebakers rather than heavy Jackson wagons—and still everyone strained. Jackson was soon facing a singular problem. As he had earlier lost his boots somewhere along the trail, he had been reduced to a pair of thin moccasins, which proved entirely unfit for such weather and road conditions. He was miserable, as he noted in his October 15 diary entry: "My feet got so benumbed & senseless that I felt but little pain in them although running over brushwood, snow, stones & such."[45]

Jackson's feet were in the throes of imminent frostbite. He soon lost feeling in them, an alarm bell in its own right. He struggled through a long day battling oxen and the weather, which did not end until 10:00 p.m. By the time he arrived at camp, the fire had gone out. But Will believed this circumstance may have ultimately saved his limbs: "I believe, though, that the lack of fire saved my feet. I have no doubt they were frozen, and had I been able to thaw them rapidly, I might well have lost them."[46]

The following day Jackson was completely spent. His feet were sore and quite swollen, which led him to remain in his wagon. Fortunately the road was a good downgrade that did not require much effort on his part. On the evening of October 18, his new wagon caravan encamped within three or four miles of the Great Salt Lake. "Darkness hid the city from view," Jackson penned in his diary, "but when morning came it was almost as if we had been magically transported while we slept." The wet, cold weather had moved on, and the sun spread out a welcome warmth. Ahead of them "lay the white houses and green trees of Brigham Young and the Latter Day Saints. I felt well again, and I drove my oxen into the city."[47] Jackson had succeeded in reaching the first true goal he had set for himself in the American West.

4

The Golden West, 1867

Jackson and his comrade, Bill Maddern, practically tumbled headlong into Salt Lake City. They entered through Parleys Canyon, a rough, rocky descent featuring sharp canyon turns and steep edges. Will was still less than 100 percent, as his "feet were so sore and swollen from being frostbitten that it was impossible to bear my weight upon them." In the back of a wagon, Jackson endured two days of jostling and pitching while "lying on top of bags of sugar and flour . . . tossed around like corn in a popper."[1] But by the time the caravan reached the Mormon city, Will's feet were recovered adequately enough to allow him to get out and explore the town he had dreamed of seeing. Jackson and Billy Maddern slept until noon the next morning, then received their pay from the wagon master. (The final accounting seemed harsh to Jackson, as his boss docked him $2 for the days he was laid up with frostbitten feet.)

As Jackson had made no real plans after diverting his path from Montana to Salt Lake City, he soon took assessment of his situation, which was not enviable. The trail had worn him and his clothes out. He was barely clothed at all, he wrote in his autobiography: "My coat was the same yellow-black hand-me-down I had got in Detroit; my trousers were so patched and torn that I wore two pairs to avoid arrest for indecent exposure . . . and my hat was recognizable as a head covering only when I had it on." To round out his "man of the road" appearance, Jackson had grown a light red, scraggly beard.[2]

The boys remained in Salt Lake City for two months. They found a cheap apartment, where they slept on the floor since there was no bed, something they had become accustomed to on the trail. The pair found work with a local farmer south of the Mormon capital tearing down one barn and raising a new one. Their employer, a middle-aged Mormon from England named Birch, allowed the boys to eat at his family table along with his three wives and his children. Birch liked having them around, since they could both read. Evenings included one or the other former bullwhacker reading to the family from old issues of the *New York Ledger*. Their time with the Birch family proved a great positive for Jackson and Maddern. The family pulled them into their circle. Evenings often included card games, with neighbors dropping in to share convivial moments. Jackson and Maddern provided accompaniment to sing-alongs, with Will on his flageolet and Billy on his cornet.

Money had proven in constant shortage since the trio of friends had left the East, and it remained so. Jackson and Maddern were working, but their income provided for their basic needs only. Jackson, failing to find more lucrative work in any photographic studio in the Mormon capital, reluctantly wrote a letter to his parents requesting $100, a query he considered "humiliating in the extreme."[3] In time he also penned another important letter. When he arrived in Salt Lake City, Jackson hoped for letters from home. They had shown up ahead of him at Fort Laramie, but Will had altered his plans from heading to Montana and had instead landed in Salt Lake City, so no letters awaited his arrival. Letters he sent home led to other letters reaching him, including one he received on November 4 from James Dyer, a friend who informed Jackson of Caddie's having written to him. The news excited him. But she had sent her missive to Virginia City, so he never received it. He chose to send a letter to her instead. She had responded to his earlier request for a letter but sent it to the wrong destination. His own feelings for her had not dimmed. Still, writing the letter brought him no joy. His November 11 diary entry reveals his frustrations: "Writing that letter to Caddie gave me a real set of blues."[4] He had no idea of her feelings—they had landed in some post office in Virginia City. But he still dreamed of reaching the gold camps of Montana, where he imagined he could accumulate thousands of dollars, his own pile in the West, and return East having found himself, his fortune, and the means to regain Caddie's love.

The men's weeks spent in Salt Lake City were pleasant, if not financially rewarding. Jackson loved to spend time enjoying the surrounding scenery. He found the eastern mountains enticing, writing that they were "very fine and picturesque. Could gaze on them for hours without tiring."[5] He was becoming a man of the West after months spent on western trails being introduced to its broad vistas, rolling prairies, and majestic mountains. But Jackson was still a restless youth in constant motion, uncertain of his future, sometimes even of his immediate tomorrow. While the West was growing on him, he had not yet found a place in it he could call home, despite the warm hospitality of the Birch family.

At some point the Birch family considered Jackson and Maddern proselyte prospects for the Mormon Church. A Brother Scott was brought in to teach them—both young men had been reading Mormon literature—but no conversion took place. As enticing as Salt Lake City had proven, both friends still looked farther west to southern California. As Jackson wrote, "According to all accounts, [California] is a perfect paradise where perpetual summer reigns." The opportunity came in December. His father sent him the $100 Jackson had requested, plus a large box of clothing. Maddern had also received family monies, so the pair of drifters had funds to join a wagon train, not as bullwhackers but as passengers. They shared their final meal with the Birches on December 21, and the three wives packed baskets of food for their visitors, including baked bread for a week, fried beef, molasses, peach preserves, potatoes, onions, beans, and one hundred cookies. The parting was emotional, as Jackson noted, "Bill and I hated to leave that kind family, and I know they all felt a real affection for us."[6]

The leader of the wagon train Jackson and Maddern signed onto was Ed Webb, a heavy drinker—he was a great lover of Mormon wine—but a pleasant sort. (Jackson notes in his autobiography how all the wagon masters in his life were named Ed.) His wife was part of the train and extremely pregnant, the only woman in the caravan, which otherwise included fifteen oxen drivers and six or so passengers. The route the caravan followed out of Salt Lake City ran south-southwest across modern-day Utah near a point where the future states of Utah, Nevada, and Arizona meet. From there the wagons crossed the southern reaches of today's Nevada into southern California and onto a great wasteland known as the Mohave. Los Angeles was the wagon train's ultimate destination, at the end of the caravan's seven-hundred-mile journey.

Heading south across Utah, the caravan reached a chain of Mormon settlements including Provo and Nephi. The trip began on good western roads that cut across the flat bottom of a long-evaporated Pleistocene lake bed, of which the Great Salt Lake was a mere remnant. All along the route, with few responsibilities otherwise, Jackson sketched drawings of the sites, including Utah Lake, framed by mountains, which the party reached on Christmas Eve. By the end of the month they reached Fillmore, which had earlier attempted to become the capital of the territory but had lost out to Salt Lake City at Brigham Young's insistence. The party's celebration of the New Year included drinking, music, and dancing until after midnight.

A few days later the wagon caravan reached Cedar, Utah. (The future national parks Zion and Bryce Canyon are close by, but those areas were largely unknown to non-Indians at that time.) Jackson's January 5 journal entry takes a stab at humor: "The settlement and creek are well named. Everything is red—the earth, the rocks and the water. The adobes that the houses are built of are red. Red cedar is used for wood work and fences. But I am sorry to say that the natives are not (well) read."[7]

On January 8 the party crossed The Rim, which was known among the Mormons as "Dixie." This marked the edge of Mormon civilization. Beyond this boundary, the land was just as nature had fashioned it thousands of years earlier, a desolate, desert environ that offered little comfort for the weary and leery travelers. Jackson described it in stark terms: "Some 8 or 10 miles over the pass [there was] a complete change in scenery. Prickly Pear and Soap Weed became almost as prevalent as the sagebrush was. As we descended into 'Dixie,' everything was as broken & wild as one could imagine. Everything appeared upheaved, torn asunder & burnt to cinders. The rocks were black, scarred & scoriated & the whole surface appeared washed to fragments."[8] This was a desolate landscape dominated by cactus.

Jackson and the caravan's other members met some of the Southern Paiute while passing through the region. Will was impressed more than most, writing in his January 16 diary entry, "Had no sooner stopped than quite a number of Pi-utes crowded into camp, begging, etc. They brought us quite a lot of wood & seemed more industrious than Indians usually are. Little & big, old & young came in [to camp] and we had great times with them, affording a good deal of amusement."[9] Perhaps Jackson felt pity for these remote Native Americans when he traded "an old shirt for a dozen arrows & an old blanket for a good bow."[10]

The train passed out of southern Utah and in a few days entered southern Nevada, following the Virgin River, near the modern-day border with Arizona. By January 17 they entered a desert more desolate than any they had seen so far, the Valley of the Vegas. (Today's Hoover Dam is located nearby.) The Vegas did not offer much comfort, as it was a stream narrow enough a man could leap across it at some spots. But it was water, and ahead of the wagon caravan lay a harsh sandy tableland—the dreaded Mojave Desert. Here the land turned as dry as bleached bone. Jackson describes the vast stretch before them: "The ground was a mixture of sand & gravel that looked as if it had been rolled & packed down hard. The only vegetation was what they called the desert weed[11] & another small plant that is at present leafless & of which I cannot learn the name. Besides these there is not so much as a spear of grass, & that brush is scattered at intervals of a rod or two apart."[12]

It was a land made for no man. No Native American group permanently populated the region, and no towns existed for many miles, Mormon or otherwise. Paiutes were seen passing along the Vegas River, as it was the only water source in the area, but they appeared to be on the move. Any buildings spotted were in ruins, long abandoned adobes left by the Spanish, who had named the region with a sense of irony: Las Vegas, the fertile plain.

Beyond the plain the caravan passed over a short range of hills into southern California, and the Mojave lay ahead of them for the next two hundred miles. In his autobiography (the 1940 version) he refers to the desert with only one sentence, mentioning only "hot red sand," Joshua trees, and thirty-foot-tall cacti. His diary presents greater detail. The Mojave crossing required ten days. Dry streams sometimes mocked the caravan. The occasional springs they encountered sometimes featured warm, sulfuric water. Mornings that might begin cool could then turn hot and windy. Still, Jackson notes some pleasant days, as he marvels at the sublime scenery. The air was so clear he could see far-off vistas in the distance, including Death Valley's Funeral Peak. Evening fires were fueled by desert weed or dead cacti, creating enough prolonged heat to bake bread. Those same evenings brought cooler temperatures and convivial interactions, including "Wills playing on his fiddle & Billy accompanying him on the bones."[13] On January 27 the wagon train entered Cajon Pass, flanked tightly on both sides by the San Gabriel and San Bernardino Mountains. Rainfall had left portions of the pass washed out, and navigating the trail became a challenge.

After negotiating the narrow pass, the wagon train saw its first expanses of green vegetation in several weeks. Things were looking up for the wagon party. They had conquered the challenges of the Mojave, and their path now put them in sight of the lush San Bernardino valley. The party spent the night of the January 28 at Cucamonga Ranch, a farming operation that included two hundred acres of grape vineyards. Jackson notes it was here "where things began to look like civilization once more."[14] The day included too much wine for several of the men in the caravan, for which they were charged $1.50 per gallon.

The next morning, Jackson awoke to the trill of a stagecoach horn "sounding melodious music in the clear morning air."[15] Will had reached the beautiful part of California, and all things seemed sweet and fresh. Five weeks had passed since he and Maddern had left Salt Lake City. The two friends had entered a new world. The air, the birds, the land, the road—everything seemed as pleasant as a June day back East, even though it was late January in the Far West. The reach of Mormon towns ended, and local communities took on a Gentile appearance, including many saloons and taverns. Jackson was "much pleased with the aspect of the country roundabout. Grass was as green as emerald & the plain extended miles off to the base of the mountain. On the plain were large herds of horses, thousands in all." (Jackson could not have known it then, but such a herd of mustangs would soon play a significant role in his future.)

The wagon train rolled into Los Angeles, and the members of the party saw their first view from atop a hill looking down into the southern California town. Jackson describes his first impressions: "The city presented a long line of low, tiled-roofed, adobe dwellings with a few more modern buildings looming up ornamentally out of the general level; the Court House with its cupola, the old Mission and one or two other churches being the most conspicuous."[16] The Los Angeles William Henry Jackson entered in early 1867 could hardly compare with today's vast metropolitan sprawl as the second largest city in the United States. It represented a mere outpost, boasting just over two thousand people during the 1830s. Thirty years later, it had become a multicultural community of Latinos, Anglos, Indians, Chinese, and Europeans. Goods entered Los Angeles through the port of Wilmington, located twenty miles south of town.

As Jackson took in the local sights, he wasted no time heading to the nearby post office in search of mail from home. He was disappointed to find no letters waiting for him. That evening he consoled himself, along with several friends and Ed Webb, at a local tavern called the Café Francais, where the party consumed several bottles of California wine. Jackson was also broke again. As he had done previously when strapped for cash, Jackson sold something, this time his rifle for $18 (he had paid $20 for it in Salt Lake City), but with greenbacks accepted at 75 percent face value, he only retained $13.50 in purchasing power. Depressed by his circumstances—including no letter from Caddie—he bought a ticket to attend the circus that evening.

Jackson and Maddern had crossed the continent and finally arrived in Los Angeles, but this southern California town was not their intended destination. They still had in mind to make their way to San Francisco, by sea if possible. Ed Webb agreed to deliver them to the port of Wilmington, then they were on their own. Wilmington offered very little other than a hotel, the Wells Fargo Office, and a scattering of saloons. The two young wanderers were further disappointed to discover no ships docked at the port and to learn that oceangoing vessels rarely docked there. After checking out another dock site at San Pedro several miles away, they were left with no option but to hoof it to San Francisco. They delayed their departure, though, since they were already out of money. They hung around Ed Webb's wagon station for several days, then headed north, in the company of a new companion named McClellan, having pooled all their funds: $1.57. Their first night on the road they slept near the location of today's Hollywood Bowl, living on little but crackers and cheese. Three days out they reached a ranch eighty miles north of Los Angeles, where they were well received and fed. The owner, Major Gordon, informed the boys of an oxen wagon train up the road that was short of a driver. When they caught up with the caravan, one job opening was all that was available, and Jackson and Maddern let McClellan take it.

The two comrades pushed on with all their earthly belongings slung over their shoulders as they crossed wide stretches of grazing valley land dotted with sage and cacti. In the distance they spotted a large herd of longhorn cattle, which seemed in confused motion and headed straight toward the pair of drifters. Only when they were twenty feet away did the herd veer away from the shouting, coat-waving youths.

The comrades continued on to Twenty Mile Ranch a few miles farther and again became dependent on the kindness of strangers. After receiving a meal, the boys settled in for an evening of conversation with the owners, Mr. and Mrs. Ward, their son Nels, and his wife. With no money and hundreds of miles before them, Jackson impulsively asked if the Wards needed an extra hand. Maddern would have none of it and, once the Wards agreed, Billy returned to the road without his comrade. Over the years, Will and Billy kept tabs on one another and even exchanged a few letters, but they never saw one another again.

The Wards were fellow easterners, hailing from New York originally. They had moved out to California to find their version of paradise and had opened Twenty Mile Ranch as a stage station and roadhouse. Jackson remained in their employ for six weeks, and the ranch proved a kinetic outpost, one where guests and travelers came and went with frequency and at all hours. Beds were constantly changing occupants so that "the house was filled to the rafters, with never less than two persons to a bed."[17] Jackson was just glad to be included in the mix, since he had a job and regular meals. He did odd chores for the Wards, including cutting wood, stoking fires, working with the mule and horse herd, helping stage passengers with their luggage, milking cows, building fences, and shoeing horses. When the family realized Will was an artist, they asked him to sketch portraits, plus a set of drawings depicting their ranch operation. During these weeks of employment, Jackson was saving some money, while his plans became as fluid as ever.

At some point he decided to give up on San Francisco and the mining camps of northern California. But he was ready for yet another change. "By the end of March," he wrote, "I had had enough of playing the part of hostler and general roustabout for the stage station and was impatient to move on again." The West had not delivered an end to Jackson's wanderlust; it seems to have whetted it instead. His wandering had not given him many answers for his future. And the East, after months of separation, seemed as enticing as ever, as he wrote: "My desire to get back east was now growing stronger."[18] In his mind, despite his having put physical distance between his home, family, and Caddie over the preceding months, they had all followed him into the West. His mind's eye could not blot out their presence. For Jackson, "Troy and Burlington, and perhaps even Rutland, would look pretty good again."[19]

Will soon settled up with Mr. Ward and received $33.50 in wages. With San Francisco no longer in his sights, Jackson turned southward to Los Angeles, where he arrived on the last day of March 1867. He took a room at the

United States Hotel, where "Spanish was heard more frequently than English, and it was a motley group of vaqueros, miners, and shopkeepers that crowded the barrooms and lined the long tables at mealtimes."[20] He soon called on the Webbs, from whom he received information regarding a Michigander named Jim Begole, who was raising a team to drive a herd of wild California broncos back east, the very direction that was calling to Jackson. When Will asked Webb about the details, his former wagon master responded: "Better see Jim."[21]

Six miles out of town, Jackson tracked down Begole's encampment but did not find the cowboy in question. "Yes, this is Jim's camp," one of his hands answered Jackson when questioned, "but he is away hunting lost horses. I will try to find him for you."[22] The hand rode off until he vanished from sight, but soon returned with Begole, who gave Jackson two important pieces of information. First, Begole was just another vaquero, not the boss, and second, the boss of the outfit, Sam McGannigan, had not yet made up his mind whether he was going to drive his herd back East or not. Over the next two weeks, Jackson daily returned to check with Jim on the status of the potential drive. Unemployed during those weeks, he spent most of the pay he had received from Webb.

While he waited for McGannigan's decision, Jackson hung around the encampment, learning as much as he could about driving horses, about becoming a vaquero. It was a task for which he was initially no more suited than he had been originally regarding oxen, but he knew he could learn.

For Jackson, driving a herd of wild horses hundreds of miles eastward represented an opportunity, his ticket back to the life he had impetuously left behind. For many young men in the West, working as a cowboy meant independence, the freedom to roam the open range, without social restrictions or family strings. But for Jackson, it represented a means to an end. "All I wanted was three squares a day and transportation in the right direction," he wrote. "The lofty ranges of the West were very fine indeed; but at the moment I longed for the restfulness of the long, low ridges in Vermont called the Green Mountains." During his western travels, Jackson had seen many mountains greater than those he had left behind. But none represented home.[23] The calendar was working against him, as well. April 4 marked his twenty-fourth birthday. Ten days later, he noted the first anniversary of his departure from Burlington and all the arrangements he and Caddie had made for their future together. These were plans he had not replaced with anything tangible in the West. He could only wonder what he might have accomplished if he had remained in Vermont. How would he have advanced himself further in his career? Save for his inexplicable separation from Caddie, he might have imagined a wedding, a happy marriage, and perhaps even a child on the way.

But he had given up all those hopes through a youthful overreaction, and the regret had not only failed to dissipate, it had borne bitter fruit.

Between his birthday and the anniversary of his departure from Burlington, Jackson finally met the elusive Sam McGannigan, a man in his late thirties, who was fairly complacent regarding Will's potential employment and any plans to drive a herd back East. Days passed into weeks as Jackson learned the ropes of working horses. He worked with several vaqueros roping wild horses for shoeing. "As a result," Jackson wrote, "I was dragged all over the corral with much damage to clothes, knuckles, and shins."[24] He learned that the work of a cowboy could be difficult, more so than bullwhacking, and danger was always a possibility. One complicating factor was the fact that various horses were brought together from divergent herds, and clashes between dominant animals could be intense.

The day soon arrived—May 3, 1867—when McGannigan announced the departure of his collected herd for the Missouri River Valley. The herd had accumulated to 150 mustangs and half-breed Morgans. The team of cowboys included McGannigan, Jim Begole, Jackson, and Johnnie, the young wagon driver. After four days heading eastward, the four men met up with another drover, Jim Kellar, a seasoned veteran of the West, who had three hired hands in tow named Dan, John, and Dilly. There was also a Mrs. Kellar, whom Jackson described as "very young and barely intelligent enough to distinguish bright objects."[25]

Jackson was once more on the road, and he was covering ground over which he had already traveled just months earlier. The challenges were more exacting than his westward trek whacking bulls. These horses were wild and unpredictable, plus Jackson was not exactly an experienced mustang wrangler. The previous weeks had offered the equivalent of a crash course, but he still had lessons to learn. One came quickly when, on the first day out, his horse— "a half-broken, bald-faced bay"[26]—went berserk when Jackson's cinch slipped out of place. As the rider dismounted, the animal snorted, tore the rope out of Will's hand, and dashed off into the sagebrush, dragging his saddle across the ground. Others had to catch up with the runaway and rope him in. McGannigan was so angry he fired Jackson on the spot, partially because he thought Will was simply not up to the challenges ahead. The next morning, though, the boss relented and allowed Jackson to stay on, having little choice, since firing Will meant McGannigan would be short a wrangler. In time, Will and his horse became more familiar with each other. As Jackson wrote, he "got along with him very well. A very mean horse though to manage."[27]

The trail became more familiar to Jackson with each passing mile. They arrived at Rancho Cucamonga the first day out and stopped to rest the herd. The most significant difference in passing along this same trail a second time was the weather. January had been a cooler month than May by far. The afternoon heat was oppressive and resting the herd a must. Such breaks gave Jackson some spare time to sketch the surrounding scenery.

Once the cowboys maneuvered the herd through Cajon Pass, they reached the edge of the formidable Mojave Desert. Again, the difference between January and May was like night and day. The passage heading westward had not been that difficult, but now it was early summer, not late winter. Not only was the desert hotter, there were also seasonal sandstorms that rose up occasionally with little warning. Such storms could camouflage the trail and cover over watering holes that were often too few and far between anyway. The trail revealed earlier victims of the desert's destructive reach. J. Ross Browne, a nineteenth-century writer and journalist, described scenes similar to those Jackson and his comrades likely witnessed: "Many indications of the dreadful sufferings of emigrant parties and drovers still mark the road; the wrecks of wagons half covered in the drifting sands, skeletons of horses and mules, and the skulls and bones of many a herd of cattle that perished by thirst on the way, or fell victims to the terrible sand storms that sweep the desert."[28]

Water, or the lack of it, sometimes turned the horses into wilder creatures than normal. The desert did not provide regular watering holes. When the herd finally sniffed out the Mojave River in the distance, "the horses, feverish with thirst . . . stampeded towards it. It was a tight race to keep up with them."[29] His own horse bolted for the river, and Jackson was soon in a maelstrom of frantic horses driven by thirst.

The trail remained rough, and McGannigan proved a harsh taskmaster. The desert was a daily challenge. After three weeks crossing its barren wastes, the cowboys reached the rim of Death Valley. Even though they drove their herd at night, the trail boss pushed them to cover as many as forty miles with only the stars to guide them. This was dangerous work, since the herd could stampede at any moment, and no one could see enough to protect themselves. Also, this relentless pace caused horses to become lame, which meant constant shoeing. Horses turned wilder, and some even died.

After three weeks spent crossing the Mojave, the cowboys and their herd reached the Las Vegas Valley, which offered no respite from the heat. It seemed a godsend when the party arrived at the Rio Virgin, but the river was so swollen from recent storms it created new problems for the men. The stream had risen far beyond its banks and spread out in every direction, hemmed in only by flanking canyon walls, requiring the cowboys to ford the river not just once, but as many as twenty times, crossings the horses often resisted. At one point a cowboy's horse lost its footing, sending the unfortunate rider into the swirling river and nearly drowning him. The weather turned from hot to cold. On May 17, Jackson recorded in his diary: "Great change in weather. Almost freezing. Herders in before daylight, froze out. Wind blew as ever, and the cold made it extremely disagreeable."[30]

By the end of May the horse wranglers entered Mormon country, covering the same route in reverse that Jackson and Maddern had traveled earlier. They passed through Santa Clara with its abundant peach orchards, then St. George, "the capital of southern Mormondom."[31] As had occurred previously on the rugged western trail, Jackson's boots were shot, prompting him to buy a new pair in town. On June 6 the caravan reached Cedar (today's Cedar City) and a trail summit that delivered a snow and sleet storm.

On June 22 the cowboys drove the herd around Salt Lake City, so Jackson had no opportunity to enjoy the Mormon capital one more time. When they reached the Birch farm, though, Will took a quick detour and paid a visit to his previous hosts. He was so disheveled after weeks on the trail, the Birches did not even recognize him initially, but once they realized it was their young friend, they all shared a batch of strawberries together. Beyond Salt Lake City, the wranglers passed into Wyoming, or back "in the States," as Jackson noted.

As the weeks on the trail drifted by, a great drama unfolded—a sexual affair between McGannigan and Mrs. Kellar. Jackson mentions it directly in his May 15 diary entry: "Scandal, big. Sam [McGannigan] has been going it rather steep with Jim's wife. She seems to be a young simple thing & Sam has completely ruined her. Sam has not taken the least precaution to conceal his maneuvers & the matter is familiar to all & completely disgusts us with both parties. Jim can't but hear of it soon &, judging from his disposition & character there'll be a big row."[32] Over the next couple of weeks, the situation became more untenable. McGannigan's behavior became quite overt. He would rendezvous with Kellar's wife at night when her husband was on horse-guard duty. When the Kellar wagon overturned and Mrs. Keller was badly bruised, Sam offered to have her ride in his wagon, which on the surface seemed a kind gesture, but all the other cowboys knew his true motives. It was an untenable situation that was just waiting to explode.

McGannigan worked up an alarm system with his cowboys. On nights Kellar was riding guard over the herd, he would meet up with Mrs. Kellar. Anyone riding with Kellar was told to fire a couple of pistol shots if Kellar started back to camp prematurely. This was to serve as a warning for Sam to clear out from where he was with Mrs. Kellar. Jackson had been so informed as early as June 6 during his turn with Kellar as herd guard. Then, on June 26, things broke open. Jackson and Kellar were once again out guarding the herd. At some point, he informed Will he was headed back to camp to "get a decent night's rest."[33] Jackson had frowned on McGannigan's overt mistreatment of Mrs. Kellar for weeks, so he followed his orders, but only technically. He did fire two pistol shots, but "in the ground so they could not be heard very far."[34] Kellar returned immediately and asked about the shots, and Jackson claimed he had fired at coyotes. As the night was pretty quiet otherwise, Jackson actually went to sleep soon afterward and rose the next morning uncertain whether there had been a confrontation between Kellar and McGannigan or not.

Indeed, there had. Jackson's tactic resulted in Sam not hearing the pistol shots, so Kellar caught him and his wife in a wagon together. An excited scene had unfolded, with shouts and curses, but no exchange of gunfire. Kellar simply took his wife back and then began separating his horses from the general herd. Sam left the camp to avoid Kellar's further wrath. Kellar went on his way with his wife and stock, but the separation was only superficial. Since both parties followed the same trail, they remained in sight of one another. The next day another confrontation unfolded, and this time guns were involved. Jackson had driven a wagon and caught up with Kellar to talk with him. Soon Sam showed up, seemingly ready for a confrontation. Jackson tells what happened next:

> Sam got out his pistol and began loading it ostentatiously. Kellar, observing this, spoke up to the effect that he had as good a pistol and horse and could shoot as straight as any other man. Nothing more was said or done; however, Sam went on with the band [of horses] while I went down to the mill and put some flour on board and followed after. . . . That was about the saddest end to weeks of suspense that anyone could imagine. All the boys felt cheated, and I have wondered ever since about the wild, wild West where men were said to shoot each other at the drop of a hat.[35]

And that was that—no gun battle, no honor redeemed, no payment in blood extracted. Both men simply went their own ways and immediately began putting the sordid chapter behind them. Whether either man had learned a lesson, Jackson never revealed in his diary or later autobiographies. One thing is clear, however. Will had become a man of the West to the point that he had become a part of its very mythology. Someone should have been shot, he thought. This is the way of the West. But instead two men who likely hated one another simply walked away, deciding it was too risky to involve guns in solving their problem.

After the final confrontation between McGannigan and Kellar on June 27, Sam halted his herd and let them roam for a few days to graze. Once back on the trail, McGannigan's outfit reached Fort Bridger on July 1 following more crossings over swollen rivers. Indians were thick at the fort, especially Utes—Jackson refers to them as the "Snakes"—and Shoshones. The cowboys traded with the Indians they encountered. Sam negotiated the purchase of five buffalo robes and a pistol in exchange for a white colt.

That evening, July 1, the men bedded down a mile or more from the fort. The next morning, they all found themselves under siege—from mosquitoes. "Musquitoes!" Jackson wrote in his diary. "O my God! What mosquitoes. They swarmed by millions & tens of millions. They followed you in swarms & as soon as you ceased active hostilities they covered every portion of you. We tried smudges, rolled up in blankets, but the heat was suffocating and they would manage to get in some way, do the best we could. . . . The mosquitoes were a torment all day. My hands are all blotched & swollen, & face & neck ditto." Only when a stiff wind blew in did the men receive any respite from the bloodthirsty insects.[36]

For Jackson, one of the most harrowing moments of the drive took place on July 9 along the banks of the Green River in Wyoming. The river was at full flood stage, an unrelenting torrent of muddy water that spanned a width of three hundred feet. A cable ferry was available, which McGannigan paid for the wagons to cross, but he was intent on saving money and driving the horses through the watery maelstrom. But it was not to be. The cowboys drove the horse herd to the river's edge, but the animals would not cooperate. Finally, Jackson attempted crossing on his horse, hoping the other horses would follow. It proved dangerous, indeed: "As soon as I struck deep water, my horse rolled over backwards, submerging me completely."[37] Given the circumstances, McGannigan had no choice but to reluctantly pay for his herd to be ferried across the uncontrollable river.

Not long afterward, the cowboys crossed over the Continental Divide and passed a couple of stations burned out by Indians. Things became more tense among the wranglers, especially at night when the herd was vulnerable to stampede or simple theft. On July 21 they reached Fort Sanders, where they heard rumors of more Indian attacks. Beyond Cheyenne Pass, at the headwaters of Pole Creek, they spotted more burned out buildings, plus new graves marked with the same message: "Killed by Indians." (Pole Creek would become the site for Cheyenne, Wyoming, in the not-too-distant future.) It is likely such attacks were unfolding due to one primary movement taking place in proximity to the Oregon Trail that summer: the advance of the Union Pacific Railroad's line across Nebraska and Wyoming. Through the late days of July, as the wranglers drove their herd from eastern Wyoming into western Nebraska, they began encountering the advance of a ribbon of steel, "the first signs of advancing civilization," in Jackson's words.[38] Everywhere along their path, the cowboys were met by great gangs of workers, Irish and German, with soldiers providing security. Makeshift tent cities dotted the land like so many Indian tepees they had seen along their way. Jackson observed hundreds of gang workers, all looking about as disheveled as the cowboys themselves. Most were armed with shovels, picks, and sledgehammers. Many were also armed with pistols and rifles.

When the cowboys arrived in Julesburg, in western Nebraska, their horse drive came to an end. From there, McGannigan negotiated with railroad bosses to hire out six rail cars to haul the herd the remaining hundreds of miles to Omaha. The loading was difficult, and many of the animals had to be roped and practically dragged into the cars' confines. The trip to Omaha took two days, and the cowboys were included to keep the animals herded, albeit in a different way than they had during the preceding months across the West. The men were worn out, as were the horses, many of which "looked thin and weak after their ride."[39]

Jackson had participated in two great drives across the American West. He had fled the East in search of a new future for himself. He had vowed not to return to Vermont and those he loved until he had made a success of himself—"I shall never return to that country, unless I can return quite rich or famous"—but during the previous year he had completed a great circuit across the West from the Mississippi River to California and back again and was no richer. He had chosen to bypass the Montana gold camps entirely and instead hired himself out as a low-paid wrangler of oxen and horses. His arrival in Omaha ended his first, great western sojourn with him still as poor as when he had begun it.

5

Progress on the Trail, 1867–1869

$\mathcal{A}$fter the completion of the horse drive, Jackson approached Sam regarding his pay and was immediately disappointed: "On Monday [August 5] I cornered Sam in the town and extracted a $20 bill from him. . . . When I think of his response, even after seventy-three years I can still work up a healthy indignation."[1] He departed McGannigan's company a couple of days later after Sam ordered him to rustle up some breakfast for him. When Jackson refused, a confrontation ensued: "I said that I didn't intend to do anything of the sort, and that if he didn't have enough men of his own to get his breakfast I certainly didn't care if he ate or not. Sam then announced that he was going to make me do it—but just about then I had my valise packed and I walked out without waiting to see how the matter would be settled."[2]

More than once over the previous year, Jackson had been forced to tolerate low wages and similar abuse at the hands of callous bosses. Not everything he experienced during those months had proven negative, of course. He had made friends, even if temporarily, and he had gained valuable experience out West. As he observed in his autobiography, "If I hadn't gone up or down in the world, I had certainly footed over a handsome piece of it by the time I settled down in Omaha."[3] The year 1866–1867 ultimately proved a starting point for years of Jackson's active interaction with the vast reaches of the American frontier, a world that was rapidly receding in the face of the advance of the American republic and the railroad.[4]

In a continuation of his life pattern over the previous year, Jackson immediately took his wages and spent nearly every dime in a matter of days. Reaching Omaha covered with months of trail dust, his clothes were once again in tatters, so he went out and purchased a new outfit for $19.50 and with the remaining two bits went for a shave and a haircut. But, as he noted in his

59

autobiography decades later, "I was a free man."[5] And he didn't have to wait long before he found new employment, a job more suited to his true talents. In Omaha he sought out the proprietors of two photographic studios. One photographer, E. L. Eaton, showed an interest but did not encourage Jackson. The other, Edric Hamilton, made Jackson a generous offer. After Will had worked in the photographer's studio for four weeks on a sliding scale starting at $15 a week and culminating at $25, Hamilton agreed to keep him on permanently "if all went well." In addition, Hamilton provided Jackson with credit at a local hotel for his first week's room and board.

Things did go well. Jackson threw himself into his work, so similar to what he had been performing back in Burlington as a studio man. In a sense, he had returned to his old life, that of a photographer's assistant, after a year's absence, except that he had traded the East for the West and left his fiancée behind in the trade. Jackson came into the Hamilton studio at just the right time. His boss was anxious to sell out and move back to his farm at Sioux City, Iowa. Events moved in that direction with celerity. Once Hamilton was convinced he had hired the right man of experience to take on responsibilities in his studio, he made an offer to Jackson to purchase the business by the fall of 1867. Will was already setting aside a few dollars as he could manage, but he was in no position to buy the business outright.

In the meantime, Jackson wrote letters to his family explaining his new, permanent circumstances—working for Hamilton restored Jackson to the life of a young, aspiring man of business—and asking for capital to buy Hamilton's studio. His father responded positively and agreed to help bankroll his son's ambitions out in prairie Nebraska. There was a catch, though. Jackson had to agree to take on his brother Ed as a partner. Although his younger brother had no experience in the photography business, Jackson had no choice but to agree. By early 1868, it was all settled. Jackson agreed to buy out Hamilton, including two galleries in Omaha. (In time, he bought up Eaton's studio as well.) A sign went up over the main studio's entrance: JACKSON BROTH-ERS, PHOTOGRAPHERS. In short order, Will had returned from the Far West after a year's hiatus; found his niche in Omaha; and become a respectable, aspiring man of business in the frontier community. Not only had he transplanted and practically reinvented himself in this midwestern venue; in doing so, he made a conscious decision to leave Caddie and her memory somewhere in a past that was ever receding from the present.

In deciding to set up shop in Omaha, he had chosen wisely. Its name came from one of the local Indian tribes. The community dated back only twenty years to 1846–1847, when Mormon emigrants crossed the river from Council Bluffs, Iowa, a location first called Miller's Hollow and later Kanesville. Iowans began making further plans for a permanent, non-Indian town on the west side of the Missouri River that would foster development of Council Bluffs. In 1853 a local Iowa businessman, William D. Brown, began operating a river ferry to deliver pioneers headed west on the Oregon Trail. There were already other jumping-off places at the eastern end of the trail— Nebraska City, Westport, St. Joseph (the latter two in Missouri)—but these offered no advantage to Council Bluffs. Later in 1853, Council Bluffs boomers formed the Council Bluffs and Nebraska Ferry Company; bought out Brown; and acquired a steamboat, the *General Marion*, to deliver folks from one side of the river to the other, with most headed west.

The following year, Iowa congressman Bernhart Henn saw to the appointment of a postmaster in the fledgling Nebraska outpost to help develop Omaha. That first postmaster, A. D. Jones—who initially gathered the mail in his hat, as there was no post office yet—was soon laying out streets one hundred feet wide, except one that measured 120 feet across—"Capitol Avenue"—named in hopes of Omaha becoming the state capital, which would help jumpstart the community. A scattering of log cabins popped up, and a newspaper was established that summer, the *Omaha Arrow*. In no time the town included twenty homes, makeshift shacks housing hotels, general stores, and saloons. It did not take long before the child, Omaha, grew larger than the parent, Council Bluffs.

By the early 1860s, with the arrival of the Union Pacific Railroad and its efforts to construct the eastern terminus of the nation's new transcontinental railroad, all bets were off regarding Omaha's future. It soon achieved boomtown status. During the five years preceding the arrival of the Jackson brothers in Omaha, the community had grown from two thousand residents to a burgeoning twelve thousand. The Union Pacific (UP) set up its headquarters in the Herndon House at the southwest corner of Farnum and Ninth Streets. Omaha was the original "Hell on Wheels." With investments pouring in, along with thousands of workers, including European immigrants from Germany and Ireland, the town gained an unsavory reputation. Sawmill hands, iron workers, hammer-wielding rail men, freighters, stevedores, quarry men— they all walked the dusty streets of Omaha on their way to or from the railheads, supporting an urban underbelly of saloons, brothels, and gaming houses. For Jackson, Omaha represented a place of opportunity, somewhere he could reinvent himself and become respectable and sedentary once again. His success came immediately. After taking over Hamilton's operation and buying out his rival Eaton, for the moment he was the town's sole photographer. By early 1868 he was a fixture in the frontier community, a professional photographer with an expanding, if local, reputation. Brother Ed ran the office, kept the books, and scheduled appointments. (Jackson's other brother, Fred, also came out to Omaha to work in the studio.) Jackson soon hired a childhood friend, Ira Johnson, to learn the photographic trade. Once Johnson became adept behind the camera, Jackson was "free to take up landscape photography."[6] Perhaps Will's months on the western trail, living almost constantly outdoors, instilled in him a need to remain on the move, in touch with the world around him. "The business paid well enough," Jackson later wrote, "but it was hardly exciting."[7] Restless, Will "was eager to be on the road again and with my camera make a record of what was happening."[8]

The world surrounding Omaha was in a sweeping state of flux. With the advancement of the railroad, technology was driving the future of the Great Plains and beyond. New farms were springing up everywhere, and the non-Indian population grew by thousands with each passing month. At the same time, the world of the Native Americans was ever shrinking, as they lost land and their old ways—the decimation of the buffalo herds by professional hunters was starting to gain traction—dispossessing them of their dignity and culture simultaneously. Jackson was aware of their decline. He could see it firsthand in and around Omaha. In every direction fanning out from the town, Indian tribes could still be reached even within a relatively short hike. South of Omaha were the Osage and Otoe. Farther west, along the Platte River, lived the Pawnee. To the north, the Winnebago made their homes, as did the Omaha nation. All these native peoples lived no more than one hundred miles from Omaha.

Jackson was conscious of the West turning into something else; he became driven to document the cultural and racial shifts before they had been completely removed from view. The technology of photography had come too late to create permanent images—other than artistic versions—of Native Americans who lived in the early nineteenth century and the centuries preceding. But the camera, Jackson's camera, could be utilized to freeze the cultural decline of the Native Americans in his neck of the Great Plains, even if only in two dimensions. His efforts in this regard were not completely altruistic. "[T]here was money there," he wrote, "both for the red man and the photographer. Those Indians would pose for me by the hour for small gifts of cash, or just for tobacco or a knife or an old waistcoat. And I in turn was able to sell the pictures through local outlets and by way of dealers in the East."[9] Both parties could gain from such an arrangement, and many Native Americans gladly did so.

Some Indians came into town often enough for Jackson to make arrangements to photograph them in front of buildings and outside his photographic studio. This was easier for Jackson, since his glass plates had to be processed immediately while still wet. But these photographs seem misplaced and devoid of context. Jackson longed to capture his Indian subjects within their own places in the West, their own villages, in front of tepees, on horseback. To take his camera "on the road," he had to devise a mobile photographic studio:

"To handle this work I devised a traveling dark room, a frame box on a buggy chassis, completely fitted out with water tank, sink, developing pan, and other gear essential to a wet-plate photographer. Soon my one-horse studio . . . ceased to be considered 'bad medicine,' and I was welcomed equally before the tepees of the Poncas and the earthen houses of the Pawnees."[10]

It was all very innovative on his part. His portable dark room included a box measuring 30 by 15 by 12 inches, in which he stored his chemicals and camera equipment. This he could attach to a folding framework covered with a black and yellow calico hood under which he could place his head and shoulders to frame and focus the photograph.

In his book, *William Henry Jackson and the Transformation of the American Landscape* (1988), author Peter B. Hales explains how photographers such as Jackson took pictures in the field and processed them on the fly. With each glass plate, it was a race against time:

> Photographing outdoors in 1868 was a complicated project requiring painstaking work. Jackson was using the then-universal wet-collodion process that required the photographer, working in complete darkness, to transform a sheet of glass and a collection of bottle chemicals into a light-sensitized plate. Once prepared, the plate had to be exposed to light while still tacky, or the light-sensitivity was eradicated. On humid days, one might have twenty minutes or more; on Nebraska summer days, the plates could dry in less than ten minutes, including the exposure, which routinely ran between one-half second and twenty minutes depending on the amount of light and choice of lens opening. Once the exposure was made, almost always with the lens cap used as shutter, the plate had to be immediately developed, or the latent image would disappear as the collodion surface hardened. Plates were developed, fixed, washed, dried over an alcohol lamp, and then varnished to protect the image—all within minutes of the exposure.[11]

Jackson shot pictures of Native Americans hailing from most of the tribes surrounding Omaha, but the Pawnee proved his favorite. He photographed some of his best Indian pictures in their villages, which were not great circles of buffalo hide tepees, but rather substantial multifamily dwellings anchored by four sturdy corner posts and heaped over with sod, houses known as earthen lodges. Jackson took several photographs of their villages, including stereoscopic prints that produced a three-dimensional image when viewed through a special stereopticon. Jackson experimented with his stereo-convertible camera during the summer of 1868. This camera could produce 3½-by-4-inch pairs of matching prints, as well as a 4-by-7-inch single image. (That same summer he also experimented with cameras producing 5-by-8-inch and

La-Roo-Chuck-A-La-Shar (Sun Chief) draped in a painted buffalo robe and wearing a peace medal outside an earthen lodge. National Museum of Natural History. National Anthropological Archives. Photo Lot 176. Item: BAE GN 01285 06250400

6½-by-8½-inch-negatives.) The stereopticon was a new technology at the time, and one that retained its popularity for decades to follow.

Through the year 1868, Jackson produced several portraits of local Indians, including pictures of chiefs, such as La-Roo-Chuck-A-La-Shar. Like so many of Jackson's Native American portraits—he made a life's work of photographing Indians all over the West—it is a poignant capture. Featured at full length, the Indian leader stands looking directly into the camera, grim faced and determined, wrapped in a great hairless buffalo robe, its surface blazoned with dozens of five-pointed stars of various colors. (The photograph is black and white, of course.) His long hair stands out from his proud face. He wears a large medallion, likely a government gift, emblazoned with the profile of one American president or another. The background is crowded with a scattering of earthen lodges that rise from the prairie like igloos fashioned from dirt. He is posing at home, in his village, the place of his prairie identity, a threatened landscape with an uncertain future. It is a scene that in a few short years would be impossible to replicate. In 1876 the Pawnee people were removed from Nebraska and relocated in Oklahoma. Their earthen lodges disappeared, and a new form of earthen house, the soddie, replaced them as non-Indian settlers claimed their land for their expanding farms.

The declining presence of the Native Americans in and around Omaha represented a microcosm of the larger demographic shift accompanying the advancement of non-Indians onto the Great Plains and beyond. The transcontinental railroad was pushing westward from Omaha during Jackson's first years in residence, and this excited him. As he later observed about the development of the West during the nineteenth century, "the main story, and the most thrilling one, was the building of the great transcontinental railroad over the plains and mountains and deserts, along historic trails and through scenes of amazing grandeur. This it was that lured me out again over the old route I had traveled as a bullwhacker and as a vaquero. I was eager to get in picture form some of these scenes and some suggestions of the activities connected with the mighty national enterprise."[12]

If Jackson fostered a personal nostalgia regarding the declining presence and status of the Native Americans on the Great Plains, he was just as intrigued with the success of the railroad and its concomitant encouragement of the nation's reach into the West. The process of laying track had accelerated of late. In July 1866 the UP line had only reached Columbus, Nebraska, about one hundred miles west of Omaha. A year later it had extended a couple of hundred more miles to Julesburg, where Jackson witnessed its arrival. In the meantime, the two railroads, the UP and the Central Pacific (CP), which had been tasked with building the western line toward the east from California, were hurtling toward one another. On January 9, 1869, UP workers laid their one-thousandth mile out of Omaha. By spring both railroads were laying track at their maximum pace, sometimes up to four miles in a single day. (Through a prearranged plan, the UP laid more than eight miles in one special day.) Only tunnel and trestle construction slowed them down.

Eventually the two rival railroads passed one another out in Utah and continued to build parallel lines, since they were paid for each mile of construction. A federally appointed commission had to step in and determine a linking point, Promontory Summit, fifty-six miles west of Ogden, Utah. A date was set for the official connecting of the two rail lines: May 8, 1869. (Ultimately, bad weather pushed the ceremonial linking forward by two days.) Learning the news, Jackson ached to take his traveling darkroom by rail out to photograph the historical event. But he already had other plans he could not cast aside. "There were two very good reasons why I was not present at Promontory Point on May 10, 1869," Jackson later explained. "One was that my business just wasn't big enough to support an expensive junket. The other had to do with Miss Mary Greer of Warren, Ohio."[13] (Jackson's reference to Promontory Point as the meeting site for the two railroad lines is incorrect. The rails actually linked at Promontory Summit. Promontory Point is a peninsula within the Great Salt Lake.)

Jackson met Mary "Mollie" Greer in Omaha just a few months after his arrival in the eastern Nebraska boomtown. She was from Ohio and was visiting her relatives, the John Campbells. Somehow, Jackson put aside his holdover emotions regarding Caddie, his former fiancée, and struck up a serious relationship with this new acquaintance, one as attractive as Caddie, much more available, and seemingly without strings. They soon became engaged and began planning the wedding to take place in Omaha, not her Ohio home. On May 10—the very day the CP and UP were linked ceremoniously with a golden spike—Will and Mollie were married in the Campbells' front parlor, with Bishop Clarkson of the local Episcopal Church officiating. The Jacksons enjoyed their honeymoon cruising the Missouri River down to St. Louis. "We had six days together, six idling days, on a boat that moved little faster than the current, a boat that tied up along the bank each night to avoid shifting sand bars. Six wonderful days on a slow boat! No, there is nothing like a Missouri River steamer."[14]

It was just as well that Jackson enjoyed his time on the river with his new bride, for once they arrived in St. Louis, he packed her onto an eastbound train back to her parents in Ohio. The timing was crucial, for Jackson would not be returning to Omaha to stay the summer anyway. Instead, he took a train back to Omaha with a new photographic commission in his pocket. Given his expanding reputation as the town's leading photographer, the UP, proud and ready to show off its newly completed line to the outside world, hired Jackson to take photos along the route designed to promote the rail-road's accomplishment and entice would-be passengers to buy tickets and take the train out to see the latest technological taming of the West. The deal the UP offered Jackson wasn't enviable. He would not be paid until he returned with photographs in hand, and when payment was finally made, it would not be much. But it offered Jackson an opportunity to return to the West he had tromped across in both directions, as well as to see some additional sights to round out the experience. Despite his newlywed status, he sent his wife to Ohio while he hit the rails for Utah.

He did not go alone. Jackson had taken on a new employee, Arundel Hull, who, like Jackson, was an itinerant photographer who had shown up in Omaha looking for work. Mostly, Jackson took him along to do the heavy lifting, but Hull was a genuine godsend. He came from St. Paul, Minnesota, but had spent 1866 through 1868 photographing out in the western territories of Colorado, Wyoming, and Utah, as well as doing photographic work in Fremont, Nebraska, and Omaha. Not only was he an accomplished photog-rapher, he also knew how to "sell" photographs, both along the various trails he crisscrossed and back in the communities he called home.

In preparation for their western trek, Jackson and Hull packed an incredible amount of equipment amounting to hundreds of pounds. Much of the material consisted of the various chemicals needed to process photo-graphs and in large enough quantities to satisfy their needs. They included two pairs of stereo lenses, a stereoscopic camera, an 8-by-10-inch camera and plate holders, tripods, processing equipment, photographic papers, and a plethora of additional equipment to round out their needs. Even after taking so much equipment and photographic supplies with them, Jackson twice had to order additional materials out West and wait for their delivery by train.

One of the most important decisions Jackson made in planning his pho-tographic excursion into the West was the taking of a stereoscopic camera. In the first generation of photography, pictures could be made in three dif-ferent forms: the daguerreotype, the paper talbotype, and the glass negative. Although Jackson worked in all three mediums by the late 1860s, he was doing most of his work as glass plates.

The stereoscopic approach to photography unfolded over a period of several years. In 1838 Sir Charles Wheatstone cobbled together an experimen-tal camera type he called the "stereoscope." When he invented this device, it was not clear what its practical application might be. In a few more years another advancement was achieved. An early photographer, Antoine Francois Claudet, who began practicing daguerrotypy in London in 1839, was work-ing on taking stereo photographs with the reflecting stereoscope Wheatstone had recently invented. His major obstacle centered on light. Daguerreotypes required light admitted from multiple sides of the camera.

Then, in 1850, an Englishman named Sir William Brewster was working with an earlier Wheatstone camera model featuring two lenses focused on the same object, but at slightly different angles. The point of the device was to replicate the way a pair of human eyes sees the world. Each eye sees something from an ever-so-slightly different angle, and when the two images come together, they create stereoscopic sight. These two combined views create a deeper perspective than one eye alone. The art of the stereoscope was further advanced in 1853 by J. F. Mascher of Philadelphia, who created a folding daguerreotype case with a pair of lenses built into the cover. When the case was opened and the two lenses aimed and sharpened, they could take two daguerreotypes stereoscopically. Initially, this camera type was used for taking portraits only.

Another innovator, Sir David Brewster, built a closed "box" stereoscope, and a model was put on display at the Great Exhibition in London in 1850, a device that so enthralled Queen Victoria and Prince Albert that it generated an interest from the general public. Stereographs of the exhibition's Crystal Palace were snapped up by the thousands. Other experimenters added their own touches to the technology during the years immediately following.

Claudet continued to experiment with stereoscopic photography and managed to patent several innovations, including a stereoscopic viewer, a pocket-sized folding stereoscope, and another model (by 1855) that featured a revolving carousel that held one hundred stereoscopic slides fed by rotation. The 1850s proved the decade that produced truly stereoscopic cameras that worked properly. The best models utilized two lenses placed 2½ inches apart situated on the exact same plane, with a partition placed inside the camera to divide the image being captured into two images, since the device was actually a double camera. The image—the stereograph—produced with such a camera resulted in a print measuring 3½ by 7 inches, which was cut at the dividing line created by the camera's internal partition. The right-hand print was mounted on the left side of a cardboard photo mount, and the left-hand side was mounted on the right, which allowed for correcting the negative's lateral inversion.

Jackson packed up most of the mobile darkroom materials, then traded the one-horse wagon—which could hardly make the trip by rail—for a tent as its replacement. The UP, while not providing funds for the road, did provide Jackson and his associate with free rail passage. The photographers' plan was to pay for their day-to-day expenses by taking photographs of anyone along their way who wanted one: other passengers, railroad workers, residents of the communities through which they passed. They lit out in June from Omaha, and Jackson began retracing his earlier steps, albeit in much more comfort than he had previously experienced. Driving oxen along the trail across Nebraska to the future location of Cheyenne had taken Jackson and his fellow bullwhackers five weeks of grueling work. The train covered the distance between Omaha and Cheyenne in a single day.

Cheyenne was another boomtown, but on a smaller scale than Omaha. It was established as the first primary division point along the line from Omaha and served as the region's section headquarters. Here, Jackson emerged from the train and saw a large, two-story station that he soon photographed. The town was home to the same wildness Jackson had seen earlier in Julesburg—prostitutes, gamblers, saloonkeepers—unsavory men and women who were all citizens of "Hell on Wheels." Before Jackson and Hull's arrival, the army had intervened to bring an end to much of the lawlessness, declaring martial law. But the unruly residents of Cheyenne represented potential customers to Jackson. He did not hesitate to make his way into town to drum up photographic business.

He soon looked up an old acquaintance, John Sumner, a resident of Cheyenne who, along with his wife, had opened up a general store in the bustling frontier town. Sumner made the empty second story of his storefront available to Jackson and Hull to set up as a photographic studio on the fly. They spent their first afternoon in Cheyenne taking pictures of the town, then "went down town and visited one or two of the gambling rooms, and watched a game of faro awhile."[15]

A local soon suggested Jackson should knock on the door of one of the town's brothels, since these working girls seemed to have money at their disposal. "Of all these positively screaming with elegance and refinement, the establishment of Madame Cleveland stood first."[16] On June 24 Jackson and Hull entered Cleveland's swanky parlor to see who might be interested in a photo. At first the girls seemed reluctant, but "I called for a bottle of wine, and soon after they began to show considerable interest in having a picture taken."[17] After another bottle, they were ready to plunk down good money for large pictures and frames. The photographer team took orders by day and processed photos at night. It was an involved process that included floating silvered albumin paper in a bath of silver nitrate, then fuming them with ammonia once dry. Six days spent in Cheyenne produced a profit for Jackson and Hull of $60.[18] Jackson used $10 to purchase an "A" tent for him and his photographic assistant to live in when they left the comfort and safety of their passenger car, plus another $15 or so for additional supplies.

Back on a train headed west, Jackson and Hull managed to network. One passenger, once he became aware he was talking to photographers, was fascinated enough with Jackson's Indian photographs that he purchased all of them, then placed an order for a thousand stereo photographs of Weber Canyon out in Utah, which Jackson had not yet even photographed. (The buyer was certain he could sell the stereo photos as souvenirs to railroad passengers.)

Although the UP did not provide the two photographers with traveling money, Jackson and Hull found the railroad's employees extremely cooperative with their venture. Once the two became known along the line, engineers would regularly stop when requested to allow the photographers the opportunity to take pictures of the sights in which they were most interested. Sometimes railroad men loaned Jackson and Hull handcars so they could proceed along stretches of track at their own pace. They were indulged to the point that the picture men were even allowed to ride on the cowcatcher of Engine No. 143.

In a sense, much of what Jackson was doing with his cameras as he rode the rods across the West was unique, even experimental. Everything was unfolding in real time, as Jackson arrived in a new location each day, sometimes several in the same day. He had to adjust his exposure times to a western sun and an open sky, not the controlled environs of an indoor studio. Exposure times had to be timed to outdoor light, and how long to leave a lens open was sometimes an uncertainty. Jackson wrote, "You prayed every time the lens was uncapped, and no picture was a safe bet until the plate had been developed. . . . Going at it in the open meant labor, patience, and the moral stamina . . . to keep on day after day, in spite of the overexposed and underdeveloped negatives, and without regard to the accidents to cameras and chemicals."[19]

The result of all this cooperation was that Jackson managed to take some superb photographs of the newly completed UP line. From Nebraska across Wyoming and farther into Utah, he took pictures combining the rugged, sublime western landscape, often in conjunction with the rail line, its support facilities and towns, and such structures as great wooden trestles built by rail workers to help level out the way for the advancing rolling stock. He photographed such outposts as Wasatch, Blue Creek, and Uintah. The line had gouged its way through massive canyons and spanned hills and valleys. Jackson understood many of the technicalities about the rail line's construction, but he was also captivated by the expansive scenery of the West, much of which he had previously witnessed during his two trips along the Oregon Trail to and from Utah. Of this he wrote, "Passing through Echo and Weber canyons, I was more than ever impressed with the scenic possibilities for the photographer in those picturesque mountain defiles. After coming out into the Salt Lake Valley, we rode through Ogden, and northward along the majestic Wasatch Range, and thence westward to Corinne." Jackson spent the final days of July in eastern Utah.

He photographed Promontory Summit, where the CP and UP had joined. But the resulting photograph could only muster so much drama. After all, Jackson's arrival was like showing up at a New Year's Eve celebration a day late—most of the excitement of the moment had already come and gone. Little remained at the spot where two engines—the CP's Jupiter and the UP's Engine No. 119—had met nearly cowcatcher to cowcatcher as proud rail workers passed a bottle of alcohol from one engine to the other amid a great crowd of spectators. In Jackson's photo, titled *Promontory Point, Utah, June 31–July 1, 1869*, a blurry stars and stripes flaps in a stiff western breeze atop a telegraph pole marking the spot of the great rail linkage back in early May. The tracks command the scene running off toward a distant mountain range, the iron rails secured to wooden ties of assorted lengths. There is little about the photograph that is either breathtaking or wild. With this picture, Jackson is not photographing the land, but rather a moment in history. In his words, "Although a stretch of empty rail is in itself a dull subject, this particular one had instantly established itself as a popular choice."[20] He is commemorating a day when American technology declared its ascendancy over the West, after having laid thousands of miles of track to the anvil chorus of two million hammer swings.[21]

After leaving Promontory Summit—Jackson continued to identify the location incorrectly as Promontory Point—the two photographers decided to remain a month in the vicinity of the Great Salt Lake Valley, operating many days out of the town of Uintah. From that western hub, they fanned out like the spokes of a wagon wheel to photograph such sights as Weber Canyon and Devil's Gate and its accompanying Devil's Slide, two massive spines of limestone running parallel along a steep hillside ending in Weber Canyon. It was a formation Jackson would photograph several times throughout his long career as a picture maker in the West.

The two photographers arrived in Salt Lake City on July 26 on a Concord stagecoach. (At that time, there were two stage lines running from Uintah to Salt Lake City.) It was a pleasant ride both men enjoyed as they "passed through farming settlements set in the midst of an abundant, ripening harvest."[22] Along the way, a smoky haze obscured some of the surrounding scenery, likely originating from regional forest fires. The boys were "one jump ahead of the sheriff."[23] They were nearly out of funds, a circumstance Jackson was accustomed to from previous experience. He had already ordered a new batch of several chemicals needed to replace his depleted stock but found he did not have the $7 needed to pay at the express office to retrieve his order. They had plenty of exposed negatives representing future orders "to pay for a dozen boxes of chemicals; but we couldn't turn the prints into cash because we lacked the ingredients to do our printing."[24] Only after a rail baggage master named McCoy loaned Jackson the money could the photographers pay for their supplies.

Jackson did make a new acquaintance in the Mormon capital: Charles R. Savage, who operated a photographic studio, Savage and Ottinger. They were Mormon photographers. Savage was one of the photographers at the laying of the final rail linking the CP and UP on May 10. Jackson only spent a half hour with the skilled photographer, but he came away with a greater understanding of the challenges of outdoor photography. He also snagged some much-needed cardboard from Savage for mounting photographs. Ultimately, the two Omaha photographers only spent a single day taking pictures of Salt Lake City's streets and buildings. The hazy smoke plagued them throughout the day. "The light was bad indeed," wrote Jackson. "A smoky yellow haziness that was very unfavorable."[25]

Following their Salt Lake City sojourn, Jackson and Hull returned to Uintah later the same day (while in Salt Lake City, Jackson took advantage of the available fruit, purchasing four dozen apricots at two bits a dozen) and spent several hours that afternoon mounting photographs. He soon delivered his most recent order of pictures to folks in the town and the rail crew that was working close by. Jackson started the day nearly broke but ended it with more than $30. He decided to return to Salt Lake City two days after his previous visit, again taking the stage, but the second and cheaper line. Once in the city, Jackson and Hull paid for lodging at the old Salt Lake House Hotel and tickets for the Salt Lake Theater, where they saw a comedy. The next day, a hot day, the photographer pair lazed around Salt Lake City, sitting in the shade of the hotel porch, eating apricots. By the time Jackson and Hull returned to Uintah, they were once again out of money.

On August 1 they packed up their portable studio and hitched a ride on a railroad handcar offered by local rail workers. They were headed to Echo Canyon. The following day, Jackson and Hull took several photographs of local rail tunnels carved through hillsides, bridges, and rail workers. They pitched their tent at evening near the entrance to Tunnel No. 3. A rainstorm rolled in overnight and nearly obliterated their encampment, tent and all. The next day (August 3), after they had photographed the tunnel, local section men gave them another handcar ride to a local landmark along the rail line, the Thousand Mile Tree, which marked the distance from Omaha.

The following morning the Omaha men once again packed up their equipment and hauled it by hand a couple of miles to Devil's Slide, one of the more dramatic locations along the new transcontinental line. Photographing in the canyon and surrounding environs presented its own set of challenges for Jackson. As he later wrote, "The scenery of Echo and Weber appeared magnificent and will keep me continually perplexed when I come to select views."[26]

Just finding a scenic vantage point from which to immortalize a scene with his camera could prove difficult, dangerous, and exhausting. The scenery inspired Jackson at every turn. Yet his venture in the West was not simply to photograph the ancient landscapes of Wyoming and Utah, but to create black-and-white visuals that framed the advance of the railroad and the sheer labor involved in conquering those landscapes. A pair of photographs stand out from Jackson's shots of Weber Canyon and the outlying region. In the photograph *West Bank of Green River [Wyoming Territory]* Jackson captures a dozen or so rail workers laboring on a steep canyon hillside in an effort to reduce the rock rubble on the surface, loose elements that could collapse and cover the single line of track at the hill's base. The rocky escarpment dwarfs the men, the track, and the rail handcar at the picture's forefront. But there they are, plugging away like ants, putting a finer edge on their efforts to tame a single hill, swinging picks and shovels and commanding the land to remain in place, out of the way of the technological advance of the UP and American civilization.

An even clearer message is found in Jackson's photo *Devil's Gate Bridge [Utah Territory]*. Here, railroad workers cooperate with Jackson as an oil-burning engine, Number 117, is parked on a massive trestle spanning Utah's

In 1869 the Union Pacific Railroad hired Jackson to take photographs along its portion of the newly constructed transcontinental railroad. The location shown here is the Devil's Gate Bridge in Summit County, UT. National Archives ID No. 516645.

Weber River. In front of the engine is a single boxcar—U.P.R.R. 1500—that is preceded by six or seven flat cars. From end to end, the train spans the bridge. Dozens of workers pose on the flats and along the bridge's edge as the river flows swiftly below them, its cascades frozen by Jackson's slow shutter speed. The photo contrasts the ancient and the new, as the rocky hill rises in the background, its perimeter breached by sheer human grit and muscle as iron, wood, and masonry work together to support this train and the many that will soon follow. A single ribbon of telegraph wire stretches across the photograph, signaling one more technology linking East and West.

When the work in both Echo and Weber Canyons was completed, Jackson felt he had accomplished something significant: "Our pictures of the craggy scenes about the Devils Gate turned out the best we had yet made. Everything seems always to work better when the scenery itself is satisfyingly attractive in every respect."[27] All along the rail line, Jackson photographed workers, railroad buildings, and rolling stock, often juxtaposed against mountains, canyons, and along rocky, lonely buttes. But the land was always in the background, providing topographical context. Devil's Slide; Weber Canyon; the Thousand Mile Tree; the reddish-brown formations known as Witches Rocks outside Echo, Utah; Wyoming's Pulpit Rock; and Echo Canyon— Jackson photographed them all and, in doing so, rediscovered places he had passed along in earlier years. Some of these landmarks he would return to many times throughout his life.

On August 23, after two months photographing in Wyoming and Utah, Hull fell sick. When Jackson went into the local town to purchase medicine, he stopped by the post office, where he "found . . . a letter from Ed [Jackson] enclosing one from a NY man who wants 10,000 of our UP views."[28] The letter gave few other details, to Jackson's irritation. The would-be purchaser was Edward Anthony, who owned the largest photographic equipment and supply house in the United States. More to Jackson's advantage, Anthony was the editor of *Anthony's Journal*, his primary venue for selling stereo pictures and other prints. Before Jackson had even returned from his western adventure, his efforts were advancing ahead of him, like news on a telegraph. The resulting contract was just the beginning of William Henry Jackson's becoming one of the nation's foremost and well-known photographers of the West.

In early September Jackson and Hull returned to Salt Lake City, where they checked in at the Salt Lake House; got cleaned up with a shave and a bath; and then bought new town clothes including shirts, collars, and neckties. After a week in the frontier Mormon capital, a local lunchroom proprietor suggested Jackson should accompany him on a fishing trip on the Bear River. The distraction was part of his final days in the Far West that fall. At the end of the month Jackson received another missive from his brother Ed, indicating the Omaha studio needed Will's attention. He left Hull in the field to take the final photographs and soon boarded a train back to Nebraska. "It had been a magnificent summer's outing for me," he later wrote. "And, as continuing sales of those western photographs demonstrated, a profitable venture for Jackson Brothers."[29] Jackson reached Omaha on October 1, carrying with him "the finest assortment of negatives that had yet come out of the West."[30]

6

Old Trail, New Lens, 1870

$\mathscr{T}$he year 1869 was nearly past and along with it, Jackson's latest adventure in the West. Upon his return to Omaha, he found his photographic business in disarray, as he notes, "Business affairs in Omaha required my immediate attention."[1] His brother, Ed, had proven inadequate to the intricacies, both professional and personal, involved in running a photographic studio. Nothing was in order when Jackson returned. The shop's finances had dwindled, as the number of customers had virtually petered out. Jackson did not manage to breathe new life into his business until the following spring and not without cutting personnel. While details are few, sometime during the final months of the year, it appears employees Ira Johnson and Arundel Hull left, as well as Jackson's brother, Fred.

On October 1, Mollie also returned to Omaha from her stay with family in Ohio while Jackson had spent the summer photographing the new UP line. They had been married a mere six days that spring before the UP commission had landed in Jackson's lap. With Jackson's departure westward within days of their wedding, the young couple had not even enjoyed a true honeymoon. With her return, they were finally reunited. They worked together to put the business back on track, and Mollie ultimately proved a loyal and capable helpmeet, one who could run the photographic studio during her husband's future absences. Jackson soon proved restless and began to ponder his next venture beyond the frontier streets of Omaha. The West continued to call him. He and fellow western photographer A. J. Russell had talked about making another trip into the Far West by 1870, but nothing had been decided between them. Jackson remained in Omaha through the spring, with no long-range plans that might deliver him back into the West.

On July 23 a new opportunity walked through the door of Jackson's studio. As Jackson writes: "During July in 1870 Dr. Hayden dropped off at Omaha on his way to join his party, then encamped near Cheyenne awaiting his arrival. He called at my studio during his stay in Omaha, partly for acquaintance' sake."[2] Dr. Ferdinand Vandeveer Hayden and Jackson had run into one another twice previously, the first time in Omaha in early 1869, when the eminent geologist had passed through during his Nebraska Survey days. They had met again the following summer when Jackson and Hull were in Cheyenne doing local photographic work. Jackson was delivering a special order of photographs to Madame Cleveland's brothel when he "was much surprised to see Dr. Hayden come in with some military friends. He acted like a cat in a strange garret."[3] But the famed geologist and western explorer had not entered Jackson's studio merely to engage in a social call, nor was he there as a customer. Rather, he came with a business proposition.

Jackson, throughout his life, remained an admirer of Dr. Ferdinand Hayden. In his second autobiography, published in 1940, Jackson quotes from Alfred Lord Tennyson's poem "Ulysses" to describe the admiration he ultimately gained for Hayden: "To strive, to seek, to find, and not to yield."[4] That summer day in the studio, Hayden once again impressed the photographer. Hayden was just weeks short of his fortieth birthday. He was the director of the US Geological Survey of the Territories, a position he had held for several years. Prior to the Civil War, he had participated in several scientific expeditions into the region of the Upper Missouri.

Hayden was raised in an unstable home marked by poverty. He was probably born illegitimate, and his father was an alcoholic. As a young man, his mother sent him to live with relatives in Ohio, where he came under the supportive guidance of an aunt and uncle who encouraged his education. In 1845 he attended Oberlin College. While at Oberlin he became acquainted with an American geologist, John Strong Newberry, who had connections Hayden needed. Newberry introduced young Hayden to Dr. James Hall, who helped him enter medical school. Following his graduation from Oberlin in 1850, Hayden attended the Medical College at Albany, New York, where he studied under Hall, a well-known geologist and paleontologist. Medical studies at that time sometimes led students into careers in the natural sciences.

Hayden received his medical degree in 1853, but medical practice was not in his future, save for a stint as a doctor during the Civil War. The geology bug had already bitten him, and he soon participated in his first geological expedition under Professor Hall's guidance. Hayden and Fielding Bradford Meek, a paleontologist, went west and explored for fossils in the Dakota Badlands, Hayden's first foray into the far frontier.[5] He ranged west of Fort Pierre, covering ground including the Dakota, Montana, and Wyoming Territories.

Hayden and Meek returned the following year—and the next—and came back with specimens and new information about that particular corner of the unknown West. In 1856–1857, Hayden participated in an expedition into Nebraska Territory under the direction of Gouverneur K. Warren. In time, Hayden became aware of his inability to accept the leadership of such mentors, vowing he would never sign on to an expedition that he did not himself lead.

In 1862 he gained further notoriety with the publication of his work "On the Geology and Natural History of the Upper Missouri" in the *Transactions of the American Philosophical Society*, in which he stated clearly his broader intentions to "lay before the public such full, accurate, and reliable information . . . as will bring from the older states the capital, skill, and enterprise necessary to develop the great natural resources of the country."[6] Hayden saw his mission not simply as a geologist but as a promoter of the exploitation of the resources in the West.

After service in the Civil War as an army surgeon, he gained an appointment as professor of geology and mineralogy at the University of Pennsylvania, which he held for seven years, even though he spent more of his time west of the Mississippi than east. During several of those years, he explored the Nebraska Territory—statehood came in 1867—and several locales in the Rocky Mountains as geologist in charge. Hayden's instructions were to discover the extent of Nebraska's "deposits of ores, coals, clays, marls, peat and such other mineral substances."[7] He discovered very little, save for some iron ore deposits and lignite coal beds near the UP's right-of-way outside Laramie, then part of the Nebraska Territory. When he reported a lack of coal deposits in Nebraska—his news was not what Nebraskans wanted to hear—the state's newspaper editors went after him, calling him a "charlatan and humbug."[8]

During his time in the West, Hayden "was a tireless collector, sometimes working alone in hostile Indian country. He was never known to carry firearms."[9] Being unarmed in the West might have presented a problem for other white men trekking through Indian country, but when the Sioux encountered Hayden, they gave him a pass, naming him by his seemingly odd behavior as "the Man Who Picks Up Stones Running." On one occasion on the Upper Missouri River, as Hayden was exploring alone, a band of hostile Indians encountered him. "Finding him armed only with a hammer, and carrying a bag of fossils," wrote Jackson in his autobiography, "which they emptied out and examined with much surprise and curiosity, they concluded that he was insane and let him alone."[10]

In time Hayden caught the eye of the federal government. Prior to the Civil War, nearly all western exploration was carried out through the US Army's elite Corps of Topographical Engineers. But the army's focus tended to be on missions that defined the young nation's western borders more clearly while seeking out the best trails, routes, and roads to facilitate the movement of Americans into the West. During the decades prior to the 1860s, the Topographical Engineers provided information and support for the advancement of railroads beyond the Trans-Mississippi region. Beginning in 1853 and continuing through 1860, the Corps carried out four large-scale railroad surveys in an effort to determine the best route for a transcontinental rail line. In time, much of the information gathered through these surveys, as well as other western missions, was combined into one large-scale map—on a scale of 1:3,000,000—by Lieutenant Gouverneur K. Warren. Through the Corps' efforts, the West began to lose its mysteries.

But Warren's great map project included pockets of the West that no government men had reached. Following the Civil War, much of the remaining work of eliminating these topographical unknowns slipped away from the military and into civilian hands. Throughout the remainder of the 1860s and into the 1870s the "Great Surveys" took place, led by four highly capable men: John Wesley Powell, Clarence King, Ferdinand Vandeveer Hayden, and George Montague Wheeler.

Between them, these individuals engaged in repeated exploratory surveys that focused on eight western states/territories, including Nebraska, Colorado, Wyoming, Utah, Nevada, California, Arizona, and New Mexico, plus limited work in Montana, Idaho, and Oregon. By the end of the 1870s, there were few places in the West that had not been reached, explored, and mapped.

Facilitating the western activities of scientists such as Ferdinand Hayden was a government agency established in 1867, the United States Geological Survey. An earlier version of the agency had begun under the direction of the General Land Office and served as a western wing of the Department of the Interior. The department recruited scientists such as Hayden, while the War Department hired its own cadre of geologists, cartographers, and paleontologists, which sometimes created artificial rivalries between professionals. During these same years, the Interior Department sponsored another western geologist, John Wesley Powell, who explored Colorado and the Southwest. In the meantime, the War Department employed Clarence King to carry out the US Geological Exploration of the Fortieth Parallel and Lieutenant Wheeler's survey of the one hundredth meridian. After several years of cross-agency rivalry, Powell finally convinced the government to consolidate the work of the two departments into one, creating the United States Geological Survey as it operates today.

By the late 1860s Hayden's western work had gained him an appointment through the federal government's General Land Office, which sponsored and funded additional exploratory surveys. (Here, the word "survey" did not refer to actual surveying and platting of western lands, but rather to a general examination, an exploration of the land.) He and his expedition went west in 1868, exploring the lands of central and southwestern Wyoming Territory, from South Pass, at the southeastern terminus of the Wind River Mountains, to Henry's Fork along the Snake River in present-day Idaho. In 1869 Hayden led a party of explorers, scientists, and military personnel on a survey of the Front Range of the Colorado Rocky Mountains, from Denver to Santa Fe, New Mexico. While his geological findings were limited, he enjoyed his summer immensely, writing, "To the geologist Colorado is almost encyclopedic in its character, containing within its borders nearly every variety of geological formation."[11] During this expedition he established the pattern of organization that set the course for all his later government-sponsored surveys, which included experts who studied all there was to study in nature, including the wildlife, plant varieties, water resources, and mineral deposits. During winter off-seasons, Hayden went to the Smithsonian Institution in Washington, D.C., where he categorized and identified specimens from his bag of rocks and wrote the academic reports that qualified him as one of the nation's preeminent geologists. This was the real reason he stopped in at Jackson's Omaha studio on that July day. His survey plans included cameras, and William Henry Jackson would hopefully agree to serve as his primary cameraman.

During his visit in the photographic studio, Hayden made his pitch to Jackson and offered him a position equal to an unpaid photographic correspondent. The expedition would cover Jackson's expenses, including outfitting him with the appropriate equipment, plus the cost of travel into the West and back again. Although Jackson had only managed to resuscitate his business during the months since his return from his previous western adventure for the UP, he had to make his decision on the fly. With the Hayden party prepared to head out from Cheyenne in a week, the clock was ticking. Virtually on the spot, Jackson made his decision. He would not miss the opportunity to serve under Dr. Hayden, even for the sake of his business.

In his second autobiography Jackson recounts the exact conversation he and Hayden had in his Omaha photographic studio:

On July 23, 1870, Dr. Hayden, on his way to Wyoming, called at my place of business in Omaha. He spent a long time studying my Union Pacific pictures and the Indian groups I had photographed near Omaha. Then, with a sigh, he remarked, "This is what I need. I wish I could offer you enough to make it worth your while to spend the summer with me."

"What could you offer?" I asked quickly.

Dr. Hayden smiled and shook his head.

"Only a summer of hard work—and the satisfaction I think you would find in contributing your art to science. Of course, all your expenses would be paid, but . . ."

At that moment my wife walked into the reception room. Our living quarters were on the floor above the gallery, and she often came in to lend a hand.

"Dr. Hayden has just been outlining his plans for Wyoming," I explained, after introducing him.

"And telling your husband how much I would like to take him with me, Mrs. Jackson," he added emphatically.

Mollie looked at Dr. Hayden for a moment, then at me. Then she laughed—and I knew that everything, so far as she was concerned, was arranged.[12]

In approaching Jackson and inviting him to join his survey into Wyoming, Hayden was sizing up a man he did not yet know with any degree of familiarity. He was aware of Jackson's photographic work, of his photos of local Native Americans and of his efforts on behalf of the UP out West. But he was taking a gamble, one that paid off handsomely in the end. Hayden was an astute judge of the men he selected for his surveys. Rarely did he pick someone who did not live up to his expectations. Hayden would eventually observe that, in picking William Henry Jackson as his primary photographer in 1870, he had rarely chosen a better man for a specific task. He and Jackson ultimately formed a friendship extending through eight years of government-sponsored exploratory surveys and beyond.

Despite Mollie's seeming acceptance of her husband's plans to leave her for another protracted period of time, William felt torn in his decision, one encouraged by the appeal of making yet another foray into the West to ply his art as a photographer. He wrote, "As an adventure, the proposition appealed to me strongly, but I did not at first see how I could profitably undertake it. . . . I had just opened a new gallery. The longer we talked it over, however, the more attractive the Doctor's proposition appeared. Finally, with my wife's consent, I agreed to go with him for the two or three months he planned to be out."[13]

Jackson's decision might appear at first glance one made in boyish haste. It meant leaving Mollie behind, again, to fend for herself and serve as the primary support of the business. The studio, Jackson believed, could function adequately in his absence, which would only be for a matter of months. But Jackson made a business arrangement with Hayden that went far beyond the immediate time he was to spend in the West as an unpaid cameraman. He managed to get the expedition's leader to allow him to retain control, including ownership rights, to all the negatives he produced during the survey. This would pave the way for Jackson to add to his personal and professional collection of photographs, and while he could not charge the survey for their use, he could make a profit off of anyone else who might want to access his work, whether another government office or the public at large. Also, as a member of the survey, Jackson could utilize that connection to facilitate the future sale of his photographs as a sort of seal of approval, giving his work an official legitimacy. That the famous government geologist Dr. Ferdinand Hayden had selected William Jackson as his primary photographer for such an important western mission would give the Jackson name greater cachet. Five days after their meeting in the studio, Jackson "received a letter from Dr. H. bidding me to come in at once."[14]

The train trip took eighteen hours from Omaha across the Nebraska plains portion of the UP line and on into Wyoming. Jackson caught up with the Hayden party at Camp Carlin, the quartermaster's rail depot supplying Fort D. A. Russell outside Cheyenne. At the camp he joined a dozen other eager members of the survey, all living in four-walled tents and supported by eight additional persons including teamsters and cooks. When Jackson arrived, Hayden was still in Denver, but the camp manager, James Stevenson, "took me in hand and soon I was on friendly terms with all." Between making preparations for their departure, several of the survey's members "were eager for photographs showing their camp life to send back home."[15]

In his hasty planning for his trip out West, Jackson had taken little time to rethink his equipment, so he took along the same cameras and supports he had utilized in 1869. Since he was to retain the rights to his photographs, he took his double-barreled stereo setup to facilitate the production of stereoscopic pictures. This required his 6½-by-8½-inch camera, which was adaptable for stereo use. His portable darkroom came along, including a large stock of chemicals and glass plates to produce four hundred images. Altogether, his equipment weighed at least three hundred pounds. Fortunately he was provided with an entire ambulance wagon to haul his complex photographic system along the trail. The 1870 survey did convince Jackson to rethink his equipment for the 1871 foray into the Yellowstone region. To capture the grand vistas of the West on that survey, Jackson went big, taking along a camera that could accommodate 11-by-14-inch glass plates. Before he completed his final survey in the late 1870s, he was lugging an oversized camera capable of capturing scenes on a 20-by-24-inch format.

Gearing up for their trip, Jackson's colleagues wrangled with a great pile of supplies including clothing and tents, scientific equipment, guns, camp chairs, portable tables, storage trunks, and stacks of canned goods. The party received support and much of their equipment from the army headquarters at Cheyenne, Fort D. A. Russell. Several of the horses provided to the expedition's members were "condemned cavalry mounts, but in the main they were fine looking, serviceable animals."[16] Along with these horses, the army provided McClellan saddles, plus a supply of ammunition and some rifles.

Jackson brought along his own Henry rifle, as well as a Remington handgun. The army's regional department commander insisted every member of the party carry firearms, since some of the local Indians were considered hostile. Whether Hayden carried a gun or not is unclear.

Meanwhile, Jackson was busy with his photographic equipment. As he noted in his original autobiography,

> It was no easy task to get my dark box and other equipment into work-ing order and carefully packed. . . . Most of my supplies were carried in an ambulance that accompanied the wagons, but I was given a crop-eared mule to carry my working kit. The little animal was at once named Hypo, a short form of the high-sounding name of a chemical used in photography. From the quartermaster I obtained a pair of parfleches, used commonly by Indians and trappers for carrying their goods on pack horses. . . . In one of these I carried my dark box with the bath holder; in the other a box of equal size containing my camera, glass plates, and chemicals for the day's work. On top, in the space between the boxes, was placed the tripod and a small keg of water to be used for plate washing when I was away from a water supply. When fast riding was the order, the whole pack was lashed securely with a cinch rope.[17]

Before the survey party departed from their initial encampment, Jackson took several photographs of the temporary village of wall tents against a scat-tering of men, some standing alone, some in pairs, while dogs wander about the camp grounds.

Dr. Hayden finally arrived at the survey encampment, along with addi-tional members of the party, a landscape painter from back East, Sanford Robinson Gifford, as well as two additional landscape artists, Worthington Whittredge and John Kensett. Although he had lined up Jackson as a photog-rapher, Hayden intended to document the lands he and his men were soon exploring through the skill of the artists. The inclusion of artists as part of such expeditions and surveys had been a long-standing practice in the West.

On the morning of August 7, 1870, with a cold, freezing rain falling, the survey members broke camp and set out, with Jackson's photographic equip-ment safely stowed away in one of the survey's wagons. The party covered sixteen miles that day and set up camp on Lodge Pole Creek, a tributary of the South Platte River.

The following day opened with the rain gone, replaced by a cloudless sky. Jackson moved some of his photographic equipment to his mule, Hypo. Soon the members of the party fanned out in various directions in search of minerals; river routes; wild game; and in Jackson's case, scenes fit for his camera. In the meantime the wagons were moved ahead to seek out a new campsite. He moved along with Dr. Hayden and a handful of comrades, following Lodge Pole Creek to its origins in the Laramie Range. At several locales, Jackson unpacked his equipment and took some photographs, especially of rock formations that Dr. Hayden pointed out. As the day grew late, Hayden and most of the small party rode out of the hills ahead of Jackson and his photographic assistant. With Hypo carrying sensitive camera equipment, there was little to do but lead the plodding animal along with a halter strap. As the two men and Hypo ambled along, the hours passed without any white tent walls looming in the distance. The sun finally set, and they continued to move under the stars until midnight. Still, they spotted no encampment. Throughout the course of the day, the men had covered a minimum of sixty miles. By 12:30 a.m., Jackson and his comrade "vented their accumulated wrath on those in charge of the wagons . . . and lay down for a supperless sleep during what was left of the night."[18] Come the dawn, they were on their way west once again and soon reached their comrades, encamped less than two miles farther along. At least they arrived in time for breakfast.

The men of the Hayden Survey continued westward, on to Laramie, then northward through today's Medicine Bow National Forest until they arrived at Fort Fetterman, near Red Butte, where they crossed the North Platte. They moved on until they camped near a hill just beyond modern-day Casper, Wyoming. The evening was punctuated by an Indian scare, prompting the men to grab their guns in defense, only to face a bear that emerged from bushes close by.

During the days ahead, as the party approached the Sweetwater River, they spotted bison. When Jackson and Gifford the artist tried to bring down a bull buffalo with their rifles, their aim was off, and the animal escaped. Then they encountered a herd of three dozen or so, but the animals "got [our] scent and were on the run before we could get near enough for a shot."[19] In time they finally succeeded in chasing down a bison while on horseback, firing their pistols into the stampeding animal. Other members of the party killed two additional bison. They slaughtered their kill for the meat—using little more than pocket knives—then removed the hides, heads, and important bones to be sent back to the Smithsonian Institution for future mounting. They made camp at Independence Rock, one of the more important mile markers on the old Oregon Trail, named by pioneers who anticipated the necessity of reaching the two-hundred-foot-tall outcropping by the Fourth of July on their journey west. Jackson took several photographs at this location. He found the slope of the famous granite mass so gradual on one side that he led Hypo to its summit. As he worked, the geologists took local rock samples.

Jackson's photographs include views focusing both inward and outward. He was careful to document not only the Wyoming West and its wide vistas, but also pictures that showed the survey's men, tents, wagons, and pack animals. Four days after departing from Cheyenne, he produced a print of their tented encampment against a vast sky spangled with clouds. In another photo, he focused his tripod-based camera toward Hypo and produced a picture of the animal fully burdened with Jackson's photographic equipment.

The party continued along the old Oregon-Mormon Trail as it followed the Sweetwater and soon reached South Pass, the wide valley in the Rockies used by earlier pioneers to cross over the Continental Divide. They saw signs of this earlier era of wagon wheels going west, as Jackson observed, "They had left a trail worn deep in the gravel, sand, and rocks, which we followed for many days." Jackson was reminded of adventures from his youth, noting "the old trail was not new to me, for I had walked along many miles of it."[20]

As they pressed on, they passed the same sites Oregon Trail pioneers had looked for on their way to California or Oregon. They reached the Devil's Gate, the great gorge where the Sweetwater runs through, then Split Rock, then Three Crossings, where they "found one of the few remaining Overland stage and telegraph stations," since most had been abandoned previously due to Indian attacks.[21] The bison evaporated along the survey's path but were replaced by great herds of antelope, shy animals that tried to remain a safe distance from the ambling party of men and wagons. Hunters bagged sage hens, which proved succulent. Nights were spent in encampments seemingly surrounded by coyotes that "kept up their yelling serenades as usual, especially in the early morning."[22]

The party reached the summit of South Pass at an elevation of seven thousand feet, having crossed the Continental Divide, then continued on to the mining community of Atlantic City, nestled in a valley between several low-lying peaks. Nearby was Camp Stambaugh, an army outpost where they camped as "the officers of the post gave us a cordial reception, entertaining us at a lunch and otherwise doing the honors in a hospitable way."[23] A band of Shoshone Indians, under the leadership of Chief Washakie, was encamped in seventy tepees nearby, to Hayden's delight, for he "was anxious to have as many photographs as possible of the Indians."[24] On September 3 Jackson took a group photograph against a tepee backdrop of three dozen Shoshone men, women, and children. According to Jackson, once Washakie agreed to have his photo taken, many of his people agreed as well.

Next, members of the survey trudged for two days across the foothills of the Wind River Mountains. Jackson's horse went lame from a pebble embedded between its hoof and shoe, so he transferred his saddle to Hypo. In time, the little mule bolted when frightened, leading him to engage in a fit of bucking, resulting in the cinch coming loose and Jackson being thrown, resulting in "getting so hard a fall that I had to ride in the ambulance the rest of the day."[25]

As they continued on, the survey members headed into the Bad Lands of southwestern Wyoming, then to Church Buttes, a well-remembered mile marker on the Old Oregon Trail. In this area, the geologists made great finds, loading into a wagon "ancient turtles, shellfish, and other creatures that lived in the great inland sea that once covered this section of the country."[26] Here Jackson took seventeen negatives in a single day, a significant number to produce in the field at that time. Soon they arrived at Fort Bridger, situated along the Blacks Fork River, not far from the Utah border near today's Interstate 80. Here was another famed stop along the Oregon Trail popular among westward emigrants of the 1840s and 1850s. At this point on the trail, the survey members had covered a great geographic arc from Cheyenne to Casper to Church Buttes.

The trail had proven hard on Jackson's delicate photographic equipment, and at Fort Bridger he examined his outfit for issues. Taking his wet plate photographs often required Jackson to clamber over rough terrain, including scaling rugged heights, all to achieve the best vantage point to produce well-framed pictures. His dark box was in poor condition, and he had the fort's carpenter make him a new one. With Salt Lake City to the southwest, some members of the party took a quick side excursion to the Mormon settlement for supplies. It was here that Sanford Gifford, Jackson's de facto assistant, left the party to go back East. Jackson was "sorry to have him go, for he had been a constant companion on all our photographic side trips."[27]

The sutler at Fort Bridger, "Judge" W. A. Carter, agreed to lead a portion of the party into the Uinta Mountains to the south, and the contingent left the fort on September 16 despite a wind-driven sleet storm, which made the excursion difficult. By early evening they reached an abandoned sawmill, where they encamped and built great fires to take the edge off the foul weather. While there, Jackson and the survey's meteorologist, John H. Beaman, continued work on the photographic dark box Jackson desperately needed to continue his work. With all things finally repaired and in working order, Jackson took a photograph on September 18 of the distant Uinta Mountains, a panoramic view of the far-off peaks, spattered with snow, a hard ridge line bisecting the photo at closer range. In the foreground the wind-battered remains of a tree stand off to the viewer's left. The photograph represents Jackson setting a tone, delivering a portrait of a sweeping western vista, unspoiled by man, daunting in lonely scale. That evening the party encamped in a grove of aspens, and the grounds were dubbed Camp Jackson in the photographer's honor.

Hayden's men remained in the vicinity of the high Uintas for several weeks. Sometimes just moving through the high country proved difficult. Judge Carter led the party to a beautiful lake at the top of a mountain. Jackson observed that the scenery was worth the difficulties of the mountainous trek, as he found "the splendid scenes of the lake and of the Uintas were ample compensation for the day's effort."[28] As Jackson spent his days taking photographs of grand vistas and mountain ranges, the geologists were constantly making discoveries less obvious to the untrained eye. As the weeks passed, they continually added to their collection of ancient fossils, including crustaceans and bivalves deposited eons earlier, until they had a wagonful.

The higher elevations—the party was camping at an altitude of between eleven thousand and twelve thousand feet—ultimately may have been rewarding, but they presented unique problems. The survey's chief cook, "Potato John" Raymond, a great tower of a man (six foot four), leathery and thin, gained his nickname from his repeated attempts to boil potatoes at such elevations. Since the temperature of boiling water is lower at higher elevations than at sea level, it proved nearly impossible to cook potatoes to a soft, edible consistency.

After weeks spent with the Uintas always in sight, Hayden's Survey members returned, by way of the Green River, back to the main base camp at Fort Bridger and the lands surrounding the Blacks Fork River along the Utah border. Often Jackson knew he was retracing his steps on the Old Overland Trail along which he had herded mustangs in 1867.

Yet another side excursion followed, this time along the Blacks Fork River, then Henrys Fork and back to the Green River to the location of Flaming Gorge. Forty-five years had passed since the first known white man, former military officer and fur trapper William H. Ashley, and his comrades had reached it by way of the Green River. Ashley described the difficulties of passing through the deep canyon: "We proceeded down the river which is closely confined between two very high mountains. . . . The rocks that fall in the river from the walls of the mountain make the passage in some places dangerous."[29] Just a year before Hayden's Survey arrived at the gorge, another western explorer with government backing, John Wesley Powell, had reached the canyon in the opening days of his 1869 triumphant voyage of discovery along the full length of the Colorado River and observed the "flaring, brilliant, red gorge, that may be seen from the north a score of miles away."[30] Jackson took a wet plate of a portion of the gorge, and he described the canyon with awe as a place "of great beauty, [that] . . . derives its principal charm from the vivid coloring. The waters of the river are of purest emerald, with banks and sandbars of glistening white. The perpendicular bluff to the left is . . . of a bright red and yellow. When illuminated by full sunlight, it readily suggests the title given to it. It is the entrance or gateway to still greater wonders and grandeurs of the famous Red Canon, that cuts its way to a depth of 3,000 feet between this point and its entrance into Brown's Hole."[31]

Upon their arrival at Brown's Hole, a side trip that took three days, Jackson and his comrades found the grounds thick with cattle, as the location was already being utilized as a winter grazing ground. During their encampment at Brown's, they "saw some thousands of them being driven in from ranges farther east."[32]

Throughout the weeks of Hayden's Survey across Wyoming in 1870, Jackson and others were reminded that the reach of the far western frontier was already shrinking. Eight years earlier, the Homestead Act had incentivized tens of thousands of American citizens—black and white alike—plus many newly arrived European immigrants to set out for the distant West to farm, ranch, and otherwise exploit and populate the Great Plains and the region of the Rockies. The signs of the advancement of the American republic were recurring, and while the reach of the government and the public had not yet tipped the West completely off its frontier axis, fewer places could be referred to as completely remote. The great transcontinental railroad had been completed the previous year, spanning ground where wagons had crossed decades earlier and where stagecoaches still rolled along. Telegraph lines represented a communication lifeline that linked West with East. When the party reached remote Granger, Wyoming, they received news from the outside world, delivered by the telegraph, that the French had lost their war with Germany.

Where the Hayden Survey moved, they encountered ranches, army forts, trading posts, and mining centers, both active and abandoned. One could still move across Wyoming and remain a lonely pilgrim, but the days of completely disconnecting from American civilization were already a thing of the past. When Jackson had passed through parts of the same region the previous year taking corporate photographs depicting the progress of the UP's reach across the West, he had seen recently established railroad depots and UP outposts, random log ranch houses, and a scattering of mining communities. In 1870 he took photographs of more substantial frontier towns, such as South Pass City and Atlantic City, along the South Pass, both signaling a movement of Americans into the West that, while not yet a tidal wave of humanity, was still enough to call any given valley or mountain draw somewhat settled. The West was changing, and Jackson knew it, in part because he had seen the frontier of earlier decades. The comparisons came easily to his mind.

Hayden, Jackson, and the party of scientists then returned to Green River City, where they followed the abandoned Overland Stage route back across southern Wyoming eastward. Throughout these weeks, Jackson took only a handful of photographs, since the weather was turning much colder. In addition, he felt "there was little of pictorial interest along drab Bitter

Situated in the midst of a Wyoming meadow, members of the 1870 Hayden Survey share a meal. Jackson stands at the far right and Ferdinand Hayden is seated, hatless, at the back of the table. "Potato John" Raymond presides at the stove on the far left. The location is Red Buttes in Natrona County, Wyoming, west of Casper. National Archives ID No. 516891.

Creek and over the Red Desert."[33] Once the party arrived at Fort Sanders, they began to disband, but not before Dr. Hayden asked Jackson to become a permanent, salaried member of his staff and participate in future surveys. Jackson had utilized his skills constantly during the weeks of the survey, having taken 150 whole plate views—of that number, more than 110 were included in the survey catalog—plus many more photos Jackson intended to utilize as possible stereo views. In all, he had produced 350 photographs. He had repeatedly proven to Hayden his own photographic eye, the capacity to frame a scene and create a landscape that represented a composition, not just one more image of one more piece of western real estate. The two men made arrangements to meet up in Washington, D.C., later. Then the geologist and the photographer parted company.

In the meantime, Jackson and Stevenson prepared to continue farther south. The army took back several items loaned to the expedition, but Jackson and his comrade retained one of the ambulances, plus a pair of good mules, and a driver, then made their way southward to Denver—which Jackson would one day call home—then on to the Pikes Peak region. Jackson took several photographs throughout the region of the Front Range as he and his comrade tromped along the foothills. In the vicinity of the great peak, they reached their farthest destination, Manitou Soda Springs, which Jackson described as "still the same as when only nomadic red men sought their sparkling waters."[34] The community of Colorado Springs did not yet exist, but a year later, when Jackson returned to the region, he observed that "men were at work plowing the lines for its streets."[35]

The men soon returned to Denver, and Jackson and his comrade took passage on the Kansas Pacific Railroad, which had only recently been completed for through traffic to the bustling Colorado mountain community. Jackson and Stevenson, worn out from their endless wanderings, boarded the train at evening, fell asleep, and did not wake up until the next morning, when they found the train slowly knifing its way through a sea of bison. In every direction, Jackson observed, "In the baggage car forward a few men engaged in the questionable sport—if such an act can be termed sport—of shooting into the thick of the herd with rifles"[36]

All through the day, Jackson's train rarely moved faster than twenty miles an hour, "often slowing down so that we could have walked alongside, occasionally stopping dead." He estimated the number of bison the train encountered that day at half a million.[37]

Before Jackson left Fort Sanders, he had taken the final photograph of the Hayden Survey, a strange, eerie pyramid of animal skulls someone had previously erected outside the fort. The pile included the bones of some of the most commonly hunted creatures of the West, including elk, deer, mountain sheep, and wolves. But the dominant number of skulls was of bison. Jackson had spent the fall of 1870 exploring lands on the verge of a new era of settlement, commercialization, and exploitation. Already, nonnative buffalo hunters, professionals encouraged by the federal government, often armed with a Sharps, Springfield, or Remington No. 1 rifle, were fanning out across the Great Plains to slaughter as many bison as they could possibly discover. This extermination went hand in glove with a policy espoused by various government officials and military personnel linking the end of the buffalo on the Plains with the ultimate demise of the Native Americans. As one US Army officer, Colonel Richard Dodge, encouraged a buffalo hunter in 1867: "Kill every buffalo you can! Every buffalo dead is an Indian Gone."[38]

William Henry Jackson was already keenly aware that summer and fall of 1870 of the shifting fortunes of the American West. While he had shot a few bison himself during his days with the Hayden Survey, what he saw from his train window looking out on the scrubby plains of western Kansas—a view punctuated and driven further home by a forlorn pile of bison bones bleaching

At the end of the 1870 Hayden Survey, Jackson took this enigmatic photo of a collection of buffalo, elk, deer, mountain sheep, and wolf skulls and bones outside Fort Sanders in Albany County, WY. National Archives ID No. 516956.

in the sun—brought into sharp focus his own sense that the West of his youth, days spent bullwhacking and horse wrangling, were unalterably evaporating. During these transitional years, Jackson would play his own part as the western drama changed from one act to another.

7

Langford's Yellowstone, 1870

$\mathcal{J}$ackson returned to Omaha following his latest sojourn into the American West a happy man. He was reunited with Mollie, his new bride, who had operated the photographic studios in Omaha as well as could be expected. But she was no photographer, so he found a backlog of business to occupy him once he set foot back in town. Ultimately, it mattered little what condition Jackson found his Omaha operation in after his return. The direction of his life was soon shifting its center of gravity.

He took a train east to Washington, D.C., where he met with Hayden. Jackson remained in the nation's capital for two months, processing his field-work, printing photos, and cataloging everything in an organized fashion before handing it all over to his geologist friend.

Jackson had gone west almost on a whim that summer—at Hayden's request, of course—and had done so in hopes the photographs he produced would serve their purpose in support of a government survey, as well as profit him financially. He observed, "My participation in the work of the Survey in 1870 was undertaken without much thought or calculation as to what might follow from it aside from a desire for adventure and to get an interesting series of negatives for use in my Omaha business."[1]

In a sense, the expedition resulted in an immediate reward for Jackson, but not in the way he had envisioned. At the 1870 expedition's conclusion, Dr. Hayden realized he had a true asset in Jackson and his photographic skills. As Jackson wrote, "Hayden decided [photographic work] must be one of the regular branches of the Survey's operations, and at our final conference in Washington I was made its official photographer."[2]

It became clear that Jackson's new position necessitated he and Mollie sell out their Omaha studios and move to Washington. Changes came fast for the reunited newlyweds, including soon expecting their first child. It was decided, considering her condition, that she would return to live with her parents while he was gone during the summer of 1871 back into the Far West. "Then in the fall [of 1871] we would move to Washington," Jackson wrote, "and enjoy a gold-braided life together until the next expedition to the mountains."[3] It was a great plan, on paper. The business did not sell immediately, so Mollie remained in Omaha to run the studio for a second summer. Although she agreed to everything to satisfy her husband's need to abandon her once again in the name of government service, she did ask to accompany her husband on his way West as far as Ogden, Utah, which would allow her to see the Rocky Mountains for the first time.

In preparation for his photographic work on the 1871 survey, Jackson reassessed his equipment, including which cameras to include. He decided to retain his whole plate, or 6½-by-8½-inch camera, as well as his stereoscopic camera. But he added an 8-by-10-inch camera, which rendered his 6½-by-8½-inch camera his second choice in the field. Knowing Hayden wanted photographs immediately available upon their return to Washington from this second survey, Jackson also packed all the materials to produce prints in the field, including the necessary chemicals.

Hayden's original intention was to return with his colleagues to southern Wyoming and pick up where they had left off at the end of the 1870 season. But he soon altered his plans, following a January lecture held at Lincoln Hall in Washington, D.C.

Throughout the earlier decades of the nineteenth century, the world of Yellowstone was shrouded in mystery. Stories were circulated, tales told by native tribesmen and non-Indian trappers, but much of what people heard—of great steam geysers, boiling mud pots, and volcanic activity—seemed unbelievable, the products of imaginations too vivid or of mountain men too drunk to separate the real from their hallucinations. In 1806 William Clark, of Lewis and Clark fame, narrowly bypassed the mysteries of Yellowstone by seventy-five miles or so during his return eastward with a portion of the members of the Corps of Discovery. (As he paddled down the Yellowstone River, he passed the future site of Livingston, Montana, today home of the Yellowstone Gateway Museum.)

At least one member of the expedition, John Colter, returned to the region during the winter of 1807–1808 and reached the Yellowstone, where he saw the geysers, sulfurous fountains, and mud pots for himself. Colter may have been the first white man to reach the lands that today make up Yellowstone National Park. He explored north around the "West Thumb" portion of Lake Yellowstone and reached the Yellowstone River near Alum Creek. But when he tried to tell comrades about what he had witnessed, he was met with

Likely in 1871, Jackson (squatting) and his assistant process wet plates from a precarious site along a cliff edge near Yellowstone National Park, WY. Library of Congress, LC-USZ62-93569.

derisive laughter. As one historian notes, Colter likely "saw too much for his reputation as a man of veracity."[4] Scoffers soon referred to the mountain man's descriptions as "Colter's Hell." No mapmaker worthy of his own reputation would include the sights Colter ascribed to the Yellowstone Plateau.[5]

In the winter of 1829, nineteen-year-old mountain man Joe Meek, working for the Rocky Mountain Fur Company, became separated from his trapping party after they were scattered by a band of Blackfoot Indians. He became disoriented, cold, and hungry, until he killed a mountain sheep for food. As he stumbled about the mountains, he wandered onto the Yellowstone Plateau and saw the legendary geysers and boiling springs. Years later he described his experience:

> The whole country beyond was smoking with the vapor from boiling springs, and burning with gasses, issuing from small craters, each of which was emitting a sharp whistling sound. . . . I have been told the sun would be blown out, and the earth burnt up. If this infernal wind keeps up, I shouldn't be surprised if the sun was blown out. If the earth is not burning up over there, then it is that place the old Methodist preacher used to threaten me with. . . . [But] the warmth of the place [was] most delightful, after the freezing cold of the mountains, [so] if this was hell, it was a more agreeable climate than [I] had been in for some time.[6]

But when he reconnoitered with his comrades and later told his stories, he was met with the usual skepticism. Such reactions helped the Yellowstone Plateau and its wonders remain secret to the outside world. As long as information was transmitted "only in the minds of illiterate men," it "perished with them. It never caught the public ear."[7]

Jim Bridger, one of the most famous of nineteenth-century mountain men, claimed to have seen the Yellowstone, but he, too, was doubted—and no wonder. He heavily sprinkled his descriptions of the region with unbelievable exaggerations and tall tales. He described finding a petrified forest in Yellowstone, home to "petrified birds that sang petrified songs." Bridger described "mountains made entirely of glass that had the property of telescopes and so transparent that a person could walk right into them if he wasn't watchful."[8] Given the actual geothermal and geological wonders in Yellowstone, it is curious why Bridger felt so compelled to exaggerate what he had actually seen.

With presumably unreliable reporters such as Colter, Meek, and Bridger, the story of Yellowstone remained a hidden gem. This proved a problem for several decades running during the nineteenth century—the reliability of those reporting on the realities of Yellowstone. Too often they were, to outsiders, the same person: a mountain man who liked to brag, frontier storytellers too often intent on entertaining instead of communicating the truth.

Thus, Yellowstone and its wonders represented a fantasy world, off the beaten path, a place shrouded in unconfirmed myth. Even as the reach of the federal government extended further into the West and Americans in increasing numbers migrated across the Great Plains and the Far West bound for Oregon, California, and various other destinations, the door to Yellowstone remained locked. Between the Lewis and Clark Expedition (1804–1806) and 1870, 110 scientific explorations crisscrossed much of the region west of the Mississippi River. Only one of them skirted the Yellowstone Plateau.

That single expedition was launched in 1859, a government operation involving the US Army. Early that year, William F. Raynolds was ordered to lead a military expedition into the Yellowstone region of Montana and Wyoming. He was sent with specific instructions to discover "as far as practicable, everything relating to . . . the Indians of the country, its agricultural and mineralogical resources . . . the navigability of its streams, its topographical features, and the facilities or obstacles which the latter present to the construction of rail or common roads."[9]

Captain Raynolds's designated party included mountain man Jim Bridger as its guide. It also included Ferdinand Hayden as the naturalist. There was a photographer in the group, James D. Hutton, who was also a topographer. The government funded the party with $60,000 of the taxpayers' money. They left St. Louis in late May on two steamboats up the Missouri River. From Fort Pierre (today's capital of South Dakota), they headed overland. Adventure stalked their path, as they encountered Crow Indians, then reached the Yellowstone River in southern Montana. Raynolds split his party in two, sending his second in command, Lt. Henry E. Maynadier, to search for a great rock formation spotted by another expedition two years earlier. He and photographer Hutton soon located Devil's Tower, likely making them the first white explorers to reach its base. Between the two parties moving separately, the expedition followed the Yellowstone River to its confluence with the Bighorn River in south-central Montana. They wintered along the Platte River at Deer Creek Station and resumed their movements in May the following year. Again, the two halves of the expedition split off. One explored the Wind River, while the other went back north to the Bighorn. They reunited at the end of June at Three Forks, Montana, the headwaters of the Missouri River. After snows held them up for a time, the reunited party arrived at Jackson Hole and the Teton Range. But rather than travel north into Yellowstone, they progressed westward to Idaho's Pierre's Hole. At Fort Benton, Montana, they boarded a steamboat headed to Omaha, their explorations ended.

The Raynolds Expedition failed to reach the region that is today Yellowstone National Park. It had made important "discoveries," of course, having tromped over 250,000 square miles of the West and traveled on foot 2,500 miles. Yellowstone and its exploration would have to wait for another day. Hayden, whom Captain Raynolds developed a strong dislike for—the geologist was always filling wagons with rocks—would return more than a decade later, with another photographer, William Henry Jackson, at his side. The opportunity to prove with photographs the existence of Yellowstone's wonders was postponed.

Western expeditions sponsored by the US government went on a virtual hiatus with the coming of the Civil War in 1861. Nearly a decade passed before another expedition headed in the direction of Yellowstone, and this one was not carried out on the government's dime. Instead, it was an entirely private venture, the brainchild of three Montana pioneers, including thirty-one-year-old David E. Folsom, who had ventured out to the gold camps of Montana in 1862. Of the other two, Charles W. Cook was a friend of Folsom, and William Peterson was a hired hand on Folsom's ranch. As they made plans for their expedition, friends warned them not to proceed, telling them their plans were "the next thing to suicide," due to the movement of renegade Indians in the territory.[10] This was a legitimate concern, especially after the US Army refused to provide the party with a military escort. The comrades took to the trail anyway, leaving Bozeman, moving down the divide between the Yellowstone and Gallatin Rivers, then crossing over the mountains to Yellowstone and the lands that today include the national park. They saw many of the sights tourists to the park seek out, including Tower Falls, the Grand Canyon of the Yellowstone, Mud Volcano, and Yellowstone Lake. They then reached Shoshone Lake and the geyser basins surrounding Firehole River. When Folsom witnessed Yellowstone's Grand Canyon, he was awestruck. He later wrote, "Language is inadequate to convey a just conception of the awful grandeur and sublimity of this masterpiece of nature's handiwork."[11] The party did encounter Indians, but they were small, friendly bands.

Their trip spanned September and stretched into October, a bit late for exploring the Yellowstone, where winter weather can come howling in at any moment, and night temperatures can dip down to freezing. The men were constantly amazed at the sights unfolding before them. Even Lake Yellowstone inspired Folsom to pen dramatic words: "[T]his inland sea . . . is a scene of transcendent beauty which has been viewed by few white men, and we felt glad to have looked upon it before its primeval solitude should be broken by the crowds of pleasure seekers which at no distant day will throng its shores."[12]

Perhaps their most important night in Yellowstone was October 1, as the three comrades huddled around a campfire on the banks of the Firehole River and considered the future of the Yellowstone Plateau. William Peterson speculated that "it would not be long before settlers and prospectors began coming into the district and taking up the land around the geysers and Canyons."[13] This inevitability concerned the three men, who had come to see the wonders of Yellowstone as national treasures that should not be exploited for private profit and exploitation. Cook expressed the opinion that the land should somehow be set aside, preserved from the plow and the miner's pick. Folsom suggested no one could guarantee Yellowstone's future but the government. In expressing their concerns, none of the three men landed on what would become the ultimate solution, as Cook later confessed, "None of us definitely suggested the idea of a national park. National parks were unknown then."[14]

When the trio of explorers emerged from the Yellowstone Plateau and returned to Helena, Folsom was reluctant to tell the story of the wonders of Yellowstone to his fellow Montanans. Others had made claims of geysers and great bubbling mud pots and been derided. In addition, he did not want to cause a stampede of the curious into the region. He did, however, decide to write an article about his adventures for an eastern magazine. Cook tried but failed to have *Scribner's Monthly* and the *New York Tribune* print his story. He then chose Lippincott's, but they did not choose him, the editors informing Cook they did not publish fiction. His article was eventually published in the *Western Monthly* of Chicago in the July 1870 issue. Little immediate change came to Yellowstone. It remained a distant mirage for nearly everyone.[15]

But word was leap-frogging from one interested party to another. When Folsom returned from his trip, he discussed his findings as well as his concerns about future exploitation of Yellowstone with General Henry D. Washburn, who was then Montana's surveyor general. Their conversation led Washburn to discuss the issue with a friend, Nathanial P. Langford. And Folsom's findings did not go completely unnoticed. Instead, his "reports of the waterfalls and canyons along the Yellowstone River as well as spectacular eruptions of geysers stimulated several acquaintances to plan a major expedition the following summer."[16]

In the fall of 1869, prominent Montanan Nathanial P. Langford became one of the "stimulated." Like Jackson, he was a native of New York and had been appointed in 1864 as the collector of internal revenue for the newly formed territory of Montana. He met with Folsom and soon began planning an exploration of his own for the 1870 season. Langford had a latent curiosity regarding the wonders of the Yellowstone Plateau, but he had other interests. As he wrote, his curiosity was mixed with a desire of "some understanding . . . concerning the usefulness of Yellowstone exploration in the grand scheme of Northern Pacific Railroad publicity."[17] Langford was interested in advancing Montana's economic interests and its expanding commercial reach.

Langford's interest in the Yellowstone Plateau was not new in 1869. In the first of two articles he penned for *Scribner's Monthly* in the spring of 1871, his debrief to the public concerning his venture into Yellowstone the previous summer, such a trip had been on his mind: "I had indulged, for several years, a great curiosity to see the wonders of the upper valley of the Yellowstone."[18]

Among those "several gentlemen" of Montana who shared "like curiosity" with Langford was Col. Samuel T. Hauser, a trained civil engineer and president of the First National Bank of Helena. (He was later appointed governor of Montana Territory by President Grover Cleveland.) Both men presented their proposed exploration to Gen. Winfield Scott Hancock, then known famously as the Union general during the Civil War whose troops met Pickett's Charge at Gettysburg. In 1870 he was the commander of the Department of Dakota, which included the territories of Minnesota, Dakota, and Montana. Langford appealed to Hancock to provide a military escort into Yellowstone, and the general complied, ordering the Second Cavalry at Fort Ellis to lead the expedition into the Yellowstone region. Maj. Gen. Henry Washburn—he was actually a former general at this point in his career—along with 2nd Lt. Gustavus Doane, took the lead, with Langford in tow. Doane's command included five cavalrymen. The party, which totaled nineteen members, also included an artist named Charles Moore. Although nineteenth-century western exploration was presumed to be a young man's game, of the leaders, Doane was the youngest at thirty. Washburn and Langford were both thirty-eight and Hauser a year younger.

Lieutenant Doane proved a crucial member of the expedition. He later wrote a report to General Hancock that included many details, and it even inspired others, including Ferdinand Hayden, who a year later referred to the document as "the remarkable report of this young officer, which he seems to have written under the inspiration of the wonderful physical phenomena around him." Hayden further added, "that for graphic descriptions and thrilling interest it has not been surpassed by any official report made to our Government since the time of Lewis and Clarke [*sic*]."

The bulk of the party departed from Helena on August 17 and soon picked up their military escort at Fort Ellis, having covered 120 miles since leaving Helena. The group did not return until late September. Nineteen men was not a large party, especially when compared to later expeditions. But Langford felt the number was advantageous, "realizing that a small body of white men can more easily elude a band of Indians than can a large party."[19]

Each man was similarly outfitted for the expedition with a horse, equipped with a California saddle, bridle, and cantinas. Most of them were armed in the manner of the earlier mountain men, including "a needle-gun, a belt filled with cartridges, a pair of revolvers, a hunting-knife."[20] Their provisions were packed on the backs of a dozen horses tended by a couple of packers. The party's two cooks were African Americans, and the staple fare was bacon, dried fruit, flour, coffee, and hardtack.

The party decided early on to make a single march each day, setting out at 8:00 a.m. and making camp by 3:00 p.m. The horses were picketed at night, with two members of the party assigned to keep guard in two separate shifts. Langford describes the party as "our little company . . . formidable [in] appearance, as by dint of whip and spur our steeds gayly wheeled across the plain towards the mountains."[21] The party made good progress and soon found itself surrounded by the very wonders they were seeking. The scenery was sublime, as Langford observed: "Following the slight Indian trail, we traveled near the bank of the [Yellowstone] river, amid the wildest imaginable scenery of river, rock, and mountain."[22]

Just beyond this scene, the party reached a curious rock formation, "two parallel vertical walls of rock, projecting from the side of a mountain to the height of 125 feet, traversing the mountain from base to summit, a distance of 1,500 feet." One of the party's members felt the formation was ethereal enough to deserve an infernal name: "The Devil's Slide." (This unusual cliff rock formation is located in today's Gallatin National Forest in Park County, Montana.) In his first *Scribner's* article (May 1871), Langford predicted the future of the strange rock formation: "In future years, when the wonders of Yellowstone are incorporated into the family of fashionable resorts, there will be few of its attractions surpassing in interest than this marvelous freak of the elements."[23]

The team swung to the eastern portion of what is today Yellowstone National Park, where they took in the sights including Tower Falls, the Grand Canyon of the Yellowstone, and Yellowstone Lake. (Through much of the Yellowstone Plateau, the Washburn-Doane-Langford party followed many of the same trails utilized by the Folsom Expedition the previous year.) Tower Falls impressed the men, with Langford referring to it as "one of the most beautiful cataracts in the world."[24] But ahead of them lay falls beyond their imaginations.

As the men continued, they witnessed some of the wonders described by previous observers and so skeptically regarded, including boiling springs. As Langford reports, "we suddenly came upon a hideous-looking glen filled with the sulphurous vapor emitted from six or eight boiling springs of great size and activity. One of our company aptly compared it to the entrance to the infernal regions."[25] (As Joe Meek and others had in the past.) The following day, the party reached a site they named "The Devil's Den," "a gloomy gorge, of abrupt descent, which on either side is filled with continuous masses of obsidian that have been worn by the water into many fantastic shapes and cavernous recesses."[26]

The men soon reached Crystal Falls, which, like Tower Falls, impressed them. Still, the best of Yellowstone's falls lay ahead. Arriving there, the explorers witnessed two of the greatest of Yellowstone's gems, the Lower and Upper Falls. Visitors today are just as awestruck as Langford and the other members of the party were in 1870. It is not just the majesty of two great falls, it is the geological context. In Langford's words, "The Great Falls are at the head of one of the most remarkable canons in the world—a gorge through volcanic rocks fifty miles long, and varying from one thousand to nearly five thousand feet in depth."

This canyon represents a vertical mile of exquisitely colored stone, a grand canyon of seemingly endless soft, melty ice cream rocks. Langford continued, "The brain reels as we gaze into this profound and solemn solitude.`. . . . We rambled around the falls and canyon two days, and left them with the unpleasant conviction that the greatest wonder of our journey had been seen."[27] At long last, the wonders of Yellowstone would be revealed to the outside world through the witness of a chronicler worthy of the plateau's most awesome scenes.

But additional sights of unbelievable beauty and scope still lay ahead. Several times along their way, unwanted grizzly bears crossed their path, with one explorer falling from his frightened horse as his mount galloped away, dragging his broken bridle. Snow also interrupted their advance, falling to a depth of two feet in some places, followed by rain that washed it all away. The party's geologist picked out a variety of rock forms including several silicious formations. They reached the massive Yellowstone Lake and skirted along its shores for miles. They arrived at several hot springs "of pure ultramarine hue—very large, and wonderfully transparent."[28]

Beyond Yellowstone Lake, traveling westward, the party discovered a location that would one day be considered the center pivot of Yellowstone National Park, the Upper Geyser Basin, featuring the sight today's tourists seek most often. Langford described this moment:

> Judge, then, what must have been our astonishment, as we entered the basin . . . to see in the clear sunlight . . . an immense volume of clear, sparkling water projected into the air to the height of one hundred and twenty-five feet. "Geysers! Geysers!" exclaimed one of our company, and, spurring our jaded horses, we soon gathered around this wonderful phenomenon. It was indeed a perfect geyser . . . elevated thirty feet above the level of the surrounding plain, and the crater rises five or six feet above the mound. It spouted at regular intervals nine times during our stay, the columns of boiling water being thrown from ninety to one hundred and twenty-five feet at each discharge, which lasted from fifteen to twenty minutes. We gave it the name of "Old Faithful."[29]

When the Hayden Survey party returned to Yellowstone in 1872, Jackson shot this photograph of the Great Falls of the Yellowstone River. Library of Congress. LC-USZ62-16709.

Jackson photographs, including this one of the Crater of the Castle Geyser taken in 1871, helped to dispel doubts concerning the geological wonders of Yellowstone. Library of Congress. LC-USZ62-27952.

The men stumbled across additional geyser basins where they took in the wonders of each as they gave them names for perpetuity: "The Grotto," "The Castle," "The Giant," and "The Giantess."

As the members of the party experienced one wonder of Yellowstone after another, they took in the unique nature of the plateau and stopped occasionally to consider what the future might hold for this astonishing landscape with its one-of-a-kind waterfalls, canyons, mud pots, and superheated geysers. On the evening of September 19, with the men sitting around a warm campfire, Langford, a comrade named Cornelius Hedges, and others shared a conversation and their personal opinions of what should be done to protect the Yellowstone Plateau from exploitation. Several men saw no problems with allowing private individuals or businesses staking "claims on the land around the geysers and waterfalls . . . in anticipation of the demand which tourists would make to see them."[30] Others, including Hedges, favored preservation and protection of the plateau by the federal government. He "did not approve of any of these plans—[he felt] that there ought to be no private ownership of any portion of that region, but the whole ought to be set apart as a great National Park."[31] This was a unique suggestion, as no national parks had yet been established in the United States. The idea gained traction among the men immediately, as Langford noted: "This suggestion met with an instantaneous and favorable response from all—except one . . . and quickly became the main theme of later conversations."[32]

In late September the party finally completed their circuitous exploration of the Yellowstone Plateau and emerged with stories to tell. They had traversed the plateau with the wonder of children, but they had also worked hard to create a scientific interpretation of what they had encountered. They had measured everything in sight, collected rock samples, took depth soundings of Yellowstone Lake, and analyzed the mineral deposits scattered around the plateau.

As concerned as they were about the future of Yellowstone, they wasted little time spreading the news of what they had seen. Newspapers printed the first accounts, including several in the pages of the *Helena Herald*. Some newspapers were uncertain of the veracity of the explorers' claims, including the *Rocky Mountain News* of Denver, with one article titled "Montana Romance" that referred to General Washburn's account of the trip as drawing "somewhat upon the powers of credulity."[33] The *New York Times* referred to Washburn's version as the "realization of a child's fairy tale." The *Times* opined further to hedge its bets: "We mean no disparagement, but the reverse."[34]

Nothing told the story of the expedition to the public better than the two articles Langford published in *Scribner's Magazine* in May and June 1871. They were engaging travelogues that presented Yellowstone through the eyes of the curious professional. These articles received wide acclaim. By the following year, a copy of both articles was placed on the desk of every member of Congress, along with photographs by William Henry Jackson. But Jackson had not been a part of the Washburn-Langford-Doane Expedition. His pivotal role had yet to play out.

Not only did Langford publish his two influential articles, he also developed a series of popular lectures, which he presented in New York City, Helena, and Washington, D.C. By arrangement with the Northern Pacific Railroad (NPRR), Langford promoted the Yellowstone Plateau as a tourist destination to help enhance business for the railroad. Jay Cooke, president of the NPRR, subsidized Langford's lecture tour. Venue halls were typically crowded with standing-room-only audiences. On January 19, 1871, Langford presented a lecture at Lincoln Hall in Washington, D.C., which was advertised in the city's newspapers, including the *Washington Star*. The paper announced to would-be attendees—admission was set at 50 cents—that they would hear of "a trip during the past season to a hitherto unexplored region at the headwaters of the Yellowstone, including discoveries of cataracts many hundred feet high, active volcanoes, fountains of boiling water 200-feet-high, and many other features of scenery, interesting and striking in the highest degree."[35] This particular lecture proved crucial in determining who would lead the next expedition into the Yellowstone Plateau. In the audience at Lincoln Hall was Dr. Ferdinand Vandeveer Hayden. As Hayden listened to Langford present his version of the wonders of Yellowstone, Hayden began to consider where, exactly, his 1871 expedition to Wyoming would explore.[36] He had not visited Yellowstone previously, although as a member of the 1859–1860 expedition with Captain Raynolds, he had come close. A late May snowstorm had blocked their entry onto the plateau. Even Jim Bridger, the expedition's guide, could not find a route beyond Togwotee Pass. The mysteries of Yellowstone had remained elusive and unreachable. Listening to Langford on that January evening in the nation's capital, Hayden began forming his plans to lead his expedition into the very heart of the lands Mother Nature had closed to outsiders. His time for exploring the Yellowstone region had arrived.

Putting together his team for the Yellowstone venture of 1871 was a lead-pipe cinch for Hayden. Seven of those who had accompanied him on previous expeditions were tapped again. There were new members as well, including various scientists, such as botanists and entomologists and others studying plant and animal life. Several other members were greenhorns, some the young sons of influential Washington officials and politicians. But if their fathers were important, most of these youths were less so for the expedition's success. They were along for the ride, treating the expedition as "very much of a lark, and the affairs concerning their horses, guns, fishing tackle, and other equipment were of greater importance than the duties assigned to them."[37] One exception among them was a lad assigned to Jackson as a photographer's assistant, whom Will later described as "an efficient helper as well as a congenial companion."[38] George B. Dixon had only recently graduated from the University of Pennsylvania medical school, where he had studied geology under Dr. Hayden. Many of the trip's details were repeats of the 1870 expedition, including the types of equipment, food stocks, wagons, and other moving parts of the expedition. Cheyenne's US Army headquarters, Fort D. A. Russell, provided much of the equipment needed, just as it had the previous year.

The various scientists chosen for the survey required a wide variety of the available scientific equipment of the day. The list included "two sextants, one artificial horizon, one sidereal chronometer, one mean solar pocket chronometer, two mercurial cistern barometers, one thermo-barometer, two aneroids, two prismatic compasses, three pocket compasses, two odometers, one pair odometer wheels, and a box of tools."[39]

One new piece of equipment for the Hayden Survey was an ingenious device, an early form of odometer. Jackson described it as "made by attaching a pair of shafts to the four wheels of an ambulance, to the spokes of which were attached the instruments that recorded their revolutions and measured the surface of the country over which we passed. These were the first wheels that were ever taken into this little-known region." A specific mule, one known to just plod along regardless of the difficulty of the landscape, dragged the device all across the Yellowstone Plateau.[40]

When Langford published the details of his explorations in the West for *Scribner's Monthly*, a magazine with "a distinct Western flavor,"[41] he included illustrations made by an artist who had not been a part of the expedition. Expedition members Charles Moore and Walter Trumbull had made the original sketches, which were then reworked by the skillful artistic hands of a young landscape painter from back East, Thomas Moran, likely at the insistence of the magazine's editor, Richard Watson Gilder, a close friend of Moran. (Moran was already a well-established artist in Philadelphia.) It is unlikely Moran had much previous interest in or knowledge of Yellowstone, but the opportunity put him on a trajectory that ultimately landed him in the Far West.

Thomas Moran was an Englishman by birth, born in Bolton in 1837. His family immigrated to the United States in 1844 and landed in Philadelphia. At the age of fifteen, Thomas was apprenticed to a wood engraver, and by 1856 he began to study art under the marine painter James Hamilton. Hamilton was a strong proponent of the British painter J. M. W. Turner, even as he advocated for a Ruskinite approach to depicting nature, including landscapes as truth. Prior to 1871, the furthest Moran had traveled west was to the Pictured Rocks of Lake Superior in 1860, where he spent an August paddling around in a canoe and camping along the lake shore, sketching constantly. This trip resulted in an early grand-scale painting, *The Wilds of Lake Superior*, which he completed in 1864, representing one of his largest and most successful works prior to his involvement in the 1871 Hayden Survey.

Following the Civil War, Moran became a commercial illustrator, which provided a steady lucrative income. He illustrated books of poetry and several articles for *Harper's New Monthly Magazine*. In time he became one of the best-known illustrators in the East. He also created paintings, which he sold in various Philadelphia galleries. Moran displayed paintings at the Pennsylvania Academy of Fine Arts. At the Exposition Universelle in Paris (1867), two of his paintings were included in the American fine arts display. In 1869 a recent painting, *The Spirit of the Indian*, which was intended as a visual representation of Longfellow's poem "Hiawatha," took a prize at New York's National Academy of Design. The painting is a dark, nearly monochromatic landscape of a bleak scene of mountains, trees, and lake featuring a larger-than-life Native American "spirit" hovering over it all. By December of the following year, Moran received the commission to provide fourteen illustrations for Langford's *Scribner's* articles, which probably incentivized Jay Cooke to promote Moran's involvement in the 1871 Hayden Survey.

When Hayden saw the Langford articles, he was immediately impressed with Moran's black-and-white illustrations. Moran soon became part of the expedition, but not directly at Hayden's request. The artist was never an official member of the 1871 survey. Instead, he arranged to have himself included through his friendship with Scribner's editor, Roswell Smith, and NPRR financier Jay Cooke. Moran struck a deal to receive $500 from Cooke in exchange for a dozen watercolor paintings of the Yellowstone. Cooke then contacted Hayden on June 7, 1871, requesting Moran be included in the expedition: "My friend, Thos. Moran, an artist of Philadelphia of rare genius has completed arrangements for spending a month or two in the Yellowstone country taking sketches for painting. . . . I have encouraged him to believe that you will be glad to have him join your party."[42] (Another well-known artist, Albert Bierstadt, had already been asked to accompany the Hayden Expedition, but he had decided not to join the party in the end. Bierstadt was already famous for his immense painting of Yosemite.) Moran would prove himself one of the most significant additions to Hayden's 1871 Survey team. He and Jackson soon became close associates and friends for life.

Will Jackson and Mollie left Omaha in late May and traveled by train out West as far as Ogden, all new territory for Jackson's wife. In the first week of June the Jacksons took their leave of one another as Mollie returned to Omaha to again run the photographic business. The trip to Ogden "made a pleasant little holiday for both of us."[43]

Jackson soon joined friends, colleagues, and strangers at the designated Ogden rendezvous. By June 10 the expedition's membership had swelled to thirty-five, fourteen or fifteen more than had participated in the Wyoming venture the previous year. Hayden wanted an accurate map produced by his survey, so he hired Antoine Schoenborn, an excellent cartographer, surveyor, and meteorologist who had previously served with the 1859–1860 Raynolds expedition. With this many men included—everyone from scientists to wranglers to the party's main cook, Potato John Raymond—Dr. Hayden had managed to wrangle a congressional appropriation of $40,000. And Jackson was aware of the role he was expected to play on this particular survey. Yellowstone had been talked about for decades, and story after story had failed to convert the skeptics. Despite the success and professionalism of the Washburn-Langford-Doane Expedition, and Langford's landmark lecture series, plus his two *Scribner's* articles, many Americans remained unconvinced regarding Yellowstone's most extraordinary wonders. They demanded more proof. Jackson had proven crucial to Hayden's 1870 venture, and he was expected to do the same in the Yellowstone region. What many doubters needed was photographic evidence. Jackson wrote, "If taxpayers and Congressmen alike wanted more evidence, none of them wanted it half so much as Dr. Hayden."[44]

As a scientist, Hayden was driven to gain more knowledge of the American West, especially the geographically obscure places, such as Yellowstone. He also knew how popular such surveys were with the American people, who were increasingly eyeing the West as either a place to resettle and seek one's place or as a tourist destination. With the railroad expanding across the Far West, linking the regions of the nation together, both goals were increasingly feasible. Plus, Hayden wanted to keep leading surveys as long as there was an unknown geography to reveal, with the federal government paying the tab. Thus, William Henry Jackson's role was crucial. As Jackson explains, "That was where I came in. No photographs had as yet been published [of the Yellowstone Plateau], and Dr. Hayden was determined that the first ones should be good."[45]

None of this took anything away from the artists who accompanied Hayden in 1871, especially Thomas Moran. Jackson referred to him as "an honored guest" and "the famous artist."[46] Photography could reveal the sights of the Yellowstone Plateau in black and white. Hand tinting could brighten up these pictures and give a semblance of natural world color and contrast for the viewer. But an oil painting or watercolor, rendered by the hand of a skilled professional—especially on the grand scale Moran would produce for some of his paintings—presented a fuller dimension, one with greater texture and depth. The photographer and artist could (and did) work together to reveal the Yellowstone to the outside world and provide at least two-dimensional artistic documents to help place the remote viewer in closer proximity to the wonders of Yellowstone without actually being there. Additionally, photographs worked as irrefutable proof that the rumored wonders were real, not the exaggerated ramblings of whiskey-soaked mountain men.

8

Jackson's Yellowstone, 1871

$\mathcal{O}$n June 10, the party set out for Yellowstone as an impressive team of twenty-one horsemen, plus seven large army wagons, each drawn by four mules. They traveled for several hundred miles before they even reached the Yellowstone and its rumored wonders. They planned to enter from the north, so their journey took them past Mormon settlements with their requisite fruit trees, just as Jackson had seen in southern Utah on his way to Los Angeles a few years earlier. At Cache Valley they crossed the Continental Divide to Idaho's Portneuf River, a tributary of the Snake, then reached Fort Hall. (This is a different Fort Hall than its predecessor, located about forty miles east of the original.) After crossing the Snake River at Taylor's Bridge, the survey party spanned the Idaho plains until they reached the Hole in the Wall stage station—future outlaws Butch Cassidy and the Sundance Kid would hide out in the region—from which they could see the Teton Mountains in the far distance, resembling, "a series of sharp pyramids of naked rock which look like sharks' teeth," according to Hayden.[1]

The party then reached Virginia City, Montana, and Jackson finally arrived at the place he had originally intended to land when he first entered the West five years earlier. Virginia City had seen its best days of mining by that time, and Jackson noted "a few Chinamen gathering the little that was left from more prosperous times."[2] After a month on the trail, the Hayden Survey reached Fort Ellis, where the Washburn–Langford–Doane Expedition had camped the previous year. Here they rested; refitted their horses; and enjoyed a side excursion, led by local cavalrymen, to a local mountain lake where the men enjoyed great fishing.

Thomas Moran had come out West to join the Hayden party as a man completely lacking experience and knowledge of the world he had entered.

A born easterner, like Jackson, to him the West was a mystery. When he joined the party at Virginia City, it was clear to nearly all the other members that they now had a greenhorn on their hands. They wondered at someone who had taken the stagecoach from Ogden and had to ask why the driver and shotgun guard had to carry weapons. It was on the stage that he learned the word "road agent" referred to a robber. He confessed soon after arriving in the Hayden encampment that he had never ridden a horse, and eventually he placed a pillow on his McClellan saddle because his backside was so sore. Moran often had digestive trouble with the trail fare, especially greasy bacon. Jackson summed him up pretty quickly. Moran, he wrote, "made the adventure with fine courage and quickly adapted himself to the new and unfamiliar conditions."[3]

At the Fort Ellis lake, Moran had his opportunity to shine. He proved an excellent fisherman, and Jackson took the artist's photograph sitting beside a rocky stream with a crowded string of large trout. Moran then baked the fish, wrapped in brown paper, buried in a bed of hot coals—Jackson refers to this as "alfresco cooking"—which produced one of the best meals the men had enjoyed in weeks. In time, Moran earned his place as a full-fledged, accepted member of the expedition, despite his lack of previous experience in the West.

After traveling thirty miles beyond Fort Ellis, the party established its base at Bottlers Ranch—today the site is known as Paradise Valley—a civilian outpost owned by three Dutch brothers, "laughing, hearty fellows who kept bachelor hall in a big log house."[4] At the ranch, the party took a few days to transfer their supplies from wagons to pack mules, all under the watchful eyes of a pair of expert mule packers, Shep Madera and Tom Cooper. (They were included in Hayden Surveys in Colorado during the 1873 and 1875 seasons.) Hayden then split his men into two groups. The first was ordered to remain at Bottlers and operate a base camp. These men were tasked with taking daily meteorological readings. But their primary responsibility was to maintain a lifeline for those entering Yellowstone by delivering supplies and the mail. This allowed the explorers to keep up their connection to the outside world even as they entered environs largely unknown to them. The men received regular deliveries of letters from home and wrote their own letters back. Some even received their magazines and journals.

Then, in late July, escorted by a small detachment of the Second Cavalry, the smaller Hayden party entered the northern reaches of what is today Yellowstone National Park. That evening, around the communal campfire, the men discussed what lay ahead, all aware of the stories of geysers and mud pots. Some of them, including several of the mule packers, claimed to have seen the Yellowstone Plateau already and told tales of what they had witnessed. The party did not have to wait long before they

Titled Successful Fisherman, *this stereoscope photo depicts painter Thomas Moran with an impressive catch of fish. The picture is from 1871, the year the survey team first entered the Yellowstone Plateau. Library of Congress. LC-DIG-stereo-1s01177.*

encountered the stuff of Yellowstone legend. They were, of course, there to scout out the plateau and gain important scientific knowledge. Ultimately, much of this information was intended for the Smithsonian Institution.

Those left behind at Bottlers, after delivering supplies and the mail, would pick up various specimens gathered by the scientists, both botanical and zoological, and deliver them to local post offices along their route for shipment to the Washington-based museum even while Hayden and his men were still working on the Plateau. At the front end of the expedition, the Smithsonian's Spencer Baird wrote a letter to Hayden expressing his desire to receive "a large collection of all kinds of skulls and skeletons: many of each, at least skulls; antelope and mountain sheep especially, 20 of each! Also any perfect bison head."[5]

The party returned to the trail and soon passed Devil's Slide, the curious parallel rock formations the Langford party had reached the year before. After another ten miles on the trail, the party reached the mouth of the Gardiner River, where the geologists had a field day. They discovered hillsides littered with volcanic debris along with older cretaceous clays that Hayden described as, "much like the refuse from an old furnace."[6] It was an eerie, bleak landscape, its knobby hills featuring great scatters of black basalt rocks and grayish conglomerate. The site was pocked with ancient volcanic vents, sometimes containing brackish water. The whole bottomland featured no trees or plants, except for a few tufts of dark green here and there. Nearby, they spotted their first hot spring in the region, where again, others had already arrived, health enthusiasts convalescing in the warm therapeutic waters.

These earlier arrivals into Yellowstone surprised some of the men, who naturally assumed they would not encounter other visitors. But in fact the Yellowstone region had already attracted three groups of interlopers, including the "invalids," as Hayden described them, those who came to Yellowstone to enjoy the therapeutic qualities of the hot springs. Several of these patients had established a small community they called "Chestnutville." (It would not be long before one site was identified by a Yellowstone entrepreneur as "McQuirk's Medicinal Springs.") One of the "invalids," A. Bart Henderson, had already begun to carve out a toll road through one stretch of Yellowstone wilderness, hoping to profit from the opening of the region to curiosity seekers. Another group was also present, including a pair of Bozeman investors who had staked a claim to the Soda Springs area. Yellowstone land was already starting to fall into the hands of those intent on profiting by their presence in the West. Similarly, another party of would-be investors had also reached the Yellowstone, including a US mining commissioner, ready to tap the region's resources for personal gain. Word had already leaked out about the wonders of the Yellowstone, and some had ideas of creating their own capitalist ventures there. Plans were forming in the minds of a few to claim this geyser or that mud pot as their own, build a wall around it to obstruct the view of outsiders, then charge an entry fee to enter the cordoned site and enjoy the wonders of the Yellowstone with each ticket purchased. All such plans caused Hayden and others to worry about how quickly the region might be carved up by investors and entrepreneurs.

Close by, after clambering over a hill, the party reached a height where they could see for miles off into the distance, where snow-white mounds and dots of hot springs "had the appearance of a frozen cascade,"[7] observed Hayden. The men set up camp near a spring-fed stream. The sights around them challenged their senses. Spring sources dotted the landscape as "great semicircular basins ornamented the steep sides, with margins varying in height from a few inches to six to eight feet."[8] In florid detail, Hayden described a landscape "so beautifully scalloped and adorned with a kind of beadwork that the beholder stands amazed at . . . nature's handiwork. Add to this, a snowy-white ground, with every variety of shade, of scarlet, green, and yellow, as brilliant as the brightness of our aniline dyes."⁹ Just as the tourists they had encountered had done, Hayden's men utilized the local warm waters for cooking, then "enjoyed the luxury of bathing in these most elegantly carved natural bathing pools . . . [featuring] water of every variety and temperature."¹⁰

The following afternoon they reached the Mammoth Hot Springs. (The Hayden party first named the springs White Mountain Hot Springs.) Jackson wrote about the arrival of the Hayden men in this portion of the Yellowstone Plateau, declaring the springs a place where no white men had previously arrived, although the claim was certainly untrue. Within a day of their arrival, Jackson took his first photographs inside the future national park, and the Mammoth Hot Springs was his subject. The photographer found the site "so rich and abundant that it was necessary to move my dark box only three or four times."¹¹

The process of taking photographs involved the usual steps of picture taking in tandem with picture processing. Jackson took time to determine the angle and position of his camera relative to the subject. He usually set up his camera in the shade, which allowed the glass plate to remain wet a bit longer.

In 1872 Jackson continued to document the exotic wonders of the Yellowstone Plateau. Pictured here is the Jupiter Terrace of Mammoth Hot Springs. National Archives ID No. 517641.

He focused the camera, moved back to the box where he would sensitize a glass plate, rushed it wet back to the camera, placed it within the camera, then exposed the plate to light by removing the lens cap. Then he retrieved the glass plate from the camera, returned it to the dark box, and developed it. If the plate photograph was acceptable, he then started the process all over again by moving the camera to a new angle or a new subject. This process usually took about forty-five minutes from beginning to end. At Mammoth Springs, since he did not have to move his camera much, he was able to accomplish it all in just over fifteen minutes. It also helped that the springs offered hot water. "By washing the plate in water that issued from the springs at 160 degrees Fahrenheit," Jackson wrote later, "we were able to cut the drying time more than half."[12]

Everyone had their roles as members of the survey. Some tended mules; others cooked; while a pair of men, Joe Clark and Jose—last name unknown—served as hunters. Jackson and his assistant remained busy taking photographs, not only of the surrounding sights of Yellowstone but of one another. He took pictures of their encampments and smaller groups of friends among the survey party, all for the folks and friends back home. Dr. Hayden supported all this peripheral picture taking, for he wanted word to spread as far as possible about his survey, and to the good doctor, there was no such thing as bad publicity.

With so many of the men responsible for different duties, the larger party typically scattered during daylight hours. Horsemen and some of the soldiers led the way along the trail, while the hunters fanned out in search of game. Some of the cavalrymen sometimes ended their days separate from the main party and established their own campsites. Mule packers were often at the end of the march.

The party left the Mammoth Hot Springs on July 24, then crossed branches of the Gardiner River as they moved southeastward to the banks of the Yellowstone River. They were in high mountains, and the meadowlands spread out like green carpets, dotted with colorful flowers and occasional copses of aspens. This was high summer for the men at Yellowstone, as Hayden wrote, "The climate was perfect and in the midst of some of the most remarkable scenery in the world, every hour of our march only increased our enthusiasm."[13] The men remained in close proximity to the Yellowstone River as they continued their passage over the Yellowstone Plateau. They took in the Devil's Den, a dark, ten-mile-long canyon that channeled Tower Creek.

Jackson and his assistant were often off on their own in search of landmarks to photograph. This meant they left the trail and the main party frequently. They spent entire days out of sight of the larger group and then stumbled into

The Hayden Survey of 1871, quite enlarged from 1870, stretches out along the banks of the Yellowstone River. Dr. Hayden is the second figure from the right. Note the party's wheeled odometer at the center of the photo. Library of Congress. LC-USZ62-20198.

base camp well into the evening. Continuing their grand circuit of the eastern portion of Yellowstone, Jackson and Dixon followed Tower Creek and then reached nearby Tower Falls, the first falls Langford had reached the previous summer that had initially impressed him so much.

But the lay of the land proved almost insurmountable for Jackson's photographic work. Clambering down the steep embankment with his equipment was difficult, since it required the transfer of all the moving parts of the process—dark box, camera, glass plates, everything—to the bottom of the defile and the creek to capture the falls from the best angle. Jackson refused to bypass the falls despite the difficulty, until he arrived at a solution. He set up his camera at the base of the gorge, then went topside, retrieved a wet plate, which he protected with wet blotting paper, then practically slid down to the bottom to slip the plate into the camera and get the shot. It was all very awkward and taxing, but Jackson managed to take four or five photographs using this method. By then he was drained: "The return trip was slower but more breath exhausting and I was 'wringing perspiration' by the time I was wrapped up in the dark box."[14]

With their photographs completed, and the larger party having finished their work, the men moved on, turning westward, leaving the Yellowstone

River behind. Everywhere they encountered more amazing sights, including additional hot springs, accompanied by vapor vents nearby and the distinctly unpleasant odor typically associated with rotten eggs, that of sulfurated hydrogen. They turned farther south and reached the Washburn Range by way of Dunraven Pass. The trail passed through more rugged terrain marked by side canyons and deep ravines festooned with eroded rock columns "resembling Gothic Spires."[15] When they arrived at Mt. Washburn, they climbed the summit to ten thousand feet, and they could see the Tetons off to the south. From this high point, they could see more than a hundred miles of black pine forests extending to the Madison Mountains, as well as the Gallatin Range to the north. To the southeast, Yellowstone Lake spread out for mile after distant mile. As they descended from the mountain, they passed through heavy pinewoods that led them out onto thick, green fields of grass and aspen. They also discovered more of the thermal wonders of the plateau, including mud pots and an extensive field of minerals including copper, alum, and sulfur.

Some thought they heard thunder rumbling in the distance. But it was the remote noise of water falling. Just like Langford, Jackson and his fellow survey members were even more impressed with the next falls they reached on their trail. Jackson wrote, "Pictorially the climax of the expedition came with our week's stay at the Falls and Grand Canyon of the Yellowstone."[16]

The Grand Canyon of the Yellowstone has remained a highlight for millions of visitors to Yellowstone National Park for more than a century and a half. Members of the Hayden party approached the deep canyon through a heavy pine forest. There, before them and spreading out for miles, was the rumbling flow of the Yellowstone River "in a serene broad valley with a floor of lush grasses spangled with red geraniums."[17] Soon they arrived within sight of the falls along the west bank of the Upper Falls, its waters streaming over high rock shelves from a height of 109 feet into a large pool at the base. (Hayden miscalculated the height of the Upper Falls at 140 feet.) But the noise of the falls was overshadowed by the thunderous sound of another waterfall in the nearby distance. The men continued along the river, which turned northeast, and within a quarter mile of coursing water they arrived at the Lower Falls, its vast mountain flow cascading downward a distance of 308 feet. (Again, Hayden overestimated the height of the Lower Falls at 350 feet.)

While all the men were mesmerized by the falls, the photographers and artists saw these sights as fodder for brush and lens. Jackson had a clear self-awareness regarding his contribution to the Hayden Survey and its implications for Yellowstone's future: "I could not help feeling a pardonable degree of pride and satisfaction in the thou't that it was my great privilege to be the first to train a camera on the 'Wonders of the Yellowstone' and that my photographs were to be the first to go forth into the world showing better than words the beauties and marvels of nature's greatest handiwork."[18]

But the responsibility of capturing Yellowstone's dramatic scenery was not entirely that of William Henry Jackson alone, for he was not the only photographer on the survey. Thomas Moran and a second artist were also tasked with producing their own types of pictures, using paints and brushes rather than cameras and wet plates. The party's second photographer was Joshua Crissman from Bozeman, Montana. Jackson and Crissman had met in Corinne, Utah, prior to the 1871 Hayden Survey. Crissman had made his darkroom available to Jackson and Hull during their 1869 trip along the newly completed UP line between Omaha and Ogden. But Crissman experienced some bad luck while creating his photographs in Yellowstone.

Crissman and Jackson often moved together, selecting camera angles to share. At one site—it is today known as Artist's Point, which clings to the canyon wall—Crissman set up his camera to take a photograph of the Lower Falls. Then the unthinkable happened, the worst calamity to befall a photographer in the field. After positioning his camera on a tripod, he took a photograph, pulled out the wet plate, and headed for the developing box set up in nearby woods, where Jackson and his associate were also working. When Crissman returned to his camera, his heart sank. In his absence, a gust of wind had upended the camera and sent it plunging two hundred feet down the cliff, dashing it to pieces on the primordial rocks below. He found his colleagues and said, "in a quiet, resigned way, 'Well, boys, my whole outfit has gone to hell a-fluking.'"[19] Crissman, Jackson, and Dixon all rushed to the cliff edge and peered over to assess the damage. There, hanging from a bush, was Crissman's black cloth under which he took his photographs. Below that, they could see the camera in fragments scattered down the ravine. This might have marked the end of Crissman's usefulness to the Hayden Survey, but Jackson stepped in and salvaged the moment by providing his old 6½-by-8½-inch format camera for Crissman's use for the remainder of the trip.

Still, the importance of Crissman to the final legacy of the Hayden exploration would remain limited. Crissman's photographs were never published nationally, which means that only Jackson's photographs managed to reach the public eye to help lift the veil of mystery regarding the wonders of Yellowstone.

The roles played by the photographers on the Hayden Survey were unique and definitive. Decades following the 1871 Hayden Survey, historian Hiram Martin Chittenden published the first edition of his famous park guidebook *The Yellowstone National Park: Historical and Descriptive*. In this seminal Yellowstone work, Chittenden expresses the importance of the photographic legacy Jackson created that summer of 1871: "The chief value of these explorations was not in the line of original discovery, but in the large collection of accurate data concerning the entire region. The photographs were of immense value. Description might exaggerate, but the camera told the truth; and in this case the truth was more remarkable than exaggeration. Unfortunately, for Captain Barlow's collection, the great Chicago fire almost destroyed it. . . . The report and collection of photographs and specimens by Dr. Hayden were therefore the principal results of this season's work, and they played a decisive part in the events of the winter of 1871–2."[20]

Once the work at the falls was completed, the party set out for Yellowstone Lake, which they had observed from the heights of Mount Washburn. Traveling from the falls to the lake took three days due to the difficult terrain, including hot springs, mud pots, steam vents, and heavy woods. Visitors to Yellowstone today simply take for granted the easy access they have to practically all the wonders of the national park. Boardwalks, bridges, protective barriers, and repeated signs warning against unsafe activities help provide a safe context for any visitor. That none of these protections were in place in 1871 goes without saying. The men of the Hayden Survey had to proceed with caution to avoid serious injury or even death. Scalding water can kill, so keeping a safe distance was a must. But what was safe? How close was too close? On several occasions, in the name of science, someone might edge up to a geyser opening or an aquamarine pool without knowing exactly how much of a risk he was taking. Between the falls and the party's arrival at Yellowstone Lake, Hayden gingerly tried to take a closer look at a grouping of mud pots, but he broke through the encrusted surface and slipped down to his knees, covering his lower legs with hot mud. Still, all the members of the expedition did emerge from their Yellowstone experience alive and well.

About ten miles above the waterfalls, the party reached a collection of springs emitting a metallic sound, similar to an "impulsive noise like a high-pressure engine," which the men named "Locomotive Jet."[21] Two miles later, beyond Locomotive Jet, the men reached the same series of hot springs the Washburn-Langford-Doane Party had arrived at the previous summer, including the Grotto and the Giant's Cauldron. Indications are that this geyser base was fairly new in origin, spewing "like an immense caldron of mush submitted to a constant, uniform, but most intense heat."[22] Hayden ordered the men to make camp nearby.

By July 28 they reached the northwest shores of Yellowstone Lake. "The Lake lay before us, a vast sheet of quiet water," wrote Hayden, "of a most delicate ultramarine hue, one of the most beautiful scenes I have ever beheld. The entire party was filled with enthusiasm. The great object of all our labors had been reached, and we were amply paid for all our toils."[23] Here the men unloaded a special piece of equipment meant just for this moment. From the backs of several mules, a collapsible boat framework was removed and pieced together, measuring 12 feet in length and 3.5 feet wide. It was covered with two layers of tarred ducking. Spars were attached, plus a sail fashioned from horse blankets. At the makeshift boat's stern, a lead line was attached to take depth soundings. James Stevenson christened the boat the *Anna*, after the daughter of a US congressman from Massachusetts, H. D. Dawes, who had supported the funding of the Hayden Survey through Congress. Early on July 29, Stevenson and the Smithsonian's Henry Elliott set out in the small craft and rowed it to an island close at hand, which they named after Congressman Dawes, the name it still retains.

The *Anna* proved an excellent lake craft for the survey. The men determined quickly how the lake changed through the course of its day, its surface remaining calm during mornings, becoming choppy by noon, followed by rough water in the afternoon hours, which meant the men ventured out farther from shore in the morning and stayed close to the lake's banks in the afternoon. Elliott and the survey's zoologist, E. Campbell Carrington, sketched the lake's dimensional shape, plus its islands. The work was not easy, as Yellowstone Lake features twenty-two miles of shoreline and measures fifteen miles across. Sometimes afternoon winds stirred up the lake waters, creating whitecaps and waves cresting at four or five feet. The men also took lots of soundings, with depths reaching up to three hundred feet. Although the lake was brimming with trout, many carried a white intestinal worm that rendered the meat inedible.

After three days Hayden, Jackson, Elliott, and a few other members of the party set out toward the geyser basin along the Firehole River, one of the headwater rivers forming the Madison. The men were soon thrashing through a maze of fallen trees that stretched on for miles, great blowdowns where trees were stacked pell-mell up to six feet in height. After more than thirty miles of difficult hiking, they reached the river, but found it was the east fork of the Madison, rather than the Firehole. Despite the mistake, they did discover several springs they would have otherwise missed. On August 1, after passing through another six miles of rugged forest, they reached Firehole Basin. The small party encamped through the nights of August 2 and 3 at a location today known as Lower Geyser Basin, surrounded by hundreds of streams of steamy smoke rising from the area's geysers and steam vents. They gave new names to a few of the geysers, including White Dome and Fountain Geyser. Over the millennium, trees had fallen amid these hot springs, creating petrified wood.

On August 4 Hayden and his small party left Lower Geyser Basin and followed the trail until they reached the Upper Geyser Basin, by evening. The Washburn–Langford–Doane Party had encamped near this same location a year earlier. Not long after the men had established their campsite, they were startled as "a tremendous rumbling was heard, shaking the ground in every direction, and soon a column of steam burst forth from a crater near the edge of the river. Following the steam, arose, by a succession of impulses, a column of water, apparently six feet in diameter, to the height of 200 feet, while the steam ascended a thousand feet more."[24] The eruption lasted between fifteen and twenty minutes, and the geyser gained the name "The Grand." Thirty-one hours later, it erupted again. In a letter Hayden wrote to the Smithsonian's Professor Baird, the survey leader expressed his pleasure at having arrived at the geyser basin, stating, "We found everything in the Geyser region even more wonderful than it has been represented."[25]

At this point, Jackson and a pair of comrades separated from Hayden and the others to explore west of the Firehole River, where no previous expedition had wandered. They went in search of an alleged geyser basin on a tributary of the Madison. With no clear idea of where they were going, they wandered until they reached the Black Sand Basin, a portion of the Upper Geyser Basin. Here Jackson managed to take a photograph of a large geyser while it was erupting. The photo is impressive, but his camera could not freeze frame the spewing water due to the required exposure time. Hayden, meanwhile, continued to explore the region he later called the Central Springs, and began naming several sites: the Bathtub, the Punch Bowl, the Dental Cup.

Jackson wrote later that the 1871 Hayden Survey did not spend much time at the Firehole Valley Basin, which meant the geysers there did not receive a significant level of attention. "But if the geysers were slighted on this expedition," he noted, "another one a year later was to do them full justice."[26] The smaller Hayden party finally left the basin and returned to Yellowstone Lake and the main party's encampment, to discover a new arrival who had caught up with them—Lieutenant Doane, along with a sergeant and four cavalrymen. He had been detained at Fort Ellis when the party left, but he soon took command of the cavalrymen assigned to the expedition. Since he had explored the region the previous year, the men were excited and hopeful the lieutenant knew some easier trails, ones that might avoid the tree entanglements that slowed their progress. It was not to be, however. As they left the lake, with Doane leading the way, they passed through the same thick underbrush until they seemed hopelessly off the trail. After hours of thrashing about, Doane led them to a fresh trail. At least that's what everyone thought until they realized the party had merely managed to double back on their previous line of travel.

During the days spent at Yellowstone Lake and the days immediately following, Jackson did not take many photographs. But once the party emerged from the heavy forests that had so impeded their path, they were out in the open once more, out into spaces where Jackson's camera could record the impressive scenery. At Signal Hills he shot photos of the lake, as well as the local mountains, one of which Doane and Langford had climbed during the previous season. Doane and Stevenson made a similar climb together up a mountain later named for the lieutenant. (Two other mounts are today named for both Stevenson and Langford.)

The weather in Yellowstone can shift on a dime, and this summer was no exception. On the morning of August 10, Hayden rose to discover his water pail was ice covered, with the temperature hovering at a frosty 15 degrees. The days offered fewer hours of sunlight, and nights remained cold. Additionally, the party's supplies were running low. Over the next few days the men frantically worked to accomplish as much as they had time to, including working around Yellowstone Lake. Hayden and a small party tried to complete their work on determining the lay of the Continental Divide. On Sunday, August 20, an earthquake startled them all, a phenomenon somewhat common to the Yellowstone Plateau.

The time was arriving for the Hayden party to abandon the Yellowstone for the season. On August 23 they moved up Pelican Creek, headed toward the northeast until they crossed the East Fork of the Yellowstone River to Bottlers Ranch, where they greeted the Dutch brothers and retrieved their wagons. The party had spent thirty-eight days in the Yellowstone and covered more than one thousand rugged miles of one of the most scenic stretches of the West.

During the final days of September, the members of the 1871 Hayden Survey reached Fort Hall and then headed east to Evanston, where they could connect with the UP railroad. By October 1 the party began to disband and scatter, with every member of the survey feeling he had made his own contribution to the expedition. In fact, the Hayden party emerged from the Yellowstone Plateau having not only seen its wonders but documented them through photography. This set things in motion for the slowly developing notion that the plateau was in need of protection. Things began to move quickly. On October 27 Hayden received an important letter from A. R. Nettleton, a representative of Jay Cooke and Company and the NPRR. In the letter Nettleton stated, "'Judge Kelley' has made a suggestion which strikes me as being an excellent one, vis. Let Congress pass a bill reserving the Great Geyser Basin as a public park forever—just as it has reserved that far inferior wonder the Yosemite Valley and big trees. If you approve this, would such a recommendation be appropriate in your official report?"[27] Elements both inside the federal government and in the private sector were coalescing to transfer the Yellowstone Plateau into a protected wilderness. (Judge Kelley was actually William Darrah, who served as a representative to Congress from Pennsylvania.)

Hayden certainly approved of the suggestion and soon began utilizing his professional gravitas to lobby for the movement favoring the protection of Yellowstone. As had Langford the previous year, he penned his own article for *Scribner's Magazine* to help further advertise the wonders of the region, wonders worth guarding. (Moran provided the illustrations for the article.) He urged the passage of a national park bill in the pages of the *American Journal of Science and Arts.*[28] Jackson's photographs played their own unique role in helping to convince members of Congress to support such a bill. The Hayden expedition had completed the most recent, as well as most accurate, description of the sights located in Yellowstone to date, and the outside world's interest had never been keener in setting aside the Yellowstone Plateau from any form of private exploitation. Newspapers joined the chorus. The *New York Times* editorialized on Lieutenant Doane's report, titling its article "The New Wonder Land." In this piece, the editors seemed reluctant to accept Doane's descriptions of Yellowstone and called for "confirmatory testimony," making reference to Hayden and his party: "The official narrative of the Hayden expedition must be deemed needful before we can altogether accept stories of wonder hardly short of fairy tales in the astounding phenomena they describe."[29] By the article's end, the *Times* made clear it was among the true believers: "We have heard enough now to be satisfied that the region in question must be among the most wonderful of this wonderful central continent of ours, and to suspect that it deserves, in this wise, absolute preeminence, Prof. Hayden's official report, which we hope, will not be long delayed, will enable us to arrive at conclusions more positive."[30]

With the end of the survey, Jackson was prepared to board the nearest train and head back to Omaha and his wife, who was pregnant. She, in his absence, had minded the photographic store. Before they parted, Hayden requested Jackson take a side trip on his way home to photograph several Pawnee villages located one hundred miles or so west of Omaha, as these Native Americans were slated for removal soon for relocation in Oklahoma. Jackson complied; he was, after all, a permanent, paid member of Hayden's geological surveys. When his work was completed, he sent prints of his photographs of the Omaha Indians to Dr. Edward Painter, who had abandoned a medical practice in Baltimore in exchange for becoming the Indian agent to the Omaha Reservation. In time the Painter family and Jackson became close friends. Jackson had already begun photographing the Omaha before he went west, and his collection of Indian pictures was expanding. Eventually Jackson's Indian photographs, taken over several decades, numbered close to two thousand.

Once back in Omaha, Jackson found Mollie in good physical condition, her pregnancy now close to full term. But she was tired and ready for her husband to take over her responsibilities. Anticipating the need to leave Omaha for Washington, Jackson got the studio into good working order and ready to sell. When a buyer came along, Jackson retained his cameras, as well as all his negatives, of his Indian subjects, his UP work, and the hundreds of photos he had shot in Yellowstone. Soon they packed up and headed east, first to Nyack, New York, and Mollie's parents, who had recently retired from their business. Will's star was starting to rise a bit higher, and it was a change he could feel in the moment, as he wrote later: "Within the next few months I was to begin to taste that little fame which comes to every man who succeeds in doing a thing before someone else."[31]

During their extended stay, Jackson received a message from Hayden calling him to the capital, where he was urgently needed. Hayden wanted Jackson to print copies of several of his pictures to hand out to every congressman as part of the effort to convince the legislators to create a new national park out of the Yellowstone Plateau. Although he had only returned to his pregnant wife a mere matter of weeks earlier, he soon left her in the care of her parents and took a train to Washington. (The original plan had been for Jackson to remain with Mollie until the birth of their child, then precede her to Washington while she recovered in the arms of her parents.) He would soon regret his premature departure.

9

The Tetons, 1872

*M*ollie's pregnancy had progressed well over the months, but she had remained very busy, rarely able to take any extended breaks or rest periods. While she appeared to be in good health—just a little tired—things went terribly wrong during the child's delivery, a premature birth. As Jackson later wistfully wrote, "She was not ever to join me again. In February, when her baby was born, Mollie died. Our child, a daughter, survived but a short while. These are matters about which, even now, I can write no more."[1] Jackson wrote these words more than sixty-five years later.

Despite his pain and loss, Jackson remained in Washington and continued his work alongside Hayden. With the question of Yellowstone's future hanging in the balance, he was in the capital to provide prints of his photographs to help "sell" the concept of setting aside the plateau—at least some portion of it—for posterity, a place maintained for future generations of Americans and other visitors to allow them to see what Hayden, Jackson, Langford, and others had already seen for themselves. This was a project the photographer embraced eagerly. (Perhaps one motivation was to provide himself with a distraction to take his mind and emotions away from the double loss of his wife and the daughter whom he would never see.) Whether Jackson retained a sense of guilt over his wife's death or not—she had likely overworked herself in his absence out West—remains uncertain. He had chosen to work for Hayden, a decision requiring a long absence from home at a time when his wife likely needed him to be available. Now she was dead. Nothing could bring her back, including any number of regrets. Just as Jackson had poured himself into his work out West for three summers running, now he concentrated on nothing but his work in Washington as a means of justifying that earlier commitment.

His photographs were crucial to the next step in designating Yellowstone as a national park. Crissman's photographs, those taken as part of the Barlow-Heap expedition, had already been destroyed by the Great Chicago Fire. To provide the ultimate evidence—irrefutable photographic evidence—that the wonders of Yellowstone were actually real was exclusively in Jackson's hands. To facilitate the production of the necessary print copies of selected photographs, Jackson was provided photo workrooms outfitted in the Hayden Survey headquarters, a dedicated building on Pennsylvania Avenue. (Since the federal government had already approved these and future surveys, such a facility was needed as a headquarters for Hayden and his team members, whose work would continue long after a given field survey was completed.) Jackson and several assistants worked tirelessly, nearly around the clock, to produce the necessary number of photographic prints.

The national park bill was crafted within a couple of months of Hayden's return from Yellowstone. Hayden was the bill's number one advocate, as he wrote of the importance of "setting aside the area as a pleasure ground for the benefit and enjoyment of the people." He warned of dire results if the bill did not pass: "Persons are now waiting for the spring to open to enter in and take possession of these remarkable curiosities, to make merchandise of these beautiful specimens, to fence in these rare wonders, so as to charge visitors a fee, as is now done at Niagara Falls, for the sight of that which ought to be as free as the air or water."[2]

The bill was introduced in both the House and the Senate on December 18. The bill's House sponsor was William H. Clagett, the territorial delegate from Montana, and in the Senate Samuel C. Pomeroy from Kansas, the chairman of the Committee on Public Lands. Pomeroy introduced to his fellow senators "a bill to set apart a certain tract of land lying near the headwaters of the Yellowstone as a public park."[3]

Over several months' time, Hayden, Langford, and others lobbied for the creation of the national park at Yellowstone. Hayden was intense in his support. After all, he knew as much about the Yellowstone Plateau as any living American, and his endorsement was significant. In late February 1872 a portion of his draft report on Yellowstone, which he wrote for the Committee on Public Lands, accompanied the final version of the proposed national park bill. In this report, Hayden predicted the future, stating, "In a few years this region will be a place for resort for all classes of people from all portions of the world."[4] Near the timing of the final vote, Hayden played his trump card. Jackson had reproduced prints of his greatest hits from the expedition, including scenes of Mammoth Hot Springs, Old Faithful, the Grand Canyon of the Yellowstone, and a host of additional views. These were placed in gilt-edged folios, with a copy placed strategically on the desk of every member of Congress.

Jackson's photographs weren't the only "evidence" of the wonders of Yellowstone mass produced and distributed to members of Congress. Four hundred copies of one of Langford's *Scribner's Monthly* articles were also disseminated to Congress the day before the vote was taken on the bill. By February 1872 Hayden's own article in the pages of *Scribner's* appeared, and his included a targeted appeal for the establishment of Yellowstone National Park. He wrote, "The intelligent American will one day point on the map to this remarkable district with the conscious pride that it has not its parallel on the face of the globe. Why will not Congress at once pass a law setting it apart as a great public park for all time to come?"[5]

Hayden's contributions in support of the creation of Yellowstone National Park are impossible to exaggerate. His survey was not just one more in a series of organized explorations, such as the Washburn-Langford-Doane mission. His was official, an act of the federal government, paid for by taxpayer monies, a scientific exploration, not simply a lark carried out by curious westerners or those searching for a means to personally profit from the Yellowstone Plateau. Hayden's stake in the game was a professional one. He was intent on his surveys serving the government and the people of the United States. And his 1871 survey helped provide some of the facts and pieces of hard evidence needed to banish all doubt among those who only knew about the Yellowstone Plateau from a degree or two of separation. Hayden had already made a personal investment in Yellowstone, and his reputation as a scientist now depended on the knowledge he and his men had gained in the West and how they presented this to the American public, as well as to hundreds of members of Congress. In this context, Jackson's photographs were a necessary piece of the puzzle.

While William Henry Jackson's photographic skills were crucial in support of the passage of the congressional bill to create the first national park in the United States, the artistic skills of Thomas Moran played their own important role. But just as he had an impact on the advancement of the concept of a national park system, his experiences in the West, starting with the 1871 survey—his first, but not his last—would help set the direction and tone for his career as a painter. He came to the Hayden Survey as a young artist. At thirty-four, his entire life to date had been spent back East, mostly in Philadelphia. His common means of travel had been by boat, stagecoach, and railroads. He came out to the Far West, recruited by Hayden with the encouragement of others, particularly Jay Cooke, the founder of the NPRR, with little concept of just how significantly the West would alter the direction of his career. (Cooke was interested in building a railroad line into Yellowstone to encourage tourism.)

His first contribution to the opening of Yellowstone was to provide illustrations for Langford's two *Scribner's* articles published in May and June 1871. Moran had not participated in the Washburn–Langford–Doane Expedition directly, and his illustrations were based on less professional renderings made by members of the expedition. Once Moran joined the Hayden Survey, he soon realized he had landed in a completely different world, one in which a talented artist could find scenic inspiration at every turn. For weeks he sketched what he saw, often alongside Jackson as the photographer took pictures. He filled sketchbooks with plenty of concepts for later paintings that would soon propel his career to new heights.

When the survey ended, and Moran returned back East once more, he set out to produce a painting destined to become one of the great masterpieces of his career, a grand rendering of the Grand Canyon of the Yellowstone, a massive canvas measuring seven by twelve feet. The canyon inspired him. Jackson wrote, "Moran's enthusiasm [for the canyon] was greater than anywhere else."[6] Moran was still at work on the painting in the spring of 1872 when Yellowstone became a national park as President Ulysses S. Grant signed the bill into law on March 1 after Congress voted unanimously in favor. Moran contributed to the multitiered campaign to create a national park through a series of watercolor sketches. When the painting was completed, Congress purchased the huge work for $10,000. For many years the great western canvas hung in the Senate Corridor of the Capitol. (Today, it hangs in the National Statuary Hall in the U.S. Capitol.)

Moran's watercolor sketches and his *Grand Canyon of the Yellowstone* provided a depth of documentation to the Hayden Survey of 1871. Hayden produced a lengthy government report chock full of details about Yellowstone, Jackson snapped hundreds of black-and-white photographs, and Moran sketched. While they both often performed their specific talents in Yellowstone in close proximity, Jackson and Moran had assumed two different tasks. Still, these two men became an unbeatable team. They shared time and effort together, sometimes documenting the same Yellowstone wonder at the same time. They developed a close professional and personal relationship that lasted until Moran's passing in 1926. Moran's journal of his days spent with the Hayden Survey that summer lacks significant detail, but there are pithy references to his working with Jackson, such as his August 9 entry, "Went to the Geysers. Helped Jackson during the day."[7]

In contrast, Jackson sometimes provided extended details explaining how the two men worked in tandem: "He [Moran] was also as interested as the photographer himself in selecting the view points for each negative, having in mind, perhaps, the good use he could make of the photographs later in some of his own compositions."[8] Jackson's point was likely well taken by Moran, who actually did consider the survey photographs a crucial aspect of the expedition, even as he utilized them to provide him with scenic perspective after he returned to the East and began framing his *Grand Canyon of the Yellowstone* composition.

Of all the works Moran produced from his participation on the Hayden Survey of 1871, his oversized Grand Canyon painting looms large. Even the way in which he arranged his painting was a complicated process that went beyond a single, on-site perspective. He remained at the falls for four days, along with Jackson, taking in the scenery from as many vantage points as could be humanly accessed. For many years, it was believed Moran utilized Yellowstone's "Artist's Point" and attempted to produce a true, accurate painting of the Lower Falls of the Yellowstone River. Certainly both Moran and Jackson utilized that specific vantage point, for there are Jackson photos and Moran sketches that serve as nearly exact footprints of one another. But a comparison of Moran's sketches, compared with the large painting he eventually completed, reveal that the artist chose to blend vantage points, thus recreating the landscape before him rather than simply copying it through paint on canvas in its natural exactitude. Even Moran had to admit he fudged the landscape to create a composition more to his own liking, resulting in a more dramatic composition of the falls than nature itself had produced. Of this he wrote:

> Every form introduced into the picture is within view from a given point, but the relations of the separate parts to one another are not always preserved. For instance, the precipitous rocks on the right were really at my back when I stood at that point, yet in the present position they are strictly true to pictorial nature; and so correct is the whole representation that every member of the expedition with which I was connected declared, when he saw the painting, that he knew the exact spot which had been reproduced. My aim was to bring before the public the character of that region. The rocks in the foreground are so carefully drawn that a geologist could determine their precise nature.[9]

The result of Moran's manipulation of the landscape of Yellowstone's Grand Canyon is that his painting and several of William Henry Jackson's photographs present subtle contrasts. In the painting, Moran has "pushed" the Lower Falls backward, telescoping the falls to a greater distance than nature had placed it. This gives Moran's version a greater depth of field, opening up his 12-foot-wide painting to reveal a grander vista based on a more fully developed V shape.

This allowed Moran to develop more pronounced flanking rock formations, including a scattering of limestone pillars on the painting's right. The right side of the painting is a contrast of brightly illuminated rock cast in varied hues of yellow, orange, and pink, offset by the dark, right foreground of jagged-edged rocks and spindly pines clinging to the thin rocky soil that flank yet another rock outcropping resembling marbled, maroon-colored raw meat. (In contrast, Jackson's best photographs of the Lower Falls do not have the option of landscape manipulation for aesthetic enhancement or even of color.) Contrast this with the expansive rock ledge dominating the left foreground. Here the colors are tones of gray and green, as the stone features various skims of moss and lichens in shades of blue and green.

The falls are exactly where they should be, but with the result that, in Jackson's photographs, based on a vertical format, the waterfall serves as a portion of a sweeping Yellowstone vista without necessarily commanding the view. The lines of Moran's painting spread out, enhanced by a muted mountain light set in contrast to grand rock formations flanking the painting's foreground while distant shadows trick the viewer into focusing on the water-fall, a dazzling, misty cascade of icy mountain water. Yes, Moran's version of Yellowstone's Grand Canyon is a color feast, a spectacular rendering of slip-pery colors running from red-rock boulders to a creamy contrast of mineral-laden limestone. The work seems to depict a fictional, rocky world left to spend eons of time alone. But Moran brings the viewer back to the realities of 1871 by placing two human figures standing in an off-center foreground on a rock ledge that did not actually exist, as it does not appear in any of Jackson's photographs. These two *repoussoir* figures are stand-ins for a Hayden explorer alongside a Native American. This represents Moran's attempt to humanize the work, to link the arrival of Hayden and the men of the survey to this exotic place and reconcile their recent arrival to an ancient landscape. In the end, Moran has appropriated the sweeping landscape of the canyon and manipulated it into the best version of itself, all according to the trained eye of the artist. These foreground human figures are juxtaposed with a trio of geysers steaming far off in the distance, revealing a scope of landscape that even a 7-by-12-foot canvas cannot fully reveal.

Compared to Jackson's black-and-white photos, Moran added something new to the emerging story of Yellowstone: color. His watercolors are awash with vivid shades emphasizing the texture of the Yellowstone landscape, which helps provide depth to the land, delineating the ancient curvature and contour of geyser basins, boiling springs of aquamarine water, and variegated color and tone palette of Yellowstone's Grand Canyon. It's all there in his watercolors, helping to mature his artistic style into a western form while revealing "the dramatic geological features, expansive vistas, and lack of lush vegetation in the West."[10]

Jackson certainly understood that Moran's sleight of hand regarding his depiction of the landscape of the falls fell within the artist's discretion. Both artist and photographer were keenly aware that photographs are accurate depictions—the picture taker has little choice, really—while the painter is allowed to distort the image to fit his own perception of the landscape.

Both a photograph and a painting could be considered their own forms of art. This was something Moran's brother, John, himself a photographer, wrote about. John would sometimes accompany his artist brother in the field and take photographs of the same nature scenes Thomas was sketching. The photographs provided Tom with visuals in creating his paintings or watercolors. John became an early advocate for photography as an art form. In 1865 he wrote that, in the right hands of one with "the instincts, feelings, and education . . . of the artist" photography became art: "True art . . . is interpretation, not imitation; the artist becomes a brilliant commentator on the book of nature, holding up to our vision harmonies and beauties that are invisible to ordinary mortals, and, giving us the power to see beyond our natural vision, he is a prophet-poet, and in an ideal sense, a creator."[11] Jackson knew the difference between the depictions of the land provided by photography and the opportunity for unique self-expression inherent in a paintbrush and canvas. In the end, of course, Jackson ultimately chose one over the other. He did not attempt to use his artistic skills to enhance an artist's career, but rather chose the opportunities for aesthetic expression through his lens.[12]

Moran spent a couple of months working on his massive Grand Canyon painting, which was unveiled at a private showing in Leavitt's Art Rooms in New York City's Clinton Hall on Thursday evening, May 2, 1872. *Scribner's* underwrote the special event, which included NPRR officials, members of the press, other artists, and a variety of pillars of New York society, plus Hayden, of course. The artist had already sent a letter to Hayden on March 3, emphasizing the importance of the painting, stating that he was "casting all his claims to being an Artist, into this one picture of the Great Canyon, and [I] am willing to abide the judgment upon it."[13]

He followed up with an additional missive to Hayden on April 6, stating, "The picture is all that I ever expected to make it, and the indication is that it will make a sensation wherever it is exhibited."[14] Moran's confidence in his work was justified. The painting was well received, accompanied by extravagant reviews. Clarence Cook, critic for the *New York Tribune*, raved: "Mr. Moran's 'Grand Canyon of the Yellowstone' [will] . . . be received by the best judges in America as the finest historical landscape yet painted in this country," and, if not, it would "rank with the great landscapes of Church, Bierstadt, and Gifford."[15] One of the painting's reviewers even quoted directly from Hayden's official report of the expedition: "The entire volume of [the waterfall] seems to be . . . hurled off the precipice with the force which it has accumulated in the rapids above . . . and as it strikes the rocky basin below, it shoots through the water."[16] Over at *Scribner's*, the reviewer paid as much attention to the sky above the landscape as to the scene itself: "There is . . . atmosphere so puzzling to the artist from the ruthlessness with which it denies him those convenient grays . . . and over all, there is the violent sky."[17]

Just as Jackson's photographs represented an important success for Hayden—not to mention Jackson's career—and the prominence of his surveys, so did Moran's watercolors and his monumental canvas. The painting added a grand element to the increasingly public documentation of the Hayden Survey's trek through Yellowstone, awakening a greater number of the American people to the wondrous realities of the plateau.

Hayden was extraordinarily pleased with the work Moran completed and the public's response to it. He understood that if Moran's star was on the rise, that fame would continue to touch the geologist if he kept the artist close by. In August 1872 Hayden wrote to Moran and stated, "There is no doubt that your reputation is made. Still you must do much to nurse it. . . . The next picture you paint must be the Tetons. . . . I have arranged for a small party to take you from Fort Hall up Snake River, thence to the Yellowstone. . . . Put in your best strokes this summer so as to be ready for a big campaign next summer."[18]

Throughout the 1870s, as Hayden led his survey teams into the West, he remained his own best advance man. Although he had already accomplished one of his grand goals—pushing through Congress the establishment of Yellowstone National Park—he continued to advance his reputation and that of his expeditions by any means necessary. He utilized the mass print media of his day, including newspaper and magazine articles. (In all, he penned three pieces extolling his surveys in the pages of *Scribner's Monthly*.) Such documentation, including his government reports, served two purposes: (1) to function as a government source providing information concerning various regions of the West, and (2) to publicize many of those same findings to an American public thirsty for information about the vast and often vacant lands on the frontier. While the written word was an effective tool for disseminating the knowledge he and his men accumulated through the surveys, he also understood, early on, the importance of photography. It is here that Jackson played an important and recurring role.

But Jackson's early photographs, those he took in Wyoming in 1870 and in Yellowstone the following year, could only reach so far. Every photograph required printing by hand in a dark room, for no technological process was in place at that time to mass-produce his photographs. Even when a photograph was used to illustrate a magazine article, it was not the actual photograph itself. In such cases, the picture first had to be copied as a woodcut or similar hand-drawn reproduction of the original. This resulted in a degree of separation between the actual photograph and the published facsimile accompanying the article. Such a reproduction could serve as a stand-in, a strong impression of the original without providing the actual photograph's true detail.

In 1872 a breakthrough technique was in the making, one Hayden intended to utilize. In New York City a local photographer and engraver, Edward Bierstadt—brother of the painter Albert Bierstadt—purchased the rights to a new prototype process developed in Germany called Albertype. The process was a form of photomechanical reproduction. With this technology, a photosensitized image originating from a glass negative was inked, resulting in images then printed from Albertype plates. The result was an image as close to the original photo as then was possible.

Hayden made arrangements with Bierstadt to provide the engraver with glass negatives from Jackson's Yellowstone pictures to print copies in large numbers, without the hand labor involved in making one print at a time. Hayden anticipated great results from the process and advertised it in 1873 by promising his next special report would "contain about one-hundred illustrations, printed by the Albertype process from photographic negatives taken by Mr. Jackson. The views will embrace some of the most remarkable scenery of the West.[19]

But alas, it was not to be; at least not as Hayden planned. On February 8, 1871, Bierstadt's 10th Street studio experienced a serious fire involving a great chemical explosion witnesses described as sounding "like the discharge of a fifteen-inch gun." The *New York Times* reported the accident had occurred when, "Mr. BIERSTADT, the brother of the painter, was bending over the box containing the negatives when the explosion, caused by the ignition of a match in the atmosphere highly charged with combustible gas, occurred."[20] Everything was destroyed. This ended Hayden's plans to utilize the photomechanical reproduction process with which he intended to further advance the reputation of himself, his surveys, and William Henry Jackson.

Not only did the US Congress pass the law creating Yellowstone National Park during the spring of 1872, but its members also voted to fund another exploration of the Yellowstone Plateau, plus the adjacent Teton Range to the south. And they funded the project at a new level of commitment: $75,000. Other surveys were also in the works at the same time, including those of John Wesley Powell and Clarence King, but in the year 1872, Hayden's surveys led the field. Hayden's projects were well known and the best funded; they utilized the most talented scientists; and especially through the photographs of Will Jackson, they were the best documented in the public mind.

The Hayden Survey for 1872 was larger than ever, including sixty or so men. But this time the larger party would not move as one, but was initially divided into two parties to cover more territory during the survey season. Hayden was to rendezvous at Fort Ellis in Montana, just as the 1871 party had, and then follow the same basic route into Yellowstone as before. The second party, led by James Stevenson, planned to originate in Ogden, Utah; travel to Fort Hall; then head eastward into the region of the Tetons, explore Pierre's Hole—otherwise known as the Teton Basin—then continue on to Jackson's Hole, enter Yellowstone through Targhee Pass—today's West Entrance to the park—and ultimately link up with Hayden's party at the Firehole Geyser Basin.

The expedition's members included several veteran hands: Stevenson, Dr. Albert Peale, Will Jackson, Shep Madera (the packer), and the cook "Potato" John Raymond. Nathaniel Langford was also invited to join them, as he had been appointed the first superintendent of Yellowstone National Park. There were new members as well, including Henry Gannett, who was included as an astronomer. (Gannett remained a member of the Hayden Surveys through the summer of 1879.) He brought along a variety of important equipment, including an astronomical transit, a zenith telescope, several barometers, and a telegraph key set. Years later Gannett became the chief topographer for the US Geological Survey and served as one of the six original founders of the National Geographic Society. Another new member was twenty-six-year-old William Henry Holmes, who was married to the daughter of the Smithsonian's Professor Henry. He chiefly worked as a topographer on the survey, along with Gustavus Bechler, a skilled mapmaker. Additional members included geologist Frank Bradley and botanist John Merle Coulter. The youngest member was an ornithologist, sixteen-year-old C. Hart Merriam, who later became a trustee of the National Geographic Society. As for Jackson, he brought along Charley Campbell, an eighteen-year-old cousin of Mollie's.

Just as on previous Hayden Surveys, Jackson was to play an important role for the 1872 expedition. With the Tetons on the agenda, the party was planning to explore yet another region previously unphotographed. His list of photographic equipment did not change much from the previous western venture, but he did add a new camera, one with an 11-by-14-inch format, to allow him to take larger photographs. This decision did affect his development process, as he described: "Since it was impossible to prepare and develop the bigger plates in my portable dark box, I now had to set up a dark tent every time I wanted to make a picture. This little tent had a cover of gray-white canvass; but inside it was lined with orange calico to cut out the actinic rays. . . . The work of this season [included] forty-five 11 by 14 views, the very first plates of this size ever to be made in the Rocky Mountains."[21]

Fortunately for Jackson, he was assigned to the Stevenson party. This group of thirty-seven men left Ogden on June 24 and proceeded to Fort Hall, then headed eastward into rugged country with hardly a road to follow. The wagons were abandoned, and the party continued with pack mules and one heavy-duty wagon. They continued for weeks until they began to notice, off in the misty distance, the jagged mountains known as the Tetons. These peaks gained their name from mountain men who had reached the area to trap beaver. No one knows the name of the French trapper who saw in their stony undulations the shapes of a woman's breasts, but the name was given: Les Grands Tetons, otherwise known as "the Paps." Hayden had seen them before, and he saw nothing feminine about them, but rather envisioned shark's teeth. But there they were, off in the distance, ready for exploration.

By mid-July the men reached Henry's Fork of the Snake River and then stuck to it for many miles. The land they passed through was largely barren, offering little vegetation for food, other than camas and Yampa plants, highly prized by the Native Americans despite their tendency to produce flatulence. On July 20 the men abandoned Henry's Fork and continued through rolling hill country to Pierre's River, the Tetons looming higher with each passing day. Jackson wrote in his 1929 autobiography that "this side trip to the Tetons was really secondary to the main object of the expedition, but by this time the Yellowstone had lost something of its novelty, and the Tetons, never before photographed, now became the first importance, so far as I was concerned."[22] Jackson took few photographs prior to his party's arrival at the western base of the Teton Range or Pierre's Hole, named for an Iroquois Indian trapper. During the heyday of the western mountain men, Pierre's Hole served as a site for their annual early summer rendezvous, a convergence point for trappers, Indians, and company men to settle up the season's beaver takings, a gathering legendary for carousing and heavy drinking. The basin featured lush meadows, where a proliferation of strawberries grew along the riverbanks. The waters and grass drew wildlife in abundance, and Stevenson's men spotted deer, antelope, and elk tracks, while hunters regularly delivered meat for the men to enjoy.

The party camped in Pierre's Hole on July 23 at the mouth of Teton Creek, the largest tributary of Pierre's River. Following the river for another fifteen or twenty miles, the men reached the base of Grand Teton, where Stevenson ordered a camp established. From here the party began its exploration and photographing of the Tetons. The party operated out of this campsite for the next ten days, and Jackson worked constantly. "I spent every daylight hour exploring canyons," he wrote, "and traversing the snowy fields above [the] timber line in search of views of the higher peaks."[23] Much of the time he was accompanied by Dr. J. M. Coulter, the botanist, plus three other men, including a mule packer. This small party of five often remained in the field on their own, separate from the larger party. Three mules—including Will's favorite, Old Molly—carried their blankets, food, and equipment, including Jackson's photographic necessities.

For three days the Jackson group made camp right on the edge of the timberline. Overall, moving up the mountains looking for photographic vantage points "was not generally difficult, as the inclination of the rocky strata was such that it afforded a gradual rise with but few breaks."[24] But high-country snows did pose a problem. At one location the party arrived at a "wall of rock over which a goat might have made its way, but which seemed impossible for a pack mule." A sheer drop flanked the narrow pass, while on the mountain side of the trail the snow lay deep, angling toward the cliff edge. But the difficult, dangerous trek paid off. Jackson and his colleagues reached a site offering "a glorious near view of the Three Tetons with the Grand Teton . . . directly in front of us." The photographer had found his sweet spot and spent the remainder of the day taking photographs with his three cameras: the 11-by-14, the 8-by-10, and his stereoscopic. Fortunately the weather was warm enough to melt snow, providing Jackson with the necessary water to process his negatives. This required the erection of his portable tent-darkroom, of course, with each photograph taking up an hour of his time.

This was Jackson at his most intrepid: surmounting treacherous mountain trails, guiding his mule to safety to avoid losing all his precious equipment. He was in the wilds of an uncharted landscape, photographing for posterity a mountain range no one had ever captured on wet plates. His work put him in difficult places, working with the exacting details of photographing and processing his pictures in a hostile environment. Sometimes he even camped alone overnight so he would be in just the right place to take a photograph at just the right time.

In the meantime, Stevenson and Langford decided to climb to the summit of the Grand Teton. They took a dozen men with them, starting at dawn on July 29. This was a foolhardy venture, for no one had the proper (and necessary) mountain-climbing equipment, only alpenstocks and a bacon sandwich for each man's lunch. But up they went, in a morning temperature of eleven degrees above zero. Despite the beauty of the high country, including white, blue, and deep red flowers, plus the occasional buttercup, the climb proved difficult. The snow complicated things immediately, and the altitude began to affect several of the men. One sprained his ankle. In time, nine of the party dropped out, leaving Stevenson, Langford, and three others. By lunchtime the men had arrived at a saddle north of the Grand Teton, where a cold wind added to their difficulties. Here the geologist Frank Bradley dropped out. The dropout rate indicates the difficulty in scaling the Grand Teton.

While the party's goal was to crest the summit of Grand Teton, it appears this goal was never achieved, despite later claims. Langford later wrote that he and Stevenson reached the summit at three o'clock, with their last two comrades dropping out three hundred feet short of the peak. At "the main

In 1872 Jackson took the first photographs of the Teton Range south of Yellowstone National Park. He took the shot from the west of the Tetons. The peaks, left to right, are Mount Owen, Grand Teton, Middle Teton, and South Teton. US Geological Survey Photographic Library. W. H. Jackson 162.

summit . . . exposure to the winds kept it free from the snow and ice, and its bald, denuded head was worn smooth by the elemental warfare waged around it. . . . [W]e were obliged to don our overcoats for protection against the cold mountain breeze."[25] Langford also wrote about a rock shelter built by a previous arrival. While Langford and Stevenson had undoubtedly accomplished a great feat of mountain climbing that day, they had certainly not reached the true summit site of Grand Teton. Today, the enclosure Langford describes is still at the site, but it is eleven hundred feet west of the actual summit and five hundred feet lower in elevation. Still, the claim of conquering Grand Teton was made, one Jackson supported for years to follow. At the time, there was no reason for the photographer to doubt the veracity of Stevenson and Langford's account.

Through their days separated from the larger group, Jackson and his associates received regular supplies of flour, bacon, and coffee through a messenger dispatched at intervals. They lived at their high elevation "in the open, without tents, depending entirely upon our tarpaulins to keep blankets dry at night when mountain storms broke loose."[26] After more than a week on their own, with the completion of Jackson's picture taking, the five-man party began their descent from Teton heights to rejoin their comrades. Unfortunately they tried to take a shortcut down the mountain and wound up late in the day stranded on a rocky ledge with no clear path in front of them. Ironically, they could see their comrades far below, a great fire lighting up the distant encampment. Jackson and his comrades could even smell coffee and bacon wafting up to their lofty perch. They shouted down but were never heard. Given the late hour, they decided to remain on the outcropping overnight and find their way down the next morning, when they rendezvoused with the larger party in time for a hearty breakfast. They arrived on August 2.

The reunited party was now in a hurry to catch up with the other half of the Hayden Survey at Firehole Basin. They headed northeast to the headwaters of Henry's Fork, then crossed easily over the Continental Divide through Targhee Pass. The trail was hardest on the mules, which were continually hemmed in by fallen trees. (One poor animal required her load to be readjusted twenty-five times along only seven miles of trail.) But it was high summer in Yellowstone once again: "It was August, and spring and fall flowers mingled in the upland meadows. Rich-colored little violets, blue, purple, and yellow monk's-hood, geraniums, and fringed gentians intermingled in the green velvety meadows. Nothing could compare with the beauty of nature's carpet. The aspens stood still, patiently awaiting summer's end, and the sky was a deeper blue."[27]

By August 14, all parties converged along the Fire-Hole River, including Shep Madera, who had made a trip to Virginia City and returned with a mule train loaded with needed supplies. All sixty-one men were present and accounted for, and together they took the opportunity to name Grand Teton after their leader as Mount Hayden. (In the long term, the name did not stick.) They also named another peak after Thomas Moran, a name it has retained until today.

The large party only remained together for a few days, then they scattered in different directions. Hayden headed for the Bottlers Ranch, while Stevenson left for Virginia City to retrieve fresh supplies. Bradley took a party on to the geyser basins. Jackson separated himself from his party after reaching Targhee Pass, as Langford joined him and led the way to the Lower Firehole. As usual, the trails were uncertain, and the men mistakenly went up the Gibbon Fork rather than the Firehole branch. Lost on the trail, the party camped in the wilderness and even managed to lose a favorite horse of Hayden's. The borrower left the animal tied up with too much rope, and it became entangled, strangling itself.

The next morning, Jackson shinnied up a pine tree to gain a better view of the surrounding countryside. Detecting steam columns in the distance, he observed the direction to the geyser basin. Soon he and his comrades found their way to the Lower Fire Hole Basin. The calendar showed it was late fall, and the temperature was dipping precipitously. Through the final weeks in the Yellowstone Plateau, Jackson spent time returning to the geyser basins he had visited the previous year, taking new photographs of the geyser craters and hot spring pools. He spent a full week at the two basins. As Hayden later wrote in his report, "Mr. Jackson, the photographer of the Survey, penetrated this region for the first time last summer and obtained from it some most marvelously beautiful views of the scenery. I doubt whether there is any other portion of the West where all the elements of landscape beauty are more happily combined."[28] Jackson photographed Old Faithful but did not produce a picture that adequately pleased him. (Not until 1883 did Jackson finally produce a satisfactory picture of Old Faithful. The issue was the difficulty of capturing the geyser spray given a long shutter exposure.) On one outing, Jackson and the botanist John M. Coulter stumbled onto a previously undocumented waterfall on the Gibbon River, about five miles east of modern-day Madison Junction. The men of the 1872 expedition named the river after General John Gibbon, who had earlier explored the region, and his name was also given to the falls.

One morning the men awoke to a frigid 4.5 degrees above zero. The Tetons were often shrouded in clouds, and snow was falling in the high country. Jackson and his party headed along the upper Snake River and then on past the mouth of Salt Creek. The heavy timber began to disappear, replaced by an emerging sagebrush plain. On October 11 the party reached Fort Hall;

days later, they arrived back at their jumping-off point of Ogden, Utah. This final leg, from Virginia City to Ogden, was completed by stagecoach, which normally covered the 550 miles in about five days. With so many men taking a pair of Concord stages—Jackson claims his stage carried twenty-two passengers, with several stuffed inside and ten riding on top, plus a half dozen sitting with the driver—each stage's six-horse team was overworked, causing the trip to take a bit longer. The adventure was heightened when highwaymen held up one of the coaches and relieved the stage of its strongbox and all the passengers of their money, watches, and jewelry. Fortunately for the Hayden men, they had not yet been paid. Once in Ogden, the men began to scatter as the Hayden Survey broke up into its individual parts.

The men had accomplished their various professional, governmental, and technical goals during this foray into the region of the Teton Mountains. Throughout the following months, several of the scientists sent papers to be included in Hayden's final report, spanning topics from fossils to dragon flies to bird lice. John Coulter's botanical studies included reports on sixty species of grasses, fifty-three of mosses, sixty-six of lichens, and a long list of twelve hundred plant species. Sixteen-year-old ornithologist C. Hart Merriam managed to collect 313 bird skins, plus 67 bird's nests, many complete with eggs. All of these specimens were subsequently stored in the Smithsonian Institution.

Jackson was pleased with the work he had accomplished as a permanent member of the Hayden Survey. He had utilized his largest photographic format to date—11-by-14 inches—in the field satisfactorily given the difficulties of his venture and the limited scope, which generally focused on the Tetons. It was not about how many photos he had taken but the quality of those he did take. And his time spent in the Tetons proved just the beginning. As he later noted in his 1929 autobiography, "The difficulties we met trying to get pictures of the lofty Tetons were but an introduction to further mountain adventures."[29]

Colorado, 1873

$\mathcal{O}$nce back in Washington, following the completion of the fieldwork in the Tetons and Yellowstone, Jackson was as busy as ever, lending a hand with Hayden's report and classifying and cataloging his photographs, while making prints for distribution among members of Congress, as well as friends and colleagues. Hayden had plans to return to the same general region of the West the following year, but poor governmental relations with the Native Americans, especially the Lakota, rendered an expedition into either Montana or Wyoming too dangerous, even with an army escort. Instead, the famed geologist began looking at another western destination, one ripe for exploration and mapping: Colorado.

Just as Montana and Wyoming were originally unknown to all except the mountain men, so Colorado was a mystery save for its miners and prospectors. Rumors had flown both east and west in 1859 excitedly announcing discoveries of gold and silver in the Pikes Peak region. New prospectors from back East, as well as Forty-Niners who had already tapped the surface gold in California, rushed out to Colorado as Fifty-Niners, a new wave of western goldmen. By 1870 the territory's non-Indian population had risen to nearly forty thousand, and mining was the consistent draw. Two regions saw concentrations of prospectors along Colorado's Front Range—one was Denver and a cluster of mining camps farther west, including Central City, Boulder, and Gold Hill, and a second was farther south, including Colorado Springs and Pueblo.

In time others joined the placer miners, including railroad entrepreneurs; eastern investors interested in deep, hard rock mining; and those seeking to establish vast ranches, including venture capitalists from England and Scotland. In 1870 the UP completed a line connecting Cheyenne with Denver. Just a few months later the Kansas Pacific also reached Denver, providing a direct link to the Missouri towns of Kansas City and St. Louis. Denver was suddenly a booming town with real estate investors grabbing up lots by the dozen. To link Denver with smaller Colorado communities, railroad promoter General William A. Palmer received a charter to construct the Denver & Rio Grande Railroad (D & RG), a narrow-gauge line. Colorado was now the scene of investment and settlement, on its way to becoming one of the most economically expansive territories in the West.

But even as the boom spread, much of Colorado remained a mystery. Few of its lands had been mapped. The Rockies, the vast mountain range that cut a chain from north to south, were unknown. With railroad expansion on the horizon, accurate maps and surveys became essential. There were vast gaps in knowledge regarding the territory's topography, mineral wealth, flora, and fauna. For Americans to fully exploit Colorado's assumed vast potential, someone would have to go out and explore its secrets. Thus Hayden, deterred from Wyoming and Montana, decided to take his men out to Colorado to see what they could find. As he later wrote in his 1873 government report, nowhere else in the West promised to "yield more useful results, both of a practical and scientific character. . . . The prospect of its rapid development within the next five years, by some of the most important railroads in the West, renders it very desirable that its resources be made known to the world at as early a date as possible."[1]

Hayden proposed a survey greater in scope than his previous ventures into the West. He anticipated a multiyear, comprehensive exploration, utilizing all the scientific fields he had previously encouraged. His men would fan out in multiple parties; study the mountains, the minerals, and the animal life; and classify as much as humanly possible. Some of this information could prove valuable to the railroads or to mining companies and, of course, to the federal government. Jackson would naturally play his usual role and capture the sights and possible wonders of the territory for the outside world. Initially, Hayden thought three or four summers might suffice. Congress bought into his vision and agreed to fund him with amounts varying from $65,000 to $95,000 per season.

Hayden intended to concentrate on the Rockies and the Front Range. He had little interest in the dry plains west of the mountains. He arranged for expert topographers to create an accurate atlas of the Colorado Territory, at least the portion he saw as having the greatest potential for settlement and exploitation. To this end, he again lined up one of the best American topographers available, William Henry Holmes, who had participated in the Teton Survey. The atlas became the grand goal of the Hayden teams that ultimately tromped over the mountains for four seasons (1873–1876).

By late spring Hayden's right-hand man, James Stevenson, had established a base of operations in the field, in the midst of a cottonwood grove near Miers Fisher's ranch at Clear Creek four miles outside Denver. This site served as ground zero for Hayden's men, some of whom were old hands, including Potato John, Shep Madera, and Tom Cooper. The scientists arrived in slow waves, and soon all were familiar with one another, ready for a season in the field.

When Jackson arrived from Washington in Denver on May 14, he was a man contemplating love. His wife, Mollie, and their newborn girl, had passed away only fifteen months earlier, a true tragedy, one made more difficult for Jackson due to his absence from her side when she died. Hayden had called him to Washington to rush print his photographs. How much her passing weighed on Jackson throughout that difficult year is unknown. Jackson wrote little about her death. How many times he found himself facing quiet moments in the Tetons as memories swirled through his head was a secret Jackson kept to himself.

But another woman was starting to capture his interest. He had first met her father, Dr. Edward Painter, the Indian agent for the Omaha Reservation, back in 1871. Jackson subsequently became a friend of the family and met Painter's daughter, Emilie. At the time Jackson was still a married man, and nothing romantic transpired between the two. Following Mollie's death, he "received a letter that was far more than a perfunctory expression of sympathy, with the result that I called on the Painters the next time I visited Omaha."[2] Following that visit, a correspondence began between Emilie and Jackson, with letters moving between them "with a frequency that would seem remarkable."[3] A long-distance relationship blossomed and, just prior to leaving for Colorado, Will asked for Emilie's hand in marriage. She accepted, "even knowing the worst—that I was a traveling man."[4] An October wedding date was soon being planned, and most of those plans unfolded with Jackson away in the backcountry of the Colorado Territory.

In an effort to cover as much territory as possible during the 1873 summer season, Hayden divided his men into several divisions or parties, terms Hayden typically used interchangeably. During their four years exploring Colorado, Hayden's men never moved as a single unit but were often divided into a half dozen or so parties, each working in its own designated region, which might put them as far afield as the Yampa River in the north and Mesa Verde in the southwest corner of the territory. For the 1873 season, the men were divided into three main divisions, each usually numbering between eight and a dozen. Each was assigned a specific piece of Colorado geography. A fourth division, one led by James Stevenson, was responsible for keeping each party supplied with food and equipment and replacements for broken or lost items. Hayden led a fifth separate division to provide overall coordination of the other moving parts, a difficult task at best. Members sometimes jumped from one party to another, but most of the groups consistently included a geologist, a mapmaker, several naturalists, mule packers, hunters, and a cook.

For the first time, Hayden placed Jackson in charge of one of the parties, a sixth division in the field. Jackson was thrilled with the assignment, as he wrote: "I felt like a general in command of an army."[5] (This was Jackson's fourth survey with Hayden and his second taking photographs in Colorado.) Jackson's men included John Coulter, the botanist; Lieutenant W. L. Carpenter, an amateur entomologist on leave from the US Army; a youth named Cole who was the son of a California senator and amateur ornithologist; veteran packers Tom Cooper and Bill Whan; and Jackson's favorite cook, Potato John Raymond. In the field the men rode horses, but they continued to rely on their steady pack mules, six in all, to carry the supplies, food, and equipment, including Jackson's all-important cameras and photographic supplies.

Jackson and his men left Clear Creek on May 24. He had received his marching orders from James Terry Gardiner, one of Hayden's favorite topographers: "First to Long's Peak, thence south along the Snowy Range to Gray's Peak, and from there work around by way of Pikes Peak to a rendezvous of all parties . . . in South Park."[6] The rendezvous was set for six weeks later at the town of Fairplay near the mining community of Leadville. Jackson's first objective was Longs Peak, located fifty miles northwest of Denver, so named for an early American explorer, Major Stephen Long, who had explored portions of Colorado in 1820. His assessment of the region specifically and the plains generally—that they amounted to an uninhabitable, great American desert—had deterred pioneers from seeking their farming fortunes in the nation's heartland as they turned west to Oregon and California instead, where prospects were considered a bit brighter. The first day featured a clear sky, soon offering a view of the distant peak. The trail was paved with nature's sandstone, then shale flats. On May 26 they reached the foothills of the Rocky Mountains at St. Vrain Canyon. They arrived at Estes Park after five days' travel, in the vicinity of Longs Peak, but on that day a stiff, cold wind blew so hard even Jackson was not willing to defy it by taking photographs. Nearby the party's campsite was a cabin, home to a family of three including a daughter who "was quite young and good looking."[7] Jackson made nice with the family, was invited for supper, and enjoyed an evening that included the attractive farm daughter.

The following day Jackson did manage to take some photographs of Longs Peak, but he needed to get closer for better shots. The party continued on until they arrived at a mining camp. Jackson and Whan decided to climb the mountain, an attempt that did not go well. They lost track of the trail and slogged through deep snow for six hours until they reached a mountain lake, where Jackson took "a fine view of the main range from Long's Peak to James [Peak]."[8] The return to their campsite was equally as difficult.

Jackson remained in the vicinity for a few days and photographed along Boulder Creek, then he and his comrades headed toward James Peak. Luckily they stumbled upon a road they knew nothing about. It was obviously abandoned, given the number of fallen trees scattered along the way, but it was passable, and the party made good progress. They then reached a small settlement site, but no one was present. It was one of those Colorado mining communities that had earlier warranted three stamp mills to process the unearthed ore, but the precious metals had since played out, leaving behind a ghost town. The party left the abandoned village without having learned its former name.

Ahead, the weather turned harsh, as "snow fell nearly every day, and two hours' work out of twenty-four was my average," Jackson later wrote.[9] But at certain moments the sky opened up, providing the photographer with the necessary opportunities to take his pictures in a region "so rich and splendid that a stock of finished plates soon piled up." The mules slogged through the snows with difficulty, but when the party reached another mining community, Georgetown, the weather had turned for the better, and the pack mules celebrated by dropping out of their usual line, "up the alleys, upon the footwalks, and even into the open doorways of stores," remembered Jackson. "Seldom has so small a pack train produced such confusion."[10]

Beyond Georgetown, Jackson's men and mules proceeded over Leavenworth Mountain and camped in Argentine Pass at 11,000 feet elevation. At Grays Peak—named for a well-known botanist of the day, Asa Gray—Jackson and the Cole youth reached the summit, their barometer reading an elevation of 14,274 feet. Next Jackson climbed nearby Torreys Peak, which came in at 10 feet shorter. There was no photographic motivation for these climbs, for it was not possible to haul equipment and process pictures under such conditions. Jackson was climbing mountains because they were there.

By June 23 the party was out of the granite heights and reached Bear Creek. They could not have known then, but the men were on top of a great dinosaur burial site that later became famous as the Morrison Formation. Some of those bones were unearthed a mere three years later. Moving south along the Front Range, they reached Colorado Springs on July 1. The town was booming due to the arrival of the D & RG in 1871. This did not mark the beginning of the community, which was originally laid out by Rufus Cable and Colonel M. F. Beach as miners rushed into the region in 1859. Through the dozen intervening years, Colorado Springs had become a destination for wealthy tourists, offering high-class hotels and spas. Pikes Peak dominated the local skyline.

Great mountains, including Pikes Peak, flank Colorado Springs to the west, but Jackson was equally intrigued by a spread of great red sandstone formations that had risen up thousands of years earlier, creating a unique landscape of tilted slabs and fantasy formations that an earlier entrepreneur had dubbed the Garden of the Gods. Jackson spent two days photographing the iron oxide–tinted formations, resulting in the earliest known pictures of this exotic landscape. Although the photographs would have to wait several years before they were tinted to reveal their natural color, the strange stone formations provided Jackson with one of his most dramatic subjects to date. On the Fourth of July, the party took a break to enjoy the baths at Manitou Springs, located just west of Colorado Springs.

All the members of Jackson's party remained constantly busy as they moved here and there, often pinballing from one site to another, as the weeks clicked down to the scheduled rendezvous with the other divergent portions of the Hayden Survey team. "My companions were as busy as I was," Jackson later wrote. "Carpenter with his bugs, Cole with his birds, and Potato John,

Jackson achieved another first with his photographs of the Garden of the Gods outside Manitou Springs, Colorado, likely taken in 1873. This image depicts the park's Cathedral Spires. Photo provided courtesy of the Museum of Fine Arts, Houston, TX. ID No. QhrA356KbcrSg.

as always, with his bacon and biscuits."[11] The cook's day began earlier than everyone else's so that breakfast was ready when the larger group arose, typically at 3:30 in the morning. They were often on the trail by first light.

The party often followed an old Ute Indian trail, which led them into the valley of the South Platte River, then north across today's Florissant Fossil Beds National Monument. A volcanic eruption had dammed up a local spring and formed a prehistoric lake, leaving many insect and fish species trapped. When the lake eventually dried up, the fossils remained for later discovery. Jackson and his men did not uncover the fossil beds, but another Hayden party did so a year later. On July 6 the party was beyond Wilkerson Pass, where they marveled at the sight of South Park, one of four intermountain natural parklands and perhaps the most scenic. Here they were surrounded by high peaks, including Mosquito and Sawatch Mountains to the west and the Thirtynine Mile volcanic field to the south. The men crossed the park's flat land and its whitened salt deposits dating back to the days when an ancient lake had occupied that same location. Local entrepreneurs had already built a bathhouse in the area for tourists, but Jackson and his men had no time to take such a break. They needed to reach Fairplay to meet their colleagues.

The following morning, they arrived on schedule. Jackson and his men had covered the seventy-two miles from South Park to Fairplay in three days. That afternoon two additional divisions met them like clockwork. Over the next few days, most of the others were also on site, but Hayden was not among them. He had sent letters to the local post office informing his men he was still on his way. This gave everyone time to enjoy a mutual encampment, where they shared stories of their adventures. As Jackson wrote later, "The day was given over to having a good time with our comrades of the other divisions and joining, in a mild way, in the diversions of the town. It was a 'wide-open' western mining camp and contained all the elements of a miners' paradise."[12]

While waiting for Hayden to arrive, many of the men fanned out to explore the local countryside, including Jackson. He ventured off toward the Park Range of mountains, from Hoosier Pass to Weston Pass, then a region being heavily mined. He was intent on photographing Mt. Lincoln, the highest of the local mountains at a height of 14,286 feet. The photographer not only shot Mt. Lincoln, he also utilized its heights to create a unique visual montage, one for which he became noted: the panoramic photograph. The mountains of the West, whether those of Colorado or Wyoming or some other frontier locale, were always enticing subjects for Jackson. They came to represent "a sort of vertical frontier, substituting for the horizontal spaces of earlier years."[13] Mountains remained the general focus for his photographs throughout the last five years of Hayden Surveys. And mountain chains gave him the opportunity to replicate, in black and white, long horizons of photographic panoramas.

With his 11-by-14-inch camera format, he sometimes linked from two to six shots together in a visual chain to present the sweep of the western landscape. He created one such panorama while atop Mt. Lincoln, titling three photos *Quandary Peak, Blue River Range in Distance, North from the Summit of Mt. Lincoln*. His vantage point revealed a boulder-strewn foreground typically found at such heights while depicting an undulating high-country landscape of deceptively soft smoothness, featuring Quandary Peak at its center and Grays Peak along the distant right. Such panoramas gave viewers a fuller perspective of the Colorado mountains by depicting their interconnected natural state, rather than showing them as separate mountains, creating a photographic depth signaling the vast scope of the land and the big sky that hovered above. None of this took away from his single 11-by-14-inch photographs from some lofty Colorado height depicting a broad valley in the distance that shrank the Arkansas River, for example, to a narrow, glistening interruptive thread. Scope, sheer scope was always a significant aspect of Jackson's Colorado photographs.

Jackson and his men returned to Fairplay by July 11 and discovered that Hayden had indeed returned, although he was away from the base camp exploring some local hills. The following day Jackson received "delightful letters" from Emilie.[14] Hayden arrived back at the camp on July 13 and informed Jackson that he was to complete his work by September 1 and the entire party would finish the season early.

Will continued to photograph several sites in the vicinity of Fairplay over the next several days, but by July 18 "we were ready to go our separate ways again."[15] Hayden's instructions to his photographer were to double back on the Sawatch Range to the Elk Mountain region between the Gunnison and Grand Rivers. (Today this portion of the Grand is identified as part of the upper Colorado River.) Then Jackson was to proceed to a region where myth and reality had yet to be scientifically separated. For years stories had filtered out of the Rockies of a great mountainside blazoned with a natural cross formation in the Sawatch Range, revealed when seasonal snows filled its vertical and horizontal arms. Hayden wanted the "cross" located and photographed.

As Jackson and his party prepared to fulfill the next phase of their work on the 1873 survey, the photographer did so with a new mount. Up to this point in the season he had ridden a horse, but the animal pulled up injured, requiring him to take on a replacement. The only animal available did not bode well: "a little white mule, with white eyes, which was considered too capricious and unmanageable for packing and was running loose."[16] But Jackson set out to rehabilitate the mule everyone called Dolly, and in short order he managed to tame her. She remained his only mount for the next five years of the Hayden Surveys.

Titled The Photographer's Assistants, *this 1873 photo shows how a mule was often burdened with Jackson's bulky camera equipment. The picture was taken on a rugged patch of Colorado landscape. Library of Congress. LC-DIG-det-4a26901.*

Refitted with fresh supplies, Jackson's party soon headed toward the Continental Divide between South Park and the Arkansas River. They reached Weston Pass and then headed upward toward the tree line. Having taken this route through the pass, the men gained a clear view of the Sawatch Range from Mt. Massive to the Collegiate Peaks, with the Arkansas flowing close to their bases and Twin Lakes framed in the middle distance. The first day turned too cold and windy for picture taking.

His men camped near one of the lakes for a couple of days. No town lay close by, but a local settler claimed a large meadow and charged Jackson and his men twenty-five cents per animal to graze on his grass, which they refused to pay. Instead, they rented his boat for $2, utilizing it for fishing. Both parties considered they had made a good trade. Botanist John Coulter loved the area around the lakes, since it teamed with wildflowers. Jackson picked some and included them in a letter he penned to Emilie.

Jackson was hiking across God's country, through some of the most beautiful mountain landscapes in the United States. He was constantly compelled to take photos; as he wrote, "there were so many pictures that I had to take. Mount Massive—Mount Harvard—Mount Elbert, highest point in Colorado—La Plata—Snowmass—these and many more fell before my camera."[17] As the men of the Hayden Survey wandered across Colorado, they occasionally named mountains, sometimes after their wives, including Mount Rosa. An alum of Princeton named a mountain after his alma mater. At one location, a group inadvertently left their coffee pot behind, inspiring them to name the local pass accordingly, Coffee Pot Pass.

As Jackson and his men moved through the mountains, weather conditions did not always allow him to take all the photographs he longed to. The cameras of the 1870s required optimum sky conditions: clear, bright, with clouds to frame the shot. He had no replacement for these conditions in his darkroom. "We have no fast emulsions to counteract the effects of overcast skies," he later penned, "or to 'stop' wind-driven foliage, and we had no filters to define clouds and horizons against the sky. If the weather was good, I could take as fine a picture as can be made today. But on bad days much patient manipulation of the chemicals was needed to produce acceptable negatives."[18]

While in the region, he and his men reached the mining outpost of Oro City, which had been the scene of gold prospecting for ten years, supporting a community of five thousand miners. But by 1873 the mines had largely been played out, leaving a shadowy remnant of a mountain town; lots of abandoned, decrepit cabins; and the remains of mining equipment and broken down sluice boxes. There was also the shell of a former general store formerly run by Horace Tabor, who later struck it rich in Leadville, became a millionaire silver magnate, was elected to political office, and eventually lost everything during the Panic of 1893.

In early August Hayden expressed his concern to Jackson: "Hurry, You are losing golden opportunities."[19] The survey's director was afraid his photographer would not be able to photograph all the sites he had planned. Then Jackson experienced his first photographic mishap during his years as the survey's chief picture taker. His party was passing along a high divide between East River and Rock Creek. "An evil mule named Gimlet slipped his pack and broke many of my exposed plates. The Doctor [Hayden] was the first person to notice what had happened. Following directly behind my party, he found plates along the trail and galloped up to learn the cause. By that time Gimlet had scattered most of his load, and it was too late to do anything except right the pack and go back to pick up the pieces. Many plates were unbroken or but slightly nicked; many more, however, all 11 x 14s, were irreparably shattered."[20]

Jackson was devastated—"I think I have never been so distressed in my life"[21]—but there was nothing for him to do but to retrace his steps and rephotograph some of the more important sights. Hayden was supportive and somehow assured Jackson that he had plenty of time. This put a finer edge on Hayden's concerns for Jackson to complete his full circuit of sites to photograph. Perhaps the survey director was primarily concerned about one sight specifically, the Mount of the Holy Cross. It was not the only goal of the survey, of course, but it was an important one.

From the outset of this particular survey, the chief goal had been to develop more accurate mapping of portions of the Colorado Rockies. Hayden had assigned survey topographer James Gardiner the daunting task, and the latter had taken up the challenge with relish and exacting organization. Early on, he had dissected the territory intended for exploration and mapping into separate parts. To the east lay the Front Range, including Longs Peak, Mount Evans, and Pikes Peak, the region's "fourteeners." To the west lay the North, Middle, and South Parks, with low-running cross-ridges separating them from one another. Then came the Sangre de Cristo Mountains, from South Park, including the San Luis Park. Across the thirty or forty miles between the parks, the Rockies rose high once more. On the northern portion lay Park Range and to the south the Gore Range—which Gardiner then called the Blue River group. Farther south of that region were South Park's Sawatch Mountains (Gardiner referred to them as the National Range). Southwest of the Sawatch Mountains were the distant Elk Mountains, noted for their lines of dark sandstone, and to their south the San Juan Mountains ran northwest by southwest. To their north the region was sliced here and there by high plateaus, river valleys, and isolated mountain ranges.

Gardiner's work often placed him apart from any one division moving in the field, but he did attach himself to the First, or Middle Park, Division for several weeks, led by Archibald Marvine, a soft-spoken geologist. After a few weeks he left the Marvine group and by August was in the field with Jackson. Dr. Hayden joined the party as well. After crossing Tennessee Pass, they followed an old Indian trail that was easy going, with the exception of a detour around Eagle River Canyon. They soon managed to reach the site of Holy Cross Mountain. Here the route became difficult, as they "found [the trail] impracticable," wrote Jackson. "The fallen timber, rocks, and bogs made such difficulties that we finally turned back and camped on the banks of the Eagle for the night."[22]

The next morning the men discussed their next step as they ate their breakfast. They decided to defer to Gardiner, who knew as much about the topography of the region as anyone among them. The party followed a stream for a while, then attempted a climb up the nearby ridge, but the way was blocked by scatterings of blowdowns, trees felled by high winds and age. Hacking their way through, they reached a narrow animal trail until they were again lost in piles of fallen trees. Through the course of the entire day, they only managed to proceed five miles. They encamped that evening in a ravine "where there was hardly more than enough room to unpack the mules."[23]

Part of the problem with the division moving through this area was their sheer number, approximately sixteen men and an equal number of animals. The decision was to jettison all nonessential personnel to accomplish the mission directly at hand: to locate the mountain and its elusive cross. The new party included Jackson and Coulter, a packer to aid them, plus Gardiner, Hayden, and William Henry Holmes, along with four mules. Three ax men were also retained, tasked with hacking a path out of the fallen tree barriers. Adding to the new strategy, the reduced party chose to abandon the ridge and try another approach up the valley. Jackson lagged behind the larger number and took photographs of the nearby mountain, then caught up with them as they followed the trail down the ridge for fifteen hundred feet. Throughout the day the party had not discovered a decent trail up the mountain, especially one the mules could reasonably tackle.

Night and another dawn later, the men were ready, with the photographers prepared to make another ascent up the rocky ridge before them. If they were successful, they anticipated finding themselves at a site from which a decent photo of the cross might be taken. "Tom [Cooper] took the cameras, Coulter the plate boxes, and I had the tent and chemicals," wrote Jackson, "a matter of forty pounds for each one. . . . It was a clear and wonderfully bracing morning."[24]

The Mount of the Holy Cross had proven elusive for so many years for two or three primary reasons, as Jackson noted in his autobiography:

> The name was a familiar one to Colorado people. Many had heard that over on the western side of the range somewhere there was a mountain with a great snow cross on one side, but we knew of no one who had ever seen the cross. The mountain itself is of such a commanding height that our topographers had located it from the surrounding, distant peaks. The cross itself can be seen under favorable conditions from far-away Grays Peak, but on nearer approach this feature of the mountain mysteriously disappears; from all usual points of observation it is not visible. It is cut off by a high ridge called Notch Mountain, which confronts the eastern face of the mountain carrying the cross. In fact, a near view can be had only from this ridge or from some higher point in the distance overlooking it.[25]

Rising on the morning of August 23, the leaders first chose a difficult route along the creek, then corrected themselves and struck up the ridge from their earlier location. It was chilly, and the fallen trees and rocks they encountered were whitened with frost, as it had rained the previous evening. Jackson usually led the way, and this time was no exception, "in advance of his assistants in order to prospect about the best points of view before they came up."[26] As he led the way, he climbed upward approximately a thousand feet, then neared the crest of the ridge. "Then I continued along it until I came out above [the] timber line at the foot of Notch Mountain, fifteen hundred feet higher yet, the attainment of which was to reveal the cross." Jackson later wrote of his ultimate moment of attainment:

> For some time I waited here for the others to come up, but as there was no sign of them, I continued on over the great masses of broken rock, eager to reach the point that would determine the success or failure of our efforts. I now began to hear faintly across the intervening gorge voices from Gardner's [sic] party, although I could not see them. They were ascending the mountain itself. Clouds began to gather, and as they drifted about among the peaks the top of the Holy Cross Mountain was hidden, except for occasional rifts and breaks. Pressing on steadily, I finally gained the summit of the ridge, and working along its crest, at last stood face to face with the Holy Cross in all of its sublime impressiveness.[27]

Jackson was the first member of the survey party to observe the Christian symbol from such a vantage point. His enthusiasm was unbounded: "It was worth all the labor of the past three months just to see it for a moment. . . . I found myself experiencing all the thrill of the old stories."[28] As Jackson waited for his companions to catch up with him, he sat down and enjoyed a sandwich, then "wrapped [my] dark tent around my shoulders as some protection from the cold wind, mist, and intermittent spats of rain."[29]

The photographer had arrived, but he postponed his picture taking and waited for his comrades to arrive—after all, they had some of his equipment—as well as for better weather before allowing himself to complete his assigned task: "Spent the night there supperles [sic] and without coats."[30] As the men huddled around their fire, they could see in the distance the fire of their comrades. Both parties could hear one another across the mountainous gulf, and they spent the evening occasionally shouting "Hellos!" to one another, helping to bridge the topographical gap between them. Jackson was anxious about his chances to photograph the cross the next day. "We were too impatient to enjoy such idle pleasures," he wrote later. "Seething inwardly, and all to no purpose. . . . We must have pictures before going down. And we would have pictures."[31]

On the morning of Sunday, August 24, the weather proved more accommodating, "without a cloud in the sky."[32] But Jackson and his comrades faced other issues. They were starting to feel sick from the altitude, in part due to their lack of food. The mountain was sapping their energy. As Jackson later wrote, "Climbing up to 13,000 ft. upon an entirely empty stomach & after the fatiguing exertions of yesterday, was no fun."[33] Another issue was a lack of water, an element absolutely required to process the wet plate photographs Jackson longed to take. The day before, the mountain had offered little streams of melting snow at every turn, but now "they were all hard & dry as flint."[34] But the Jackson party was fortunate to find a small reservoir in a large hollow rock well. (As the day went on, the sun also melted additional snow, according to Jackson.) His was a race against time and the weather: "It was a perfect day for the making of the first photographs of the Mountain of the Holy Cross. The early morning is the best time for this particular subject."[35]

Jackson was pleased with himself—working speedily under pressure, a bit light-headed from altitude sickness, and having missed breakfast—as he managed to coat, sensitize, expose, and develop eight 11-by-14- and 5-by-8-inch plates of the elusive Mount of the Holy Cross. It marked another first for the frontier photographer. (The cross in the snow is immense, with its upright measuring 1,500 feet in length and its arms reaching out for 750 feet.) Throughout the decades that followed, Jackson made at least three additional visits to the remote cross site, utilizing more modern equipment and cameras. "I have snapped my shutter morning, noon, and afternoon," he later wrote. "And I have never come close to matching those first plates."[36]

One reason Jackson was able to take such good photographs on that August 24 morning in 1873 was that he was already on site the evening before. This put him in the right place, at the right time, as he explained in a letter to Fritiof M. Fryxell, an American geologist and mountaineer who wrote extensively on the Teton Range in Wyoming: "The fine effect obtained in those old first negatives of the mountain and the cross was due mainly to their being taken soon after sunrise. . . . It is only by the early morning light that the strong lines of the mountain and cross are clearly brought out. Few photographers cared to spend the night on Notch Mountain to secure this effect." When Grand Teton National Park was established in 1929, Fryxell was named the park's first naturalist. He wrote scholarly works on both William Henry Jackson and Thomas Moran, including the brief study *William H. Jackson: Photographer, Artist, Explorer* (1939).[37]

In a typed letter—Jackson had recently purchased a Corona typewriter—to Thomas F. Dawson, then a historian at the Colorado State Historical Society, dated January 30, 1922, Jackson alludes to his first photographic venture to the Holy Cross site in 1873, then adds: "I photographed it again in '80 and '91 after I had gone into business for myself in Denver. In 1905 . . . I made a four or five day trip from Red Cliffs up Homestake to the Holy Cross Camp, then over the divide to Rock Creek, which we followed down to the Eagle again." Obviously, as with many other sites across the West, Jackson often returned to his earlier haunts to take additional photographs.[38]

Over the years, Jackson's photographs of the Mount of the Holy Cross remained some of his most popular pictures. The vast majority of Americans

Jackson took the first photograph of the Mount of the Holy Cross in 1873 after spending a supperless night on an adjacent mountain. National Archives. ID No. 517691.

were faithful Christians, and for nature to produce such a vivid symbol of their faith seemed more than simply natural happenstance. To them, it was a sign from above, God's personal seal of approval regarding Manifest Destiny and the movement into and settlement of the West. Even congressmen were inspired by the photos, which may have actually encouraged them to fund additional Hayden Surveys. Inspiration came in many forms, including artistic, with its discovery leading Thomas Moran to come out to Colorado the following year to paint one of his grand paintings of yet another wonder of the West. In 1879 New England poet Henry Wadsworth Longfellow referred to the cross in one of his poems.

Photographing the Mount of the Holy Cross was the culmination of Jackson's work during the 1873 survey season. While other members of the survey continued their work, including Hayden, Gardiner, and his geologists, Jackson headed for home. Emilie had set October 1 as their wedding day. In a sense, the West had separated them over the past several months, but Indians had brought them together, as Will had met his future bride while photographing the Omaha Native Americans with her father, Dr. Painter. Jackson soon headed across Tennessee Pass and then Mosquito Pass to South Park and on to Denver by way of Kenosha Pass and Turkey Creek Canyon. There he packed his luggage, his equipment, and his precious glass negatives for shipment back East, as he boarded a Pullman car for a train ride to Washington, D.C., and the Maryland girl he intended to marry.

II

Colorado, 1874

The wedding was a simple affair. Jackson married Emilie Painter, a young girl whom he barely knew, in Cincinnati, at the home of her brother, Samuel. Early in the nuptial plans, all parties—bride, groom, bride's parents—had agreed on a quiet ceremony with family, since Will was a fairly recent widower. (As they were also Quakers, they did not put high value on anything even remotely ostentatious.) The Jacksons honeymooned for a few days even farther east in New York City, staying at the Metropolitan Hotel on Broadway, below Twenty-Third Street. Then they took a train to Baltimore, where Will met additional members of Emilie's family. Dr. Painter, her father, was the Indian agent for the Omaha Reservation, the catalyst for Jackson's earliest contact with the Painter family.

Emilie's mother—her maiden name was Louisa Gilpin—was a frugal, gentle Quaker matron who worked alongside her husband at the reservation. Emilie's older brother, William, was an engineer of sorts, who was granted a patent for his development of a device that improved rail passenger seats. He was also credited with inventing the "crown seal" that is still utilized today to seal beer and soft drink bottles. Mrs. Painter's cousin, William Gilpin, was a man of the West for many years. A graduate of the University of Pennsylvania and West Point, he had fought alongside General Andrew Jackson during the Seminole War. He accompanied John C. Fremont all the way to California during his western explorations in 1843 and subsequently fought in the Mexican War. In later years he moved to Colorado as one of its original Fifty-Niners and was subsequently elected its first territorial governor in 1879. By that time, Will and Emilie were living in Denver, where they spent many evenings hosting Emilie's famous uncle, with the governor regaling the Jackson children with stories of the Old West. Following the honeymoon and the kindling of family connections, the new couple began their young lives together in Washington, D.C., where they took up residence at Mrs. Ryan's boarding house on H Street near its intersection with Seventh Street. Here the Jacksons slipped comfortably into a domestic routine that both husband and wife found mutually satisfying.

But there was more to Jackson's life than simply quiet evenings and Sunday excursions to visit family and friends. Washington was, when Jackson was there, the photographer's home base, as his permanent member status with the Hayden Survey demanded. At $175 per month, the survey was his primary source of income. The surveys tended to require only two or three months of fieldwork, so Jackson was expected to lend a hand in a variety of tasks, including classifying, cataloging, and copying his photographs, plus other Hayden materials. Jackson often gave assistance to those survey members who wanted to publish their findings.

The nation's capital offered a certain amount of allure to Jackson as the center pivot of the federal government and the Hayden Survey's permanent headquarters, but he had long ago grown beyond his eastern roots—includ-ing those of New York and Vermont—and had since become a full-fledged man of the American West. He had seen more of the frontier and its environs than most Americans ever would, including some of its more mysterious parts. He had traveled from Nebraska to California and back again and over many places in between, including Wyoming and Colorado. The West represented repeated opportunities for the young photographer—in 1874, he turned thirty-one—to make his mark professionally. He had become accustomed to its grand vistas and open skies, and the idea of plying his photographic skills in the confines of a one- or two-room studio held less and less appeal. Jackson had found adventure in the West, and he assumed future adventures awaited him. Will and Emilie's marriage was split between two worlds. For most of the year, part of his job kept him close to his young bride, working out of a building located within walking distance of home. But Emilie understood that from summer to fall she would lose her husband to the West, where he was to work a frontier world away from her. It was a trade-off, and one that for the most part seemed to work for both the new bride and her wandering husband.

For a moment in late 1873, it appeared the next Hayden Survey might be in jeopardy. When Congress convened in December, the nation was in the midst of a severe depression, the Panic of 1873. Money was tight, even for the government, and budgets were regularly cut. Months went by before Con-gress voted to approve yet another Hayden Survey for the summer of 1874. But the appropriation came so late that everything was still up in the air at the end of June. Soon, however, the men of the next Colorado expedition were on their way to Denver, arriving from a variety of points of origin.

Jackson arrived in the territorial capital on July 15. This year's survey proved similar to previous models, especially the 1873 Colorado venture. Once again, Hayden chose to divide his men into six divisions (or parties) and placed Jackson at the head of his own seven-man photographic unit. Joining him was newspaper correspondent Ernest Ingersoll of the *New York Tribune*. Ingersoll had already written supportive articles about previous Hayden Surveys and had been asked to take a front row seat with the 1874 outing. Jackson developed a strong friendship with the young eastern reporter, who came out West an experienced naturalist, having studied under a famous scientist of the day, Louis Agassiz of Harvard fame. Other members of Jackson's party included veteran mule packers Bob Mitchell and Steve Stevens, plus a pair of young assistants, Frank Smart and Ed Anthony, whose father was an important New York photographic supply dealer. Gone was Potato John, the cook, replaced by a former waiter at Denver's famous Charpiot's restaurant. Jackson was reunited with a nonhuman veteran of the 1873 survey, his white mule, Dolly. The team was supplied similarly to the 1873 survey, including all of Jackson's usual equipment. A couple of changes were made. For this venture, all the pack mules were fitted with aparejos—a type of Mexican saddlebag— except for the one designated to carry the photographic equipment. He was provided with a sawbuck saddle, "as it was more convenient for a light pack and quick work."[1] Perhaps Jackson's most fateful decision was to reduce his number of cameras to just his 5-by-8-inch model, which did double duty producing regular prints as well as stereoscopic pictures. The smaller camera also allowed Jackson to revert to using the more compact, more portable, folding development box he had taken west in 1870 and 1871 during his first two Hayden Surveys.

The photographer's division left Clear Creek on July 21 and headed directly west. Jackson and his men were expected to follow a predetermined route, along Clear Creek through Berthoud Pass to Middle Park, then south into San Luis Park and west along the Rio Grande to its headwaters in the San Juan Mountains. In time, he and his party were to reconnoiter with the remainder of the Hayden men. Then, if time and weather permitted, they might extend their work into New Mexico and even Arizona. Jackson was given a certain amount of discretion in following this general route and could deviate slightly at any time. Jackson may have started out with a specific diversion in mind. "I had my heart set on getting some fine Indian pictures before the summer was over," he wrote, "and with this in mind even the gorgeous landscapes of the Rockies failed to stir me greatly."[2]

The Jackson men followed the trail for a month, remaining busy, with the focus largely on the photographic work. Along the route, he photographed Longs Peak once again. Along Berthoud Pass, at 11,300 feet elevation, Jackson shot a picture destined to become an iconic image of the American West, a panoramic photo of Berthoud Pass, mountains commanding the background with a lone figure standing in the foreground, Harry Yount, who served several Hayden Surveys as a guide and hunter. (He was directly assigned to the party led by geologist Archibald Marvine.) Yount represents every American mountain man who ever preceded him: heavily bearded, wearing a heavy coat and tricornered hat, and cradling his rifle as he scans the distant horizon. Yount would one day be appointed the first game warden in Yellowstone National Park. Horace Albright, the second director of the National Park Service, later referred to Yount as "the father of the ranger service, as well as the first national park ranger."[3]

At Grand Lake, lying along the western flank of Longs Peak, the Jackson men stumbled upon a lone cabin where a fisherman rented them a boat. "It was a delightful ride," penned Jackson later. "The early morning light shimmering over the surface of the deep dark waters of the lake, the low hanging wreathing clouds clinging about the mountain peaks and the exhilarating air made one feel all the enthusiasm such scenes inspire." Reaching the opposite lake bank, the party explored some local river cataracts, where they consumed their lunch, including a bottle of brandy.[4]

Come August, the Jackson team was moving along the Colorado River toward Hot Springs. At a local town they enjoyed hot baths, then returned to the river and to its confluence with the Blue River, its waters tainted with a yellowish mud caused by chemical drainage from a mining operation upriver. Jackson took several photographs, then the party continued to Hoosier Pass, where they crossed the Continental Divide and landed in the mining town of Alma, through which they had passed the previous year, and later arrived in Fairplay, which was already declining as a mining community. At the small frontier outpost of Granite, Jackson's men linked up with Hayden and his party, where they enjoyed a "jolly time."[5]

The next morning the Jackson party continued south, following the Arkansas River until it took a bend to the east. They crossed the Continental Divide again, this time at Poncha Pass, then reached the settlement of Saguache in the San Luis Valley. Along the Saguache River, the survey team passed several ranches, both American and Mexican, and Jackson noted how they all had "Mexican senoritas about them."[6] It was here Jackson saw his first opportunity to photograph the Indians he seemed so intent on immortalizing, those living on the Los Pinos Agency, including a large party of Uncompahgre Ute families who were encamped nearby to receive their annual allotment of food and supplies from the federal government. At the confluence of Cochetopa Creek and Los Pinos Creek, the party encountered a collection of seventy tepees dotting the landscape around the local Indian agency. With the prospect

This iconic 1874 photograph features mountain guide and hunter Harry Yount with Colorado's Berthoud Pass in the background. Yount served as guide for several Hayden Surveys and would one day be appointed Yellowstone National Park's first game warden. National Archives. ID No. 517126.

of seeing Indian women in the village, several of Jackson's men washed up in a local creek.

The agency featured a dozen or so log buildings, plastered with mud and whitewashed, all arranged in a great quadrangle with a one-room schoolhouse at its center. The local Indian agent was a Unitarian minister, Rev. Henry Bond, who lived on site with his wife and children. Jackson informed Bond he and his men were intent on photographing the Indians, and Bond soon escorted Jackson and Ingersoll to meet the local Ute chief, Ouray. He was such an important leader that he lived not in one of the tepees but in one of the agency's whitewashed log houses.

Ouray had assimilated significantly on the reservation. He usually wore the white man's suits, including a derby hat, and had joined the Methodist Church. On the day Jackson met Ouray, he entered the Ute chief's house, where he "found him . . . alone, reclining on a rude couch covered with blankets."[7] He was not dressed in his "white man" clothes, as Ingersoll later described, but instead wore a "buckskin costume of native cut, full and flowing, with long fringes trailing from his arms and shoulders, skirts, and leggings, until they dragged upon the ground. . . . [H]e looked every inch a monarch."[8] Ouray's wife was dressed resplendently: "The doeskin of which her dress was made was almost as white as cotton, and nearly as soft as silk."[9]

Ouray spoke several languages, including English, so he and Jackson spent much of the afternoon talking. This was the photographer insinuating himself with the Ute chief so he could take his picture. Jackson first took some photos of the Bond family, then asked the chief and his wife to pose. Both cooperated, posing both together and separately. Plans were made for Jackson to take his camera into the Ute tepee village for additional photographs of other willing Native American subjects. The following day, Jackson, Ingersoll, and Reverend Bond arrived and presented themselves to Chiefs Shavano and Guerro, with whom they shared a ceremonial pipe. But when Jackson asked about taking photographs, he received a curt, "No bueno." An argument ensued as Jackson insisted. The subchiefs would have none of it, offering their reasons as best they could: "Make Injun heap sick," "Squaw die," "Papoose die," "Pony die," "All die." Only after Jackson offered to purchase some blankets from a third chief, Peah (or Tushaquinot), did the photographer find a willing Native American subject.

Jackson took some photos, then a storm came up, and Peah invited Jackson to take shelter in his tepee. But when Will attempted to take a photo of Peah's papoose without asking permission—Jackson described his efforts as "a little sharp practice"—an incident ensued that surprised Jackson: "Peah and some half dozen others came up, protesting vehemently, taking hold of the camera and preventing me from either focusing or making an exposure. Peah kept on exclaiming that the Indians 'no sabe' pictures [which make] Indians heap sick, tapping his head."[10]

Although Jackson remained at the Indian agency for three or four more days, he did not take any more photographs of the Ute. When he set up his tripod, even to take a photo of the Ute tepee village, "three or four Indians were detailed to get in my way. As I attempted to focus, one of them would snatch the cloth from my head; or toss a blanket over the camera."[11] While Jackson became rather indignant at the uncooperative behavior of the Utes, including Peah, he also continued to make himself a nuisance, refusing to leave the village until he believed he had taken as many photographs as he wanted. This was Jackson at his most uncharacteristically obnoxious, likely appearing to the very Native Americans he was intent on documenting as just one more insistent, demanding white man. When Peah asked the photographer to return all his negatives to him, Jackson refused and even ordered a couple of his survey members to put on a demonstration of their pistol and rifle skills as an intimidation. In time his welcome was worn out, and Jackson left the agency, taking his men south along a well-defined Ute trail. This route led them along a pass through the San Juan Mountains to the Rio Grande, which they followed westward until they reached another Indian trail leading to Lost Trail Creek.

After spending the evening at a remote ranch house with a young woman whose husband was gone fishing—Jackson describes her as "extremely good

Ute Chief Peah poses with fellow chiefs in this 1874 stereoscope image taken at Los Pinos, Colorado. Photo provided courtesy of the Amon Carter Museum of American Art, Fort Worth, TX. Fred and Jo Mazzulla Collection. Accession no. P1971.23.70.

Jackson took this photo of the San Juan Mountains during the Hayden Survey's foray into Colorado in 1874. The range is located in the southwestern region of Colorado and northwestern New Mexico. Library of Congress. LC-USZ62-47747.

looking . . . with many smiles & dimples"[12]—the men continued west over the San Juan Mountains. Jackson had already shot many photographs of great mountains throughout Colorado, but he was impressed with this range: "On the summit, we had a glorious view of the grand old mountains which contain the mineral wealth of the San Juan mines. Each new turn in our zigzag trail opening up new vistas that rendered our admiration speechless."[13]

The following day the men arrived in the small mining town of Silverton, nestled in the mountains in the valley of the Animas River. The narrow-gauge railroad had not yet reached Silverton, so the only way in was by packhorse. (Once the railroad arrived a few years later, Jackson would return several times to take astonishing photographs of the canyon, the Animas River, and trains sitting precariously on a cliff-side shelf.) Here the Jackson party met up with another Hayden division. Some of the men, including Jackson, decided to climb nearby Sultan Mountain, where they could take scientific readings, and when the trail proved too difficult for the mules, the men shouldered their packs and continued up. Jackson shot fourteen pictures at the peak, despite the weather, which was sharp and cold, and Will later noted that his hands nearly froze. "I with my coat was shivering all the time," he wrote.[14]

While Jackson and his companions were knocking around in the general vicinity of the Four Corners, his old friend, artist Thomas Moran, took a train out to Denver, where he hooked up with Stevenson and a small party of Hayden men for the singular purpose of visiting the Mount of the Holy

Cross. This venture reveals how much Hayden respected Moran's previous contributions to the legacies of the surveys, especially his work in Yellow-stone a few years earlier. The special party set out to the west with Moran excited about what lay ahead and the possibilities for his producing a large painting depicting the cross, like his earlier work, *The Grand Canyon of the Yellowstone.* Some of the details of Moran's trip to the site may be gleaned from a handful of letters he penned to his wife while in the field. He wrote the first on August 10, stating, "We left Denver on Saturday [August 8] & made 12 miles to a village called Morrison on the edge of the mountains. . . . We shall get to Fairplay on Wednesday night or Thursday morning. . . . We all have splendid horses & first rate bedding. Our eating is first rate."[15] The party continued on for another ten days before they arrived in sight of the Mount of the Holy Cross.

The next day Moran, Woods, and Stevenson continued their climb, ascending up Notch Mountain. Just as Jackson had discovered the previous year, this mount provided the only aesthetic view of the cross. The trio climbed for four hours that morning, covering three miles. The climb was difficult due to felled trees. By noon, they had reached 12,000 feet, where they "were in clear view of the Cross and although still 800 feet below where we intended to reach, we were all so tired that we concluded we had gone far enough." After a half hour rest, the survey members started back down the mountain.[16]

Moran's pilgrimage to the Mount of the Holy Cross fell short of Jackson's experience the previous year. The photographer had been forced to linger on Notch Mountain more than a full day just to gain the right sunlight to produce quality photographs of the cross. Moran seems to have drawn some preliminary sketches while in view of the cross—his trip out to Colorado was necessary for him to gain a firsthand artist's view for his future picture—but he may have already decided to utilize Jackson's photographs of the cross as a guide. One of his early sketches seems to have been lost, but a photograph of it still exists, dated 1874.

He also produced a watercolor, which may have had its origins in a preliminary sketch. Moran would ultimately blend the two works—and the unique angle each represents—into his large-scale oil painting. In creating this painting, Moran once more recreated the landscape, just as he had with his *Grand Canyon of the Yellowstone.* He completed the painting in 1875; it measures approximately 5-by-7 feet, less than half the size of his Yellowstone painting. Just as he had altered the vast foreground framing the Lower Falls, so Moran recreated the lay of the land in the cross painting. The cross is a distant image in Moran's work, a far-off, holy mirage trapped on a distant mountainside shrouded in misty light. Jackson's photographs fail to include any of the forest primeval sloping hills dotted with forlorn greenery and trees, likely because he photographed the cross at a higher elevation than Moran allowed himself to climb on that single day in August. Such juxtapositions between actual nature and the recreated landscape Moran chose to compose for his painting mattered little in the end. The painting was considered another masterpiece by the American artist.

As they left Silverton, Jackson's men followed the Animas Canyon, spotting along the way a pine tree Chief Ouray had burned to mark the southernmost boundary of the land he bequeathed to the US government. Farther on, the party was entering land the Utes still claimed as their own. Soon, in fact, at the future site of Durango, Colorado, a band of Ute warriors warned the Americans off their land. But Jackson and his men continued in spite of the threat. The men were entering a different sort of landscape, leaving the high mountains behind as the land became flatter, with scattered mesas dotting the horizon. The high-country timber also receded in the face of an arid land boasting occasional outcroppings of stunted junipers and pinon pines. Perhaps the Utes had threatened other white interlopers on their land, for the Jackson party reached an abandoned ranch site where the crops were ready to harvest. The men gladly performed the task and soon left with their packs filled with corn, potatoes, and watermelons.

Then Jackson had an unlikely encounter with an old friend from his Omaha days. E. H. Cooper had come out West to Colorado to seek his fortune in precious metals. On the day of his reunion with Jackson, members of his party watched with amusement as Cooper drove balky burros with a stick to encourage them to keep moving. He eventually came over and introduced himself to the survey men, and Jackson recognized his old comrade. That evening, sitting around a campfire, Cooper intrigued the men with stories of his earlier prospecting days along the La Plata River. He began describing a region unknown to most outsiders. "He told us of the Mesa Verde," explained Jackson later, "where he said there were cliff dwellings and other ruins more wonderful than any yet discovered."[17] Cooper admitted he had not seen these wonders himself, but his traveling companion, John Moss, had. Moss knew the region as well as any non-Indian, since he had traveled extensively "all over the Southwest from the San Juan [River] to California and knew the location of all the principal ruins."[18] Jackson was enticed to divert his path into the unknown, with Moss as his party's guide. Moss warned Jackson and his men the Ute were then driving whites off their land in earnest. But Jackson and his comrades decided to continue on. They passed additional abandoned homesteads with crops waiting in the fields, and again the survey men took advantage of the opportunity to gather the food.

Jackson picked a few comrades to follow him farther across Ute lands into the heart of Mesa Verde, including Ingersoll and packers Steve Hovey and Bob Mitchell. Between them they carried three packs of supplies and equipment. The party followed Bear Creek Trail into the Sultan Mountains. At Castle Springs they encountered another party of white men leaving Animas Valley, who said the Utes had encouraged them to leave.

Within a few days, Jackson and his men could see off in the distance the Mesa Verde bluff, featuring layers of white and red sandstone. As they continued along the valley, the men began spotting pieces of Indian pottery, white clay shards, many decorated with black paint. They began noticing Indian mounds and small cave shelters long abandoned. The men did not have to wait long before they spotted their first ancient Indian ruins, occupied by Southwest natives a millennium ago. Although no one knew what name they had called themselves, the Navajo had their own name for them—the Anasazi, "the ancient people who are not of us."[19]

The ancient Anasazi developed through various cultural phases, shifting ultimately from hunter-gatherers to primitive agriculturalists. By the third stage of Anasazi development (AD 700–1000), these mysterious Native Americans were building elaborate pueblo systems featuring multistoried structures, with dozens of interconnected apartments and rooms for social gathering. The upper stories of such pueblos were only accessible by ladders. Eventually the Anasazi began building new, round subterranean spiritual centers known today as kivas, which were typically more elaborate than their own homes.

One of the most intriguing of the pueblos built during the third Anasazi stage was constructed out in the desert of northwestern New Mexico, in Chaco Canyon, a site called Pueblo Bonito, only one of a beehive of interconnected Anasazi structures, the center pivot of the Anasazi world. In time a prolonged drought cycle—plus the destruction of all the useable trees within a fifty-mile radius—drove the ancient residents at Pueblo Bonito and its satellite settlements to abandon their villages and migrate en masse northward, where they took up residence along such life-sustaining river systems as the Rio Grande, the Salt, and the Gila. It was in this region, near the Four Corners, that an Anasazi remnant built new pueblo complexes, including those located at Mesa Verde. Here these ancient peoples built homes similar to those at Chaco, but now they erected their shelters under overhanging rock ledges, including the most elaborate site, Cliff Palace. These more significant sites— Pueblo Bonito, Cliff Palace—would remain hidden from Jackson and his men during the 1874 exploring season, but their secrets would not remain obscured from the outside for much longer. (Two-Story House, which Jackson and his men would soon discover, is located south of today's Mesa Verde National Park in the Ute Mountain Tribal Park.)

Along Mesa Verde bluff, Jackson and Ingersoll, with Moss leading the way, reached a site still hidden from their view. But Moss signaled his comrades and pointed up to the heights above. "There it is," he said. Between the layers of rock, eight hundred feet above them, Jackson and his team could discern a man-made structure of ancient origin—a small, two-story cliff dwelling set into the recesses of the cliff wall. Excitedly they began to scale the vertical wall, but after six hundred feet everyone dropped out except for Jackson and Ingersoll. They continued their climb with care as the sun reached its western horizon. The hour was an exciting one for Jackson and journalist comrade Ingersoll, but too late in the day for taking photographs. Besides, Will had not brought his equipment to the site. The next morning, September 10, he was back on the scene, taking the first ever photographs of an Anasazi-era cliff dwelling, one tucked away for centuries in Mancos Canyon. No pictures were taken until the photographer's bulky equipment had been hauled gingerly up the cliff. Not only did he document the ancient ruins with his camera, Jackson also described the ruins with the eye of an archaeologist: "A two-story house of hewn stone, built in a narrow crevice of the sandstone mesa 800 feet above the valley at its feet. It is in a fair state of preservation, the overhanging rock protecting it from the weather."[20] After centuries of abandonment, the structure was still livable, although the cedar timbers that had at one time held up the second floor were now deteriorated.

On September 12, with the photographic work completed, the party hit the trail snaking its way along the Mancos Valley. The men hoped to locate additional ancient structures. The two-story house on the cliff represented only the tip of the iceberg. When the Jackson men encountered a party of Ute warriors—fortunately they were intent on raiding a local group of Navajos to the south—Moss, who was familiar with the Ute language, inquired about the identities of the long-vanished peoples who had built the ruined house, but the Utes knew nothing of them.

In time the Mancos Valley pathway broadened until it reached the San Juan River, which Jackson's men followed, and soon they were nearly at the actual point where the modern-day states of Colorado, Utah, New Mexico, and Arizona intersect. The land was as inhospitable as ever, producing only scattered outcroppings of sage and greasewood. Along the Hovenweep, a tributary of the San Juan, the men spotted additional Anasazi houses in ruins, including a series of shallow caves situated along a cliff wall, with two containing houses, including "a well preserved little square building about 6 feet high & 8 long, hid back under a broad shallow cave or niche in the bluff, about 30 feet above its foot & safe [from] harm."[21] Reaching dry springs along McElmo Creek, Jackson spotted an anomaly on the horizon, a dark stone tower rising above the mesa. "It wound and turreted among the rocks in a very unusual

Jackson often placed people in his photos to provide a comparative scale. In this 1874 photo of the Anasazi-era Two-Story House, dated September 7, located in Mancos Canyon, Colorado, the photographer included Captain John Moss (left) and journalist Ernest Ingersoll. Library of Congress. LC-USZ62-56180.

manner," he later wrote. "It evidently guards the way to a large city or settlement back upon a higher level."[22] As the men investigated, they discovered the tower was close to eight feet square and nearly ten feet high, situated on top of a large rock formation. Again, Jackson took his photos, measured the structure, and made sketches. He wanted to spend more time at this and other Anasazi sites discovered that day, but he and his men were running out of water and time.

From the Hovenweep, the men hiked for three days before returning to the La Plata. They remained busy, with Jackson taking photographs and exploring the region. Ingersoll located some fossils and for a time fell behind the remainder of the party. He became disoriented, then lost the trail and spent the night in a canyon later named Lost Canyon. The following day, he picked up the trail again and soon joined his comrades at Merritt's Ranch.

The party soon parted ways with Moss, but not before making semipermanent plans for him to rejoin them next year for the next Hayden Survey. The division remained on the trail for several more weeks before returning to Colorado Springs and subsequently to Denver on October 11.

While Jackson and his men had located and photographed several smaller Anasazi sites, including those located in Mancos Canyon, he had managed to bypass the ancient wonders of today's Mesa Verde National Park, including Cliff Palace and Balcony House. The canyon is situated approximately twenty miles southwest of the southern rim of the national park. Non-Indian outsiders did not discover the site until 1888. It is certain Jackson's photographs played a singular role in helping promote interest in Mesa Verde, which gained national park status in 1906. Hayden and his team of dedicated scientists and support staff had accomplished one more successful reconnaissance in the West. Jackson had photographed some cooperative Native American subjects, and he was destined to photograph others the following year when Hayden and company returned to the Southwest once again.

12

Land of the Anasazi, 1875

$\mathscr{H}$ayden, Jackson, Stevenson, and all their comrades had completed one more successful venture into the West. Jackson had photographed the mountains, rivers, and mesas of southern Colorado and produced images of nature previously undocumented. He had also taken pictures of the ruins of ancient peoples who were all but completely unknown to both Native Americans and nonnatives alike. He could not have known it then, but there were greater, more elaborate ruins that remained hidden for another intrepid soul to discover at a later time. Still, Hayden emphasized Jackson's work that summer in his government report, spending several pages on the efforts of Jackson and the Photographic Division of his surveys. "The first trip [into Colorado] proving so successful," he wrote, "Mr. Jackson was dispatched again this season with instructions to ascertain, as far as possible, the extent and distribution of these ruins north of the present Moqui [Hopi] pueblos."[1]

Jackson understood Hayden's expectations completely. "The main purpose of my 1875 expedition was to follow up my work among the cliff ruins in '74 by another trip to the Southwest."[2] This mission was not Jackson's only goal that summer as the party returned to Colorado. If there were mountains or other sights to photograph, he would capture them as well. As to his equipment, he packed his trusty 5-by-8-inch camera, as well as his 11-by-14-inch model. But given that he was returning to the vast mountain expanses of the Front Range, he thought bigger than ever, including in his equipment a camera capable of photographing 20-by-24-inch prints, representing the largest format—480 square inches per print—he could reasonably haul across the rugged landscape without too much difficulty.

Such cameras were not yet readily available. Jackson could find none to purchase in Washington and had to order a model from a company in New

York. As things turned out, it proved a difficult format to use on the trail. In later years he wistfully regretted the limited photographic technologies during the years of the Hayden Surveys. "Nowadays bromide papers furnish ready means of enlargement to almost any extent from small negatives," he noted in his 1929 autobiography. "In the seventies, however, such papers were not in general use, and large photographs were made from equally large negatives." In addition, "there were no ready-made dry plates at this time and also no pre-pared printing papers; the photographer purchased plain paper and sensitized it himself as required."[3]

His new camera arrived in late May, and Jackson soon bade another goodbye to his wife, Emilie, and boarded a train to Denver, where he arrived on June 6. He then headed straight south to Parrott City, at the headwaters of the Rio La Plata, just north of the Colorado–New Mexico border. He entered the field with Bill Shaw, his cook, plus a pair of his veteran packers, Bob Mitchell and Bill Whan, and Harry Lee—whom Jackson later compared in appearance to Buffalo Bill Cody—who had a far-flung reputation as a trail guide. Yet another journalist was included to trumpet the accomplishments of the Hayden Surveys—E. A. Barber, who wrote for the *New York Times*. (According to the survey report, he was listed as a "naturalist.")

At the outset of the survey, Hayden only included two divisions—Jackson's and another led by William Henry Holmes, the skilled topographer. His primary interest was to examine the geology of the San Juan country, but Hayden was so interested in the mysteries of the region's cliff dwellings that Holmes functioned largely as an archaeologist during this trip. (Years later, Holmes became one of America's preeminent authorities on early Indians, an interest the survey of 1875 likely kindled.) Both parties moved in the field together until around August 1. At that point Lee, Barber, and Jackson continued westward into Utah following the San Juan River.

Jackson's initial movements in the field followed the Rio Grande to Bakers Park. He tried out his 20-by-24-inch camera near Lake San Cristobal and managed to get some good photographs. He then shot images of the Uncompahgre Mountains, one of the highest peaks in the San Juan Range. As they continued through the foothills just a few miles from Lake City, Jackson found the climbing rough. One of his mules lost its footing and fell off the trail. The animal might have been killed if several trees had not blocked it from tumbling downward farther. The mule, Old Maggie, soon seemed to shake off the fall "with no greater damage than the delay."[4]

The following day, Jackson attempted some photographs of lands along the Uncompahgre Mountains, but the weather was uncooperative. The sky remained overcast, and the wind came up brisk just as he was in position to take some shots of the long plateau before him. He took pictures under these difficult conditions and was disappointed with the results. When he processed his negatives in his portable darkroom, they came out blurry, as the wind had shaken the camera ceaselessly. With long exposures a necessity, Jackson could not change the conditions to produce decent pictures. The day ended with the arrival of a full-blown rainstorm. The following morning dawned brightly, though, the Fourth of July. Jackson returned to his mountain perch and took a good negative, even as snow flurries flitted around him.

Beyond Bakers Park, Jackson once again photographed Sultan Mountain, although he was forced to wait more than a day for rains to cycle out of the region. On several occasions, Jackson rephotographed sights he had shot previously because his larger camera could produce larger, more dramatic compositions. On July 11 he photographed Arrastra Gulch and captured yet another of his sweeping scenes, featuring a scatter field of scraggly trees in the foreground against a backdrop of undulating, snow-streaked mountains, all capped by a sky bursting with billowy clouds. While his composition depicts a pristine natural world, the nearby vicinity had already been heavily mined. Of this prospecting detritus, Jackson wrote later: "The wrecks of the old arrastras [small circular ore crushers, usually operated with mules or horses] that were put in some twelve or fourteen years ago . . . have given the gulch its name. It was also worked in that time for placers, but with no success. It is now more favorably known through its silver mines, which are among the richest of this region."[5] The following day, Jackson and his party reached a remote encampment of miners, those working "the North Star and Mountaineer lodes, on King Solomon Mountain, above Cunningham Gulch."[6] As the men passed up the trail to the top of King Solomon Mountain, Jackson and his party reached an unbelievably narrow mountain pass, as the photographer describes: "Within half a mile of the camp we came to a place where the trail had been blasted out of the perpendicular face of a spur of the mountain deep enough for the burros with bags of ore, but hardly commodious enough for our larger animals. We finally got around however by taking off the packs & saddles and compelling the animals to crouch down and crowding them through."[7]

At Trout Lake, near the San Miguel River, Jackson and his men slipped through the thirteen-thousand-foot pass and soon located a high waterfall that Jackson wanted to photograph. Just getting himself and his camera into position proved difficult: "I had to go nearly half a mile and then make a precipitous descent of some four hundred feet down into the gorge. . . . The exposure was made all right; but as a result of the effort to get down and back in the shortest possible time. . . . It was too late to make another exposure so we returned to camp."[8]

No other opportunity presented itself to photograph the falls, for the weather turned cold, and snows soon began to fall. Jackson's party trudged its way across the Continental Divide back to Bakers Park. The men were headed toward Denver, and the last leg of their journey included a return to the Animas River, where the trail was so narrow due to previous rock slides that the men had to dismantle their wagon for the mules to pack out the parts. The trails beyond were decent, taking them over Cochetopa Pass into the San Luis Valley and back to the Arkansas River. There, Jackson sent three of his men, along with the wagon, straight to Denver, while he and one of his packers searched for a few more subjects to photograph. They crossed over Hoosier Pass and Argentine Pass, where Jackson took pictures of places he had visited the previous year, including Grays Peak, Georgetown, and several other mountains. From Georgetown, the pair crossed the mountains to Idaho Springs, where they made rail connections to deliver the bulk of their supplies back to Denver. Jackson and his associate then drove their mules the remaining fifty-two miles to Denver.

Jackson was then sent out on another venture, one of Hayden's side trips that summer. Returning to follow various lengths of the San Juan River, Jackson's and Holmes's parties split off from one another at Montezuma Wash, with Jackson and his men remaining on the San Juan. Throughout this region, high bluffs flanked the river, and several contained cliff ruins, just as Jackson had hoped. They dotted the landscape, some hidden away under rock shelters, while others were discovered in caves. A short distance from the wash, Jackson's men spotted a large circular cave that seemed carved into the entire bluff site. Jackson describes the scene: "Midway around the cave a shelf of harder rock supported a row of small connecting rooms extending around more than half the entire circle. The great dome over all echoed and reechoed with marvelous distinctness every word we said."[9] (Today the site is known as Seventeen—or Sixteen—Room Ruin or Fourteen Window Ruin and is located near Bluff, Utah.)

Once Jackson had taken photographs of this enigmatic Anasazi hideaway—including a stereoscopic version—the party moved on and discovered that the river ran through a difficult canyon, forcing them up onto the plateau, where they walked along on "upturned edges of red and white stratified sandstones, following in the tracks of sheep and goats that a band of Indians had taken across the mesa the day before."[10]

In time they returned to the San Juan and reached Chinle Wash, where they camped at the confluence of the wash and the San Juan. It proved a miserable campsite featuring little but sand and sagebrush and red rock outcroppings. Jackson did manage a few photographs, but the weather was unbearably warm. Even in the coolest shade, the temperature registered at 100 degrees, compared to "125 in the sun, where we were most of the time; and 140 when it [the thermometer] was placed in the sand."[11] Even the river water was a warm 88 degrees.

Despite the heat, the party continued to the south, headed for the pueblos of the Moquis, native peoples known today as the Hopis. The Moqui village venture required the Jackson men to detour two hundred miles from their river course, but Jackson desperately wanted to photograph these peoples of the Southwest. This route took them into the canyon of Chinle Wash. They then struck a trail leading them toward the Colorado Canyon and on to Monument Valley, which features the great sandstone monoliths later featured in the western motion pictures filmed by director Howard Hawks. Jackson wanted to reach the valley, but the trail forked, and his packers were so far ahead of him that he could not catch up and reroute them. Instead, in Jackson's words, "we were headed for an equally interesting place."[12]

Soon they gained sight of a series of bluffs situated along the Chinle Wash. Below were copses of green cottonwood trees, signaling good water. The men discovered a cool spring and enjoyed a satisfying drink. They made camp by the spring, and then Jackson and Harry Lee began to explore the area, searching for cliff ruins. They soon hit pay dirt, "finding the largest and most important one I [Jackson] had seen so far."[13] Jackson described the find in his 1929 autobiography: "This was in a long, shallow cave about fifty feet above the base of a bluff, two or three hundred feet high, with the deep arroyo of the wash sweeping close under it. The ruin was really a compactly built town."[14]

The party was soon back on the trail. It was early August. Fifteen miles beyond the ruins of Chinle Wash, the men crossed a field of white sandstone and undulating piles of sand. The men picked a few handfuls of garnets in the area, but they did not otherwise linger, since "the sun beat down upon [us] with such intensity."[15] They soon reached Laguna, which slashed its way across the rocky plateau.[16] It proved a hidden paradise, a site featuring "abundant green grass, with a long line of the tall, reedy growth common to damp lands."[17] The grass provided welcome fodder for the pack mules. Once the men emerged from the canyon, they were again on the Chinle, where they noticed the fecal remains of a large flock of sheep and goats that Navajo shepherds had recently led through the wash. The area featured more ancient ruins, and Jackson photographed several.

The Jackson party was now in Arizona, in the land of the Navajo Indians. The Navajo offered no resistance, but instead traded with the survey men when they entered their villages. "We bought a lot of green corn and melons from them," remembered Jackson, "paying in silver, but what they wanted more than anything else was leather. They looked with covetous eyes upon our equipment of saddles, cantinas, and aparejos."[18] When the men encamped near a Navajo village, they were extra careful to guard their leather items for fear of theft.

In mid-August, Jackson decided to split his small party and continue with only Harry Lee and E. A. Barber, while sending the remainder of his men back to wait at Laguna Creek (Canyon Bonito Chiquito). Jackson made this decision based on his lack of knowledge about availability of water. If the trail ahead offered little water, the larger party might be jeopardized.

With a smaller number of companions, Jackson continued passing through the land of the Navajo. They reached a large farming area where cornfields went on for miles, accompanied by several small homes, called hogans, a Navajo version of an earthen lodge. Natives greeted the Americans as they passed. This was mesa country, and the men moved past the high ground of the Great White Mesa. That evening they encamped with a group of Navajo, plus a large number of yelping dogs that, fortunately, settled down after dark so everyone was able to sleep. The next morning the Natives asked the visitors to remain and celebrate their corn dance with them, but Jackson begged off, feeling time was too short.

That day the survey men reached a broad valley surrounded by high, flat-topped mesas including Tewa, "the first of the Moqui towns." This is the mesa known to the modern-day Hopi as First Mesa. The town dates back to the 1780s. There was little to distinguish the Indian town on the mesa at first glance. Jackson even suggests the party "might have passed it without noticing the line of rock-built houses upon its summit, so like are they to their surroundings."[19] At the base of the mesa, the Americans encountered friendly Moquis (Hopis) tending their cornfields, as well as their flocks of sheep. One shepherd pointed out the nearest watering hole, a man-made reservoir lined with rocks. Jackson saw a photo opportunity at the mesa village, and his party was directed to the trail leading upward, cut into the bluff like a steep staircase. Jackson noted the ease with which he and his men climbed up four hundred feet to the summit of the mesa. As they ascended, the men likely perceived the heavy scent of sheep manure in the air, as the Hopi burned the animals' dried dung for cooking and heat. At the top, a pair of Hopi men greeted them and began giving a tour: "[W]e were bidden to be seated on a raised platform at one side of the room. . . . Behind us a maiden was grinding corn in the primitive manner of the Moquis. Scarcely had we become seated when a beautiful girl approached and placed before us a large mat heaped with pee-kee, or bread."[20] As hungry as the men likely were after a day on the trail, the young Hopi girl who served them captured their attention immediately.

This young girl, one who eventually brought honor and fame to herself and her people through her skills as a potter, captivated Jackson's men. Jackson identified her as "Num-Pa-Yu," which today is written as Nampeyo. This Hopi girl of the Tewa Pueblo on First Mesa drew Jackson's attention.

Jackson returned to the Southwest several times following his visit in 1875. He continued to take photos of the Hopi over the years, including this one of a Hopi potter. Library of Congress. LC-USZ62-104604

He sketched her and even had her pose for a 20-by-24-inch photograph, an oversized format for such an intimate portrait. He posed her in several different photographs, so intent was he on capturing the image of this fifteen-year-old Indian maiden. His fascination with Nampeyo continued through the next sixty years. He returned to First Mesa several times during the decades that followed and with each visit reacquainted himself with the Hopi artist, as he captured various stages of her long life with his cameras. (Another famous American photographer, Edward Sheriff Curtis, would also pose Nampeyo on several occasions, starting in 1900.)

Jackson and his men did not tarry more than a couple of days at First Mesa. They were on their way by August 15, headed to yet more Hopi villages, including three on Second Mesa: Shungopavi, Sipaulovi, and Mishongnovi. They bypassed the Hopi village of Oraibi (Jackson spells it "Oraybi") at Third Mesa, again due to time restraints. Everywhere the Hayden Survey men went, they experienced the same grand hospitality, which usually included meals of piki and stewed peaches from the Hopi orchards located at the bases of their mesas. When the men swung back around, retracing their footsteps on their return trip, they again visited Tewa, where they met the newly arrived Indian agent, W. B. Truax. Jackson then shot yet another photograph of Nampeyo, and before leaving the village, the men purchased pieces of pottery, native baskets, and other "fetishes and small idols."[21] On their last night in the village, the villagers treated the Jackson men to a dinner of piki tortillas and stewed pumpkin, with everyone eating out of the same bowls and containers, all using their fingers in lieu of tableware. The days ahead saw their return to several previously visited sites including Bonito Chiquito and the cave complex at Chinle Wash. Jackson shot several more photographs during these second visits.

By this time August was nearly over, and Jackson and his men finished out the final weeks of their 1875 season. Their next major objective on the trail was the Blue Mountains of eastern Utah. "It was a mysterious region," Jackson wrote later, "reputed to be the haunt of a band of outlawed, renegade Indians, recruited from the surrounding Utes, Navajos, and Apaches."[22] What Jackson and his men did not know as they approached this region was that one party of the Hayden Survey, led by topographer James Terry Gardiner, had been attacked a week earlier in the vicinity of Cold Spring along the Old Spanish Trail by a party of one hundred warriors. The survey party was pinned down behind rocky alcoves and escaped without any loss of life—four party members were wounded—while losing all their equipment and supplies, plus two mules killed and two wounded.

Subsequent to the battle, Gardiner was intent to warn Jackson and his men of the encounter by writing him a letter and posting it at Parrott City, hoping the photographer would find the missive and avoid the same general region.

Unaware of this incident, Jackson and his party continued marching through the area, following the trail parallel to Sierra Abajo Mountain, past modern-day Monticello, Utah, and then on to Dry Valley. The party soon encountered a band of Paiute Indians, but they were only interested in trading. Both parties spent the night encamped near one another. Over the next few days the party skirted around the eastern portion of Abajo Peak, where they passed out of the desert lands and into mountainous country marked by "a fine grove of scrub oaks, where there was luxuriant feed for our animals and plenty of clear cool water."[23] Jackson chose to separate from his party, along with Harry Lee and Bill Whan, to investigate the lands between the Abajo and La Sal Mountains. Following the Old Spanish Trail, they reached a shallow canyon where they located an abundant spring of cold water. (This was Casa Colorado Rock, the site Gardiner's men were headed toward when they were attacked.) Jackson photographed the location. Following the trail, Jackson and his comrades reached a broad canyon and spotted a unique rock formation called La Tinaja (large jar). They continued their search for additional ancient cliff ruins, but none rose up to meet them. Instead, Jackson photographed a set of red sandstone bluffs fitted with rounded caves he described as "a fine place for cliff dwellings."[24]

The men soon reached a new trail, which directed them to the east around white sandstone bluffs. They saw horse and mule tracks along this route that were definitely not Indian, but who had passed ahead of them they never discovered. After completing a circle, the Jackson party returned to their rendezvous camp along the banks of the La Plata, then headed toward Montezuma Canyon. When they camped that evening in yet another canyon, the men discovered several cliff ruins long abandoned by the Anasazi. The following morning, the trail revealed new ruins, "so numerous now that frequently one or more were in view as we rode along."[25] The ground was littered with so many arrowheads that the men made a competition out of finding the most. Pottery shards were everywhere, along with beads and other items. Jackson took several photographs here. While many of the ruins Jackson and his men discovered were nestled into cliff sides and underneath rock shelters, some were not. The party also reached several surface ruins originally erected on the canyon floors or on top of mesa sites. Many of these ruins were older and in poor condition, leading Jackson to refer to them usually as "mounds." Most were not photograph worthy.

After camping in this valley, the men set out on a late August day and soon spotted "a cloud of dust down the trail, and out of it came some fifteen to twenty Indians on ponies, rushing full tilt toward us."[26] The warriors were shouting as they rode, swinging their rifles above their heads, then pulled up their ponies as they surrounded Jackson and his two comrades, Harry Lee and Bill Whan. But the Indians soon greeted the Americans, asking them who they were and where they were headed. Lee lied—the men were uncertain how the warriors might take the news they were working for the federal government—and told the Indians they were prospectors. The natives proved friendly and announced they would accompany the Jackson men to their rendezvous site at La Plata. Soon they were driving the Americans' horses and mules at breakneck speed all the way to their village. Jackson was concerned the drive might damage his cameras and other equipment, "for if anything had gone wrong, that would have been the last of it."[27]

In the Indian village, the Americans met the chief, Pogonobogwint, who greeted them enthusiastically and offered them a meal of boiled green corn. He encouraged the visitors to stay in his village for the night, since the trail ahead offered little water. But Jackson insisted he and his men keep to the trail, despite the warning. As the Americans continued on—they had not informed the Indians of their other comrades in the vicinity—Jackson noticed a pair of warriors following them on horseback. To evade them, the men ducked into a small side canyon that led them to the top of a mesa.

Over the following days, as August became September, Jackson and his men typically repeated their previous days, trekking through new canyons and reaching new cliff ruins. In time the trio found no way out of Montezuma Canyon and had to backtrack to the Indian village, where they were again well received and given more boiled corn. Jackson searched for another trail to take them in the direction they wanted to go without simply retracing all their previous steps. This proved difficult. The men began tacking back and forth through canyon slots and following difficult uphill paths, as the mules struggled along, worn out and suffering from a lack of water. Then an unfortunate accident occurred, as Jackson later described: "Old Mag, carrying a load of bedding in which was packed some of our pottery collections, fell backwards on a steep incline. The mule rolled heels over head, making a clear leap of about forty feet over a perpendicular ledge, and landed on her back in the top of a thick scrub cedar."[28] Fortunately, Old Mag's fall did not involve the destruction of any of Jackson's glass plates or photographic equipment.

Through much effort, the Jackson men finally found their way out of the nearly trackless wilderness, but not before they passed through an Indian village they had visited earlier. The Indians there protested that the Americans' mules had trampled their cornfields. Jackson had nothing to offer to placate them, so a short standoff ensued until the survey party made their escape. They eventually reached the Hovenweep and then arrived at La Plata, where they ended up at a local ranch and received word of Gardiner's earlier skirmish with the Native Americans. Here they also reconnoitered with several other Hayden Survey men, resulting in "a regular jubilee for a time."[29] The men heard multiple versions of the Gardiner battle in detail. Jackson learned of the letter Gardiner had posted for him as a warning. He was also informed that Gardiner had sent a pair of his men from Parrott City to locate him and his comrades, but they had lost the trail before reaching them. This had led Gardiner to send a larger contingent of men to locate Jackson and his comrades "or our remains."[30] All rejoiced that everyone had finally returned safe and sound.

While the work of many of the participants of that summer's Hayden Survey was completed by mid-September, Jackson remained in the field for an additional month, hiking and photographing his way across western Colorado, even as snow fell. He did not return to Denver until October 13, with a new collection of glass plates to show for his months crisscrossing portions of the American Southwest.

Jackson had now participated in six Hayden Surveys and had proven himself a crucial member of these government-sponsored explorations of the American West. His photographs became synonymous with the surveys and provided a means of advertising Hayden's missions, as well as himself as a photographer. His photographs, as well as his sketches, were often duplicated as lithographic prints included in Hayden's official survey reports. Jackson, by 1875, was a well-known man of the West, and his photographs had gained an international reputation. He sold thousands of his photographs as stereoscopic cards, which could be found in the collections of countless American parlors and beyond. The 1875 survey proved to be one of the best for Jackson. Although he would venture into the West under the Hayden banner again, he could not have known that fall that his best days in the field were already past.

13

Adventures and Misadventures, 1876–1877

*W*illiam Henry Jackson was ready to get home. After months exploring and photographing some of the most inhospitable lands of the Southwest, while facing Indian difficulties, lost trails, tropical temperatures, and mule mishaps, he was ready to return to "the comforts of mechanized civilization that appeared so agreeable as I started for Washington."[1] He returned to a domestic world that was about to change dramatically. Throughout his time in the field, Emilie had stayed as the houseguest of a close Gilpin cousin in Sandy Springs, Maryland, as an expectant mother. With Jackson's return back East, he and Emilie returned to Washington to a house they rented on Eighteenth Street, not far from DuPont Circle. This was their home for the next three years—the period of the last of his Hayden Surveys—before Jackson moved his family out West to open a new business in Denver. On February 2, 1876, the expected child arrived, the Jacksons' first, a boy they named Clarence Seymour Jackson. As a family man, Jackson could not have been happier, the by-product of "enjoying the blended satisfaction that comes to him who has a charming wife, a sturdy son, and a house of his own to return to at the day's end."[2]

Although he was back home, Jackson was extremely busy with his professional work for Hayden. Not only did he have the usual darkroom work and writing to perform as part of his duties working for the Hayden and Geological Surveys, he was also handed a special assignment, one that soon dominated months of his time and expertise. The year 1876 marked the one hundredth anniversary of the founding of the American republic, a gala celebration intended not simply to mark the revolutionary separation of the United States from Great Britain, but also to extol the progress of that republic, including its advancements in science and industry.

The focal point of the country's centennial celebration was Philadelphia, ground zero for the Founding Fathers, who had gathered in the Pennsylvania State House (Independence Hall) and signed their names to the Declaration of Independence. The great planned fair would serve as a showcase of American ingenuity and inventiveness, while lauding the development of the republic into the West, the very part of the United States Jackson had spent six summers documenting and advertising to the American people. Hayden's Surveys had proven so popular—including Jackson's photographs—the centennial committee had granted exhibition space to Hayden. The director then turned to Jackson to collect the necessary materials for such an exhibit, which would provide an ideal opportunity for Jackson to tout his photographic accomplishments before millions of visitors to Philadelphia that centennial summer.

Jackson began work on the survey's display within weeks of his return to Washington. Hayden assigned him four assistants to help in preparing the materials to include in the exhibit. The photographer wanted to put the survey's best foot forward, including the lengths to which its participants had scattered across parts of the West, then somewhat unknown to the outside world. The project became, for Jackson, "as absorbing a piece of work as I ever hope to tackle."[3] Topographer William Henry Holmes worked alongside Jackson as well.

One of the genius aspects of his display was a 3D model of some of the cliff ruins he had photographed during the 1874 and 1875 surveys. That Jackson had often photographed some of these ruins from multiple angles gave him the opportunity to recreate a scale model of one set of ruins specifically, an ancient cave village located on the Rio De Chelly in Arizona. Not only had he photographed the ruins, he had also measured them with the precision of an archaeologist. He had all the information he needed to construct a model so exact it would provide the average exhibition visitor a secondhand experience just short of actually being there. Jackson and his assistants designed clay models of the Anasazi town, then cast them in plaster, followed by a coloring process to replicate the village in shades of brown adobe even Jackson's photographs could not reveal. (Following the summer centennial celebration, some of the plaster ruin models were loaned for display in several leading museums around the country.)

In addition to the model ruins, Jackson sorted through many collections of fossils and rocks, dried plants, taxidermied animals, and other items to round out the Hayden Surveys exhibit, not to mention his own photographs depicting the West, including its mountains, deserts, unique formations, and Native Americans.

When the Centennial Exposition opened its doors in Philadelphia on May 10, 1876—seven years to the day after the transatlantic railroad dedication at Promontory Summit—the Hayden Survey exhibit drew large crowds, intrigued by Jackson's hand-painted, hand-cast Anasazi ruins. Among the exposition's thirty thousand displays, which were housed in five large buildings, were such technological marvels as Alexander Graham Bell's telephone. The exposition wowed visitors, who could move from one part of the fairgrounds to another on elevated steam trains. Commanding the exposition's skyline was a 185-foot observation platform accessible by an elevator capable of delivering forty visitors in a single car. Still, Jackson's displays and photographs drew countless attendees, who were captivated by the wonders of Yellowstone and the vast mountain chains of Colorado. Indians stared back at viewers through Jackson's photos. Visitors were introduced to a West they had only read about in newspapers and books. They found inspiration in what they saw, the seedlings of motivations feeding ten thousand desires to board a train and take a trip to see the West firsthand. Jackson remained on scene through the summer, riding herd over his precious survey exhibit, which he claimed "drew almost as many visitors as Dr. Alexander Graham Bell's improbable telephone."[4]

In a sense, Jackson was himself part of the display. He had been a participant in six Hayden Surveys, and he was more than willing to provide informal talks and answer visitor questions, "about the cliff dwellings, the flavor of buffalo hump (one meat of which I never got enough), the geysers of Yellowstone Park, and the domestic habits of the American Indian."[5] Jackson's work paid off. The centennial committee awarded him a bronze medal for the survey's exhibit, quite an accomplishment considering the centennial exhibition included tens of thousands of displays. Jackson's involvement came at a cost, however. Since he remained at the exhibit through the summer of 1876, he did not participate in that year's Hayden Survey.

Jackson's time spent at the 1876 exhibition provided him with an opportunity to visit displays by other photographers and the latest photographic equipment and cameras. He saw new cameras from Europe and became familiar with everything innovative in the world of photo taking. He observed the lack of a type of camera he had been thinking about since his time in the West. Of this he wrote, "Many times while photographing the encircling mountain ranges from some lofty peak I had wished for an instrument that would take the entire horizon with one continuous sweep instead of making separate plates and then joining them together to complete a panorama."[6] Jackson had worked in the great outdoors, the big sky country of Wyoming and Colorado, which featured vistas that seemed endless. What about a camera capable of capturing this vast landscape from a 360-degree viewpoint? Jackson put his own innovative skills into play and believed he had arrived at a solution:

Mechanically it was no great trick to construct a camera that would rotate at constant speed through an angle of 360 degrees; that was merely a matter of cogs and clockwork. The real snag was a sensitized surface to move at the same speed across the focal plane. A glass plate obviously was impossible. Roll film was hardly past the laboratory stage. Finally, after studying all the data available, I hit upon the idea of coating ordinary paper with a collodion emulsion on a substratum of thin rubber. It worked, and I was (so far as I know) the only photographer in the world capable of making a satisfactory 360 degree picture.[7]

Jackson actually built a working model of his panoramic camera design, which involved a revolving camera sitting on a tripod. He cannibalized the works of an eight-day clock to provide the motive power that drove the camera. Jackson "made several experimental exposures with the paper film, getting negatives of nearly 360 deg. radius that were everything desired as to definition but the difficulties in making, developing and striping the films in addition to their being no immediate need for such work, induced me to lay it aside for the time being."[8]

The Centennial Exposition proved a glorious success, but organizers only operated the fair for one season, then closed its doors. This meant Jackson was available for the 1877 survey season. In Jackson's absence, Hayden had led the 1876 survey back into Colorado. That June, the US Army's Seventh Cavalry, led by the impulsive Col. George Armstrong Custer, had faced annihilation on the rolling plains of Montana's Little Bighorn River, startling the nation. While the Centennial Exposition touted America's advancement into the West, the Lakota and Cheyenne reminded all that they had not yet been fully subdued. But by 1877 the army had largely rounded up nearly all Indian roamers on the northern Great Plains, so the government had no objections to Hayden leading his next survey back into Wyoming, with plans to "pick up where he had left off at the end of 1872."[9] But as events transpired, his chief photographer did not join him that summer. Other plans were in the works that included Jackson. While in Washington during the winter of 1876–1877, Jackson met Rev. Sheldon Jackson, the superintendent of the Board of Home Missions of the Presbyterian Church. Reverend Jackson—no relation to William Henry—planned to visit all the church's mission posts in the West between Santa Fe and the Hopi pueblos, some of which Jackson had visited during the 1875 survey. Jackson felt he had photographed enough of Wyoming and, as he wanted to return to the Southwest, became intent on joining the Presbyterian minister instead. Hayden made arrangements for just that. Therefore Jackson did not accompany Hayden into the West either in 1876 or 1877. Instead, he explored in a completely different region, even if it was in the name of the Hayden Survey.

With Jackson and the minister set to travel largely on their own, the photographer saw the opportunity to reinvent his approach to the West. The two men could travel faster, and Jackson chose to lighten his load. This meant he decided to switch photographic technologies, abandoning his heavy, bulky equipment and its cumbersome wet plate process—including his portable darkroom—for a camera that shot photographs on dry film, a relatively recent innovation at the time. Jackson had never really worked with this type of film, but he chose to order enough rolls from a London photographic house to allow him to take four hundred photographs with his 8-by-10-inch format camera during his weeks in the Southwest, all of which he ordered for delivery to the rail depot in Santa Fe, New Mexico.

Jackson left home and Emilie, excited about his latest venture into the Southwest. "My heart was as light as my burden when I stepped off the train in Trinidad, Colorado, then the closest rail connection for Santa Fe."[10] From Trinidad, Jackson took a mud wagon over Raton Pass, site of the Santa Fe Trail a generation earlier, and traveled through the Sangre de Cristo Mountains. He soon met Reverend Jackson in Santa Fe, the territorial capital of New Mexico and home to Fort Marcy. Within days his film arrived. Jackson had ordered his "experimental" film from L. Warnerke of London. When he did so, he did not purchase the film holders that Warnerke sold to accompany his film, but bought holders from a pair of American companies. Since he was new to such film, he meticulously followed all the directions provided by the suppliers.

Jackson does not seem to have had any significant anxiety concerning his decision to use dry film for the first time, especially in the context of yet another important Hayden Survey. From Fort Defiance he sent off a letter to William Henry Holmes, his geologist companion from earlier surveys, in which he expressed his confidence: "My paper film seems to be working all right, although I have developed one small lot only, but that came up so well, so easily and uniformly that I have banished all fears as to the final result. The only fault I found was that I had been over exposing."[11]

On March 23 Jackson and the reverend reached Fort Garland, Colorado, west of the Sangre de Cristo on the western edge of San Luis Park. Instructions had been sent to the fort commander to provide the two men with the necessary transportation and supplies for their journey into the Southwest. They headed back south into New Mexico and reached Taos and its pueblo, which Jackson photographed and measured, keeping exact records of his findings. Within a few days the two Jacksons arrived again in Santa Fe.

The two companions soon set out in the buckboard wagon—actually an ambulance—that the army had provided, which contained their bedrolls, supplies, personal luggage, and cooking equipment, as well as Jackson's photographic gear. They followed the Rio Grande Valley, sometimes retracing the steps of Spanish explorer Francisco Coronado, who had arrived in the region in 1542, searching for cities of gold he never found. After three days they reached the Laguna pueblo high atop a mesa, the village dominated by an adobe church built by villagers under Spanish supervision. Here they were hosted by the Marmon brothers, who ran a local trading post. While in the region, the Jacksons visited the pueblo at Acoma, known locally as Sky City, situated on top of a 350-foot-high mesa. The region's historic Pueblo peoples had often built their towns high above the valley floor for protection, given they were surrounded by more hostile Native American nations, including the Utes, Apaches, Navajos, and Comanches.

Jackson and the reverend then headed west and soon reached the Zuni Pueblo—Coronado had also reached this native town—where the two Americans were well treated, perhaps due to one being a man of the cloth. Jackson would one day return to the Zuni Pueblo and take photos of hundreds of men and women engaging in sacred, ritualistic dancing. On this trip, he drew a sketch of three Zuni drinking cups in the shapes of an owl, a spotted bird, and a duck.

After passing through Fort Wingate in southwestern New Mexico, the Jacksons proceeded northward to Fort Defiance, located in Arizona Territory. They happened to arrive just as the Navajos had turned up at the fort for their annual distribution from the government.

Jackson reached the fort to experience this great scene of expectant Indians, numbering perhaps up to ten thousand, all camped around Fort Defiance in brush wickiups and canvas shelters. Animals grazed away from the encampments in every direction. Evenings at the fort were cold due to the high elevation (seven thousand feet). One evening Jackson witnessed the following: "The snow was falling fast, and through the veil of feathery flakes the innumerable camp fires—thousands of them scattered over the hillsides overlooking the post—twinkled and gleamed redly in varying, fitful intensities."[12] By day, Jackson took several photos of the sweeping Indian encampment using his innovative dry film. Since he had not brought along his portable darkroom, he did not have the advantage he had become accustomed to of processing his plates in real time and seeing his finished photographs while still on location.

While working near Fort Defiance, Jackson found his prized .45 Smith and Wesson revolver missing, presumably pilfered by some Indians. He reported the loss to the local Indian agent, who sprang into action and assigned a pair of Indian policemen to locate the thief. Four days later, after the pair of Jacksons had left the fort and made their way to Canyon de Chelly, the native policemen caught up with them and returned the missing revolver.

After a few days at Fort Defiance, Jackson left his minister-companion behind and, with the help of a Navajo guide, took a side trip of forty miles one way by mule to the spectacular Canyon de Chelly. Although he was a veteran of hundreds of Southwest canyons, this one astonished Jackson. He arrived late one afternoon and walked around, taking in the rows of high sandstone mesas, streaked with iron oxide—known locally as "desert varnish"—as the sun set, casting dancing light across the canyon. This had been yet another site the ancient Anasazi had called home. These early Indian peoples had long moved on from the canyon when the Navajos arrived and claimed the land as their own.

Jackson soon returned to meet up with Reverend Jackson, and the two returned to Fort Defiance. They then returned to the trail and covered the one hundred miles to the Hopi pueblos Jackson had visited two years earlier, where he reacquainted himself with several tribal leaders and the young woman, Num-pa-yu (Nampeyo). He took photographs and sketched the figures of several wooden kachina dolls, which the Hopi considered powerful figures providing them with protection from evil spirits. They then returned to the Rio Grande, with the minister bidding Jackson one last farewell and returning to Santa Fe. Jackson had already heard stories that intrigued him of another Anasazi site barely known outside of local circles, one located in Chaco Canyon in northwest New Mexico. An army officer, Lt. James Simpson, had explored the site thirty years earlier, but Jackson wanted to see the place for himself.

He set out for Chaco Canyon in early May along with a pair of companions: Hosta, an older Mexican guide who was nearly blind, and his twelve-year-old grandson. (As a younger man, Hosta had accompanied the army during the 1849 military campaign during which Lieutenant Simpson had reached Chaco Canyon.) The weather was already hot as the small party began crossing the deserts of western New Mexico. "Looking across its desolate waste," Jackson later wrote, "a mirage danced constantly on the horizon, magnifying the insignificant sage bushes and the low, rolling hills into great oaks and distant mountains."[13] The journey proved difficult, as the trio of companions left the Rio Grande and passed through narrow canyons on the way to Chaco Canyon. They first spotted Penasco Blanca while still five miles away. Jackson soon arrived in the midst of Anasazi ruins, including Pueblo Bonito, where the ancient Puebloans had built a great, D-shaped town complex complete with four- or five-story high apartments and rounded, stone-lined kivas excavated into the ground, sites utilized by Anasazi men for special ceremonies. The place was in a state of disrepair, with wooden timbers having rotted out of place long ago. Stone walls had collapsed here and there, as the site had been abandoned and left to the elements more than seven hundred years earlier. Behind the Pueblo Bonito complex was a high line of sandstone bluffs, a portion of which had collapsed and caused further destruction at the site. Everywhere Jackson walked he was surrounded by mystery. As he had done previously at other Anasazi sites, he carefully measured the ruins and made sketches.

Of course, Jackson took photographs with his trusty 8-by-10-inch camera loaded with dry film. As he explored the ruins at Penasco Blanca (Jackson refers to them as Pueblo Pintado), he noticed something intriguing: "Back of the Pueblo Chettro Kettle [Chetro Ketl] . . . I saw some steps and handholds cut into the rock. . . . Easily gaining the summit, I walked back over the bluffs, ascending by terraces some 200 or 300 feet above the bottom of the canyon."[14] At the top of the cliff Jackson gained a new perspective, a panoramic view of the canyon that revealed even more ruins. He also discovered "a series of potholes in a deep crevice, containing hundreds of gallons of cool, sweet water. . . . The vexatious part of it was that I could take only one long, satisfying drink of it."[15] Due to Jackson's "discovery" of the Anasazi staircase ascending the cliff wall, the system of foot and handholds is known today as the Jackson Staircase.

Jackson and his comrades spent three days in Chaco Canyon while he examined the ancient sites. They set up a base camp, explored each day, and returned to the camp at night. Chaco Canyon, even today, is a desolate, remote site, generally accessible only by fifteen miles of rough gravel road. Today's visitor can easily lose his or her sense of the modern world and feel transported back into ancient time. There are no non-natural noises, such as traffic or contemporary machinery. Save for the visitors and the visitor center, Chaco Canyon remains a throwback to a world long gone. Jackson likely felt the sense of remoteness and removal as he tromped around the cliffs and ruins searching for answers to questions that still baffle today's visitors.

During his days at Chaco, Jackson employed all his dominant skill sets. After all, he was not in the company of other scientists, including topographers, botanists, geologists, and the like. Everything to be discovered was in his hands. He became all things for the moment—a photographer, yes, but also a topographer, archaeologist, and cartographer—as he utilized a knowledge of mapmaking he had learned during his days as a soldier during the Civil War.

Leaving Chaco Canyon and feeling he had accomplished something unique in the name of the Hayden Survey, he and his native guides headed to the Jemez Pueblo and San Ysidro, which they reached without incident. From San Ysidro, Jackson covered the sixty miles southwestward to the Laguna Pueblo, even though he had to follow a barely perceptible trail at best, given he was still driving a wagon. Not only was the trail poor, he had to maneuver his way across a nearly unoccupied desert, the course cut laterally with arroyos and intimidating valleys. Jackson felt fortunate his buckboard wagon did not experience a complete breakdown. At the pueblo, the Marmon brothers hosted his return, then led him back to the Acoma Pueblo, where Will spent another couple of days taking photographs and measurements. His plan was to make a model of Sky City when he returned to Washington. During his return to Santa Fe, Jackson visited additional pueblos and took more photographs. He entered the New Mexican capital at the end of May, handed over his government-issued items, including the wagon, and was soon on his way back East.

Jackson had accomplished yeoman's work from March through May. He had single-handedly explored a region of the Southwest on behalf of Hayden, and his efforts were included in the government report issued later. He had mapped and charted and measured and photographed his way throughout the Four Corners region, visiting active pueblos and sites long abandoned by the ancient Puebloan peoples. He still had not reached the lands of the future Mesa Verde National Park, but his travels had exposed him to a wide variety of ancient ruins. In the end, though, following his return to Hayden headquarters in Washington, he faced a crushing blow. He had used dry film for the first time in the field, and something had gone wrong. He wrote later describing what had happened: "It was not until I got back to Washington and began development that I could make sure of the results of the costly experiment. There I met with the bitter disappointment of getting only my test negatives for all my long journey and earnest efforts."[16]

This technological failure was Jackson's greatest disappointment involving his photography since back in 1873 when a wayward mule had slipped its load, breaking many of Jackson's glass plates. But he had been aware of that accident in real time, which allowed him to hurriedly retrace some of his steps and take replacement photographs of several key sites. This time he had discovered his problem too late. His 1877 Southwest venture was not a total failure, though. He had made significant measurements of such sites as Chaco Canyon, although, as he later noted, this "didn't comfort me much."[17] Whatever roles Jackson performed that spring in New Mexico and Arizona, he saw his first and foremost service to the Hayden Surveys as that of a photographer. His was a professional failure and a personal disappointment.

He was uncertain exactly what had gone wrong. Perhaps it was a matter of exposure or an unacceptable lag time between taking a photograph and processing the negative. Jackson had traveled light this time across the Southwest, and he did not have his portable darkroom. But something failed. Writing more than sixty years later, in his 1940 autobiography, Jackson still expressed disappointment: "My feelings were beyond the repair of Dr. Hayden's praise. They still are. I can never replace those lost pictures."[18]

14

The Last of the Surveys, 1878

$\mathcal{F}$or seven summers, William Henry Jackson had packed up his cameras and his photographic equipment, kissed one wife or another goodbye, and trekked across the American West, performing his unique responsibilities as a part of the Hayden Surveys. His final trip, in 1878, marked the beginning of the end of the Hayden Surveys sponsored by the federal government. When Jackson signed on for one more survey that year, he had no indication it was to be the last for himself and Hayden, even though the allotment from Congress for that summer was held up for months until late July. Only then was Hayden given the green light to head out West again with his corps of scientists and support staff.

The focus of the 1878 survey included ground previously covered several years earlier, perhaps indicating that Hayden and his men had reached the end of their exploratory possibilities. They were to return to Wyoming, to Jackson's satisfaction: "I was . . . happy to be going over Wyoming, where my first work with the Survey began."[1] Jackson took the UP out to Cheyenne, and plans were soon framed for him to photograph Wyoming's Wind River Mountains and ascend Fremont Peak. The last time he had participated directly with other Hayden men on the frontier was three years earlier in 1875, and he was glad to be back. This time he did not intend to rely on dry film, at least, not exclusively.

He and the others met up, as they had in 1870, at Fort D. A. Russell outside Cheyenne, where they drew their supplies, which were then shipped by rail to Point of Rocks, located approximately twenty-five miles east of today's Rock Springs, Wyoming. On July 24 the Hayden party headed for the Wind River Mountains. (Until recently, these mountains had been part of Lakota country, but the Lakota Indians had been subdued during the previous two or three years and placed on reservations.) The men were concerned they were starting too late for the season, a fear that became reality. They did not all travel together, as had become the practice over the past few years. They moved toward different destinations with plans to reconnoiter in Yellowstone, which was now a national park. As for Jackson, he traveled with various divisions of the survey. He took no photographs during the opening days of travel, until his party had moved beyond South Pass.

The next location where Jackson took pictures he considered important was near Wind River Peak, along the headwaters of the Little Popo Agie River, approximately fifteen miles south of Lander, Wyoming. The mountain borders today's Shoshone and Bridger National Forests. On August 2 he framed a photograph with the mountain in the background and a pretty lake scene in the foreground. Jackson was soon reminded that the best pictures in this western region were those taken in the morning, as the mountains were often shrouded with low-lying clouds in the afternoons. The mountain almost became a mere backdrop to the lake that dominates the lower half of his photo, framed with scattered rocks, a steep, rocky hill, and rough timber. As was often Jackson's practice, he included a member of the party in the scene to provide scale. For these photos, he relied on his 5-by-8-inch format camera.

The party moved on, crossing the lowlands to the west of the Wind River Range beyond Wind River Peak. Then a portion of the men, including Jackson, prepared to climb to the summit of Fremont Peak—named for the famed nineteenth-century American explorer and US Army officer, Capt. John C. Fremont, who had explored the region thirty years earlier—which loomed larger with each passing day. The mountain is located fifteen miles south of Lander. Will did not attempt to take his camera and equipment up the mountain, since the climb promised to be a difficult one, but instead decided to try making some dry plates using "a recently perfected collodio-bromide emulsion."[2] Mindful of his photographic failure in New Mexico the previous year, he knew he might be taking a risk, but "in this instance I had more confidence in my material and was prepared for development soon after exposure."[3] To prepare for his picture taking on the mountain, Jackson spent his evening coating half a dozen plates and allowing them to dry, using a heated shovel from the campfire to speed up the process. "Then," Jackson later wrote, "dreaming of New Mexico and Arizona and all those black films of 1877, I slept."[4]

The next day Jackson and several comrades climbed up Fremont Peak, a difficult climb impeded by several blocking ridgelines, forcing the men to zigzag up the peak to bypass the ridges. But ultimately they reached the summit, where they enjoyed a grand view of the surrounding landscape, which included mountains in nearly every direction. Off to the west, they could

Likely shot in 1878, this Jackson photo features Wyoming's Wind River Peak in the background. At the photo's center is Hayden Survey member A. D. Wilson, who on one occasion barely escaped being struck by lightning while on a mountaintop. National Archives. ID No. 517694.

barely make out the faint images of the Tetons and the Absarokas. As for the Big Horns, they were out of visual range. Jackson took several photographs from the summit, including a group picture of five of the men and a panoramic compilation of several mountain chains. The day was fantastic picture-taking weather—virtually no wind, no clouds. The weather, of course, did not always cooperate with the photographer. Jackson could become frustrated with repeated weather issues, as well as the basic, even primitive conditions under which he attempted to create photographs that reflected his own professionalism.

Back in camp, the party packed up and prepared to move on toward the headwaters of the Green River, which they soon reached, followed by Hoback Canyon, then the sweeping valley everyone knew as Jackson Hole, named for Dave Jackson, who had trapped with mountain man Jim Bridger decades earlier as employees of the Rocky Mountain Fur Company. While the canyon and the surrounding environs were extremely scenic, the trail was a challenge, including steep rises that made progress difficult for the mules. At one point a mule slipped down the canyon for two hundred feet before landing in a cold stream. (The animal was shaken but not seriously harmed.) While crossing Jackson Hole, Jackson did not take photos because the valley was shrouded in a hazy smoke. But when the party reached the Upper Gros Ventre Butte, he snapped his first photos of the Tetons since the original ones he had shot back in 1872.

The party continued on toward the Upper Snake River, following dim trails and sometimes no trail at all until they reached the banks of Heart Lake with Mt. Sheridan looming high above. (Hayden men had named the peak back in 1871 after Civil War Union general Philip Sheridan.) The men encountered an abundance of wild animals in this region, including "elk, particularly, coming out into the open and gazing curiously at our little encampment, entirely oblivious of the danger lurking behind the strange intruders."[5]

The Hayden men continued their trek across western Wyoming for more than a month, reaching Fire Hole and the Madison and Gallatin Rivers, both headwaters of the Missouri, and passing through lands many of them had explored previously until they entered Yellowstone National Park—which the Hayden men had helped encourage and create—then arrived at Mammoth Hot Springs around mid-September, where the party rendezvoused with Gen. Nelson Miles, who had until recently been engaged in fighting various Plains tribes, including the Kiowa, Comanche, and Cheyenne. Miles was in the region on an inspection tour of western military facilities. There was a certain tension in Yellowstone during the summer of 1878. The previous year, the US Army had chased down the Nez Perce people and forced them to surrender their ancestral lands. Indian roamers were still in the region, and some had killed a pair of Yellowstone tourists and wounded others. Stories swirled that Indians were wandering the park, and the army had sent in cavalry units to see for themselves. As for the Hayden men, they had no contact with hostile Indians that summer, except for a brief encounter with Ada D. Wilson's subparty. Throughout the brief ambush, no members of the Hayden party were killed or wounded.

Otherwise, while the Hayden men were in the park, it was obvious to all that Yellowstone had changed fairly dramatically. It had become a tourist destination where uniformed park rangers greeted groups of tourists from across the country and beyond. It was still a place where nature ruled supreme, but its previous frontier edginess—the attack on Wilson's party aside—had receded significantly. The Hayden men encountered visitors of all ages, including young women who came to see the very geysers and mud pots Jackson had helped reveal to the outside world just a few short years earlier. Visitors, though, meant something else to Jackson, who took photographs with his stereoscopic camera to produce sellable 3D picture sets to those interested in Yellowstone, whether actual tourists or armchair enthusiasts.

By late September the Hayden party had completed their work and prepared to leave. Snow was starting to fall, and the temperature was dropping, conditions familiar to those who had participated in previous surveys in Yellowstone. Following old, previously covered trails, the men passed over Mt. Washburn during a true snowstorm, then proceeded to Yellowstone Falls, where Jackson spent two or three days taking new photographs. He also, for the first time, descended to the bottom of Yellowstone's Grand Canyon along the east side for a unique perspective of the Lower Falls. It was a perilous descent:

> A coating of ice on rocks and slopes from the drifting spray of the falls made the undertaking hazardous. By using the packers' lash ropes and letting ourselves down over the steep places with the photographic outfit strapped to our backs, we managed finally to get to the bottom of the colorful gorge. There was a little difficulty in finding a smooth and level place for the dark tent. With that set up, conditions were as fine as they could be for our getting a successful series of negatives of the scene that has since thrilled thousands of visitors to this wonderland.[6]

After their time at the falls, the Hayden party crossed the river near Sulphur Hills and lit upon an old trail they had used before to pass around the eastern portion of Yellowstone Lake. The snow came down heavy and stranded the men for a few days. Once back on the trail, they passed an Indian camp, recently abandoned, with no Native Americans in sight. At some points the snow obscured the trail so thoroughly the men had to depend on the marks blazed into the trees by previous expeditions to stay on course.

One afternoon Jackson had a unique adventure. As the men were searching for a viable campsite, he and Hayden were riding ahead and noticed bear tracks. Hayden suggested they follow the tracks, which took them off the trail. After a half-mile detour, the men caught sight of the grizzly, which appeared to have caught their scent. They continued to follow until the bear leaped over a fallen log, then turned to face them. Jackson later wrote of the encounter: "Soon we caught a glimpse of him lumbering ahead through the woods. . . . I threw back the cape of my heavy coat, dropped to one knee, and fired. Without sound or struggle the grizzly crumpled in the snow."[7] It was Jackson's first grizzly bear kill. He asked the survey packers to skin the animal, which they did, with Jackson intending to deliver the skin to the Indian Agency at Camp Brown on the Wind River for a proper tanning as a trophy, the proverbial bearskin rug. But the party did not arrive at the agency for ten days and by that time, as the weather turned warmer, the skin had decomposed too much for proper tanning. All Jackson managed to salvage was a handful of claws.

The warm temperatures that had helped to ruin Jackson's bear skin continued throughout the days that followed. The party reached a site called Two-Ocean Pass, so named following an earlier claim made by mountain man Jim Bridger that the pass on the Continental Divide allowed the waters from a local spring to flow in two directions, toward both the Pacific and Atlantic Oceans. Hayden was intent on determining if the pass existed and where it was located. Gaining a higher elevation, the party encountered snow, leading the men to sleep on their tents rather than in them. The following morning they found "everything was frozen up as tight as a drumhead."[8] But Hayden instructed half a dozen of his men to search the area—including a whopping forty acres!—in search of any streams under the ice and determine their direction. Bridger's claim was ultimately vindicated, as the Hayden men discovered waters flowing eastward into the Yellowstone and westward into the Snake River. Indeed, Two-Ocean Pass had been accurately named.

They then proceeded to the headwaters of Buffalo Fork, leaving the snow behind as they descended, until they reached a vast grassland filled with large herds of elk. Off in the distance stood the peaks of the Three Tetons, well defined against a clear western skyline. Here Jackson shot some photographs of the mountain he had immortalized several years earlier. Sublime scenery remained the Hayden party's constant companion, as the men crossed Togwotee Pass, climbing up poor trails and returning to the high-country snow. Jackson continued setting up his camera and taking more shots, focusing on "the castellated volcanic rocks that are a prominent feature of that region."[9] The party then descended into the Wind River Valley, where they reached Camp Brown and the Washakie Indian Agency, the forced home of the Shoshones—whose ancestors had so famously aided Lewis and Clark in their advance to the west by providing them with horses—many of whom were absent on fall hunting forays. Other Native Americans at the agency included the Bannack, who had recently been rounded up by army campaigns. Jackson took several photographs of these Indians, including one man with whom he was familiar. Beaver Dick Leigh had served as a guide for Jackson during his 1872 sojourn through the Tetons and on into Yellowstone. He agreed to pose for Jackson's camera along with his wife, a teenager named Susan Tadpole, a Bannack.

This visit at the Indian agency marked the end of the Hayden Survey in the field for the summer of 1878. The party began moving toward the closest railhead to ship out of the region. Their trek placed them near Three Crossings on the Sweetwater River. Snow was beginning to accumulate as they passed through Muddy Gap, a site located today at the intersection of Wyoming Route 220 and US 287. From there the party took two days to cross a wide-open plain covered with heavy snow, which led them to Rawlins,

Wyoming, then on to Fort Steele, located fifteen miles farther east. The remaining supplies and government equipment the Hayden party had "borrowed" were returned, and the following day most of the men were enjoying the comforts of a Pullman car, headed back to Washington.

Jackson's days in the field that summer marked not only the end of his latest season with Hayden and his merry band but also the last of the surveys on behalf of the US Geological Survey. They also signaled the end of Jackson's pioneering days as a western photographer, one who had carried bulky, heavy cameras across Wyoming and through the Rocky Mountains year after year, taking wet plate negatives and developing them on the fly in makeshift darkrooms of canvas. He was not done taking photographs of the West, but his days as a photographer reliant on these primitive, sometimes unreliable technologies were over. Despite his failed experiment with dry plate photography in 1877, it represented the next phase of photographic advancement. He would no longer roam the West as a Hayden man, but on his own or in the employ of others, including the D & RG. These experiences, though, never rose to the level of excitement Jackson had felt during his Hayden years. As he concluded his 1929 autobiography, "None of these later experiences . . . can ever bring more delightful memories than those of earlier days, when I was doing my part to help reveal the scenic and other wonders of our Rocky Mountain region to the world."[10]

15

Beyond the Surveys, 1879–1893

𝒯he last of the Hayden Survey seasons in the field had proven short and final. The year 1878 marked the end of the congressional bankrolling of Dr. Hayden's explorations of the American West, as control of the Geological Survey slipped into other, firmer federal hands. Jackson produced fewer photographs than he often had on earlier surveys, perhaps in part due to the survey retracing many of its earlier steps. Jackson had already photographed the Wind River Range, the Tetons, and the wonders of Yellowstone. He still produced good photographs, but he did so by photographing not new places but new angles of old ones. (In fact, he produced seemingly better pictures with his smaller, 5-by-8-inch camera than with his 11-by-14-inch format.)

The return to Yellowstone did open the eyes of the men of the survey to what their earlier explorations in 1871 and 1872 had produced. Hayden had almost nostalgically returned to the plateau in 1878 and was disturbed by what he witnessed, as was Jackson. Yellowstone was no longer a frontier wonder of nature; it was a tourist destination like so many others. As historian Peter Hales notes, "They found it not an escape from civilization, but an escape into civilization: accommodations had been built on the site and tourists were ensconced, riding the trails, staring at the fountains, taking the water, bathing in the pools."[1] And the transformation had happened so quickly. As early as 1874, Secretary of the Interior Columbus Delano, writing to President Grant, lamented that "the park has been visited during the past summer by many persons, and . . . has been despoiled by them of great quantities of its mineral deposits and other curiosities." He warned of the need for government "protection of this great natural wonder from the vandalism of curiosity-hunters."[2] Delano had received some of his insights directly from Nathaniel Langford, the first superintendent of Yellowstone National Park, who had explored the region before Hayden had entered with his survey team in 1871.

With the end of the Hayden Surveys, Jackson's life took a decided turn. He was no longer a paid member of the survey. But he was not simply an unemployed photographer. Jackson later insisted he had already made the decision to resign from the survey and future picture taking even before the end was made official. Just as his first child, Clarence, was born following Jackson's trek west with the 1875 survey, so a second child came along following his 1878 venture. On November 23 a daughter named Louise was born in their house in Washington, D.C. The birth, in tandem with the culmination of the Hayden Surveys, led Jackson to "sit down and do some heavy thinking."[3] Jackson had participated in the surveys through nine seasons, including the 1876 season when he did not travel out West but instead rode herd over the Hayden exhibit at the Centennial Exposition in Philadelphia. Although his 1877 trip had culminated in the disaster of ending pictureless due to dry film issues, he considered each a success in its own way. He had served as a unique member of the surveys, and his photographs had graced multiple reports through woodcuts, making him one of the most well-known photographers in America, especially of western landscapes. He had enjoyed himself throughout these years despite the myriad challenges he faced traveling across rugged mountains and through formidable deserts. "I loved my work," he wrote later. "I could ask nothing more."[4]

But that chapter of his life was now closing, and Jackson was still a young man with a long career ahead of him: "I was thirty-five years old. I was the head of a family—a growing family. Soon there would be schools to consider. And there was my wife. Emilie, always loyal and comprehending, surely deserved something better of marriage than a husband who was away five, six, seven months every year."[5] But Jackson's concerns were not merely familial. No longer employed as a Hayden man, he faced the consideration of money. The survey had provided him with a decent base of support at $175 a month, but Jackson had not grown rich on his government job. He had always supplemented his salary with sales of his photographs, including the popular stereoscopic pictures of his scenes of the American West, which increased his total annual income to between $2,500 and $3,000, a decent income at that time, but not "a very high scale of living for a man who had reached the front rank in his field."[6] Had he remained on the government payroll for future surveys, his financial situation likely would not have improved much, at least not in the immediate future. With the surveys over, Jackson was now on his own hook, free to chart his own destiny separate from that of Dr. Ferdinand Hayden. He soon began to consider that destiny and that future represented a return to his earlier days as a commercial photographer.

The redirection did not happen all at once. He continued to receive his monthly stipend through the fiscal year ending July 1, 1879. Jackson had time to methodically ponder where his career might take him next. Would he remain in Washington or return to the West permanently as a resident rather than an exploring photographer? He soon landed on Denver as a viable option for a new photographic studio: "I liked the way the place had grown, from a raw town of 5,000 when I first saw it in 1870, to a flourishing city seven times that size."[7]

Denver was the place, the decision was made, and Will Jackson never looked back. But he was not the same man he had been when he first hung out his photographer's shingle over a storefront in Omaha in the late 1860s. Now his name was a bankable commodity, one known in many corners of the country by those familiar with his photography, including customers who had purchased his stereoscopic visions.

To that end, before packing up his young family and moving west, as he had so impulsively done following the Civil War and his breakup with his fiancée, Caddie, Jackson took a train to New York City. His first priority was to visit photographic supply houses to learn about the latest camera innovations and talk to those who represented the vanguard of American photography. He also wanted to meet the directors of American railway companies, as he had a specific gambit in mind. Just as he had worked for the UP in the summer of 1869 documenting the construction of the eastern line of the transcontinental railroad, he now sought audience with other rail tycoons who might be interested in hiring him to document their own, newer western lines. If he could secure such an agreement, it would provide him with an instant business venture upon his arrival, with his family in tow, in Denver. His old survey pal, James Stevenson, helped open initial doors. He knew several of the railroad movers and shakers, including his personal friend Commodore Vanderbilt, who had recently passed away, as well as Jay Gould.

Few men in America were known in more significant circles at that time than the American railroad magnate and financial speculator Jay Gould, who would one day become the virtual poster image for the robber barons of the Gilded Age, at least as it related to railroads. He had gained a controlling interest in the UP when its stock tumbled in value during the Panic of 1873, and had expanded its footprint, providing rail service to farmers and ranchers in remote corners of the West.

Jackson was introduced to Gould in his office in the New York Opera House, with Jim Stevenson serving as the go-between. On that June day, Jackson found Gould and, "as I walked toward his desk," Jackson later wrote, "I felt as if I were being X-rayed by the blackest, most piercing eyes in the world."[8] Gould was only seven years older than Jackson, small framed and dark complected, with black hair and an accompanying black beard. The railroad tycoon was soft spoken and seemed to be listening absent-mindedly to both Stevenson, his friend, and Jackson, whom he likely did not even know by reputation. Only when Jackson moved the conversation to photography did Gould perk up.

"Tell me, Mr. Jackson," he queried. "Are you the man who took those Union Pacific pictures a few years ago?"[9]

When Jackson confirmed Gould's curiosity, the conversation took a decided turn. Now Gould had put a name with a reputation, and he began peppering Jackson with questions about his work out West, including with the Hayden Surveys in Colorado and Yellowstone. He even asked Jackson some questions about western flora, as the tycoon was a bit of a gardening enthusiast. From this point on, Jackson's encounter with Gould proved golden. The men talked for an hour, and the conversation ended with Gould promising to write letters to several railroad officials out in Denver, a promise he followed up on. "I am grateful for that kindness," Jackson later wrote.[10]

Given his connections with the survey, Jackson managed to convince government officials to sell him some of the leftover equipment, including four cameras and a variety of lenses, all at a vast discount, as Jackson only paid $200 for the whole lot, about 20 percent of its market value. He soon moved out to Denver, where he set up his new photographic enterprise with a single assistant, Frank Smart, the son of a photographer acquaintance of Jackson's, at 413 Larimer Street in a two-story building then under construction. The photographer only needed the second-floor space and managed to get the builders to add a skylight to their design. Jackson went to Denver without his wife and children. He called for them to come once things were fully established.

Denverites greeted the latest arrival with open arms. Jackson already had a reputation in the community as Hayden's photographer. The professor had included a correspondent for the *Rocky Mountain News* in the 1873 expedition to photograph the Mount of the Holy Cross. That reporter was none other than the newspaper's editor and publisher, William Byers, who became an advocate for Jackson, along with several other influential Denver men, including Emilie Painter Jackson's uncle, William Gilpin, Colorado's first governor, who proved a repeat visitor at the Jackson dinner table over the years. Just as these influencers promoted Jackson in Colorado, so Jackson was expected to promote Colorado. And just as Denver had served repeatedly as the operational base for Hayden's expeditions in Colorado, so the town became Jackson's photographic hub.

Jackson did not hang around Denver long. He was intent on traveling across parts of Colorado, not as a survey man but as an entrepreneur, taking photographs of sights would-be customers might be willing to pay to own. The photographer and his assistant were soon on the road in a two-seater wagon bound for the booming silver town of Leadville, which Jackson had visited in 1874. On his previous visit, Jackson had encountered storekeeper Horace Tabor, who was now the mayor of the growing mining town. Tabor was on his way to becoming one of the richest men in Colorado, with enough money to buy himself a seat in the US Senate.

Jackson's first railroad sponsor since the summer of 1869, when the UP had hired him to take photographs, was the Colorado & Southern, which had only recently been gobbled up by the UP. This was a line linking the mining communities of Central City and Black Hawk, Georgetown, and Idaho City to the line running between Golden and Denver. Will Jackson took photographs in nearly all these mining towns, sometimes conjuring up memories of earlier days when he had passed through the area by pack mule. Outside Georgetown, a tidy Victorian community featuring gingerbread mansions, he photographed the famous Georgetown Loop.

A couple of miles out of the town, situated at an elevation hundreds of feet higher, was the mining camp of Silver Plume. Silver ores were initially removed by mule teams, until a rail line was laid that included the Loop, an engineering marvel based on four and one-half miles of spiraling lines that crossed over one another on trestles, the tracks perched high above the canyon floor. Building the Loop had proven a difficult task, indeed. For Jackson, just photographing the Loop had its own challenges, including locating a safe high canyon perch where he could set up his camera and capture the sweeping scale of this complicated engineering project.

In his travels around Colorado that summer, Jackson replicated commonplace experiences from the Hayden Surveys. He and his assistant slept outdoors and cooked their own food, only occasionally paying for a hotel room. The photographic pair traveled through Clear Creek Canyon and into additional mining towns, with Jackson taking pictures along the way. Many of these prospecting communities were short-lived ventures, which, Jackson hoped, might lend value to his photographs as scenes of a transitory reality.

When he returned to Denver, Will was intent on getting his new business in order, ready to profit from his reputation as a photographer of grand, sweeping landscapes. He waited until the spring of 1880 to encourage his family to join him in Denver, where they lived at 488 Champa, close to Jackson's studio.

His venture to Leadville and the mining camps did pay off as Jackson had hoped. He sold enough print orders to justify adding more personnel, including a cameraman named Hosier, a print maker, and a female receptionist. Jackson's move to Denver was producing immediate benefits, and profits

Jackson posed his family circle in this mid-1880s photograph featuring his wife Emilie and his three children: Clarence (born 1876), Louise, (1878), and Hallie (1882). Library of Congress. LC-D419-30.

continued throughout the 1880s. A pair of significant business opportunities came Jackson's way in 1881. He managed to convince one of Denver's leading photographers, Albert E. Rinehart, to go into business with Jackson rather than compete with him. The combination proved quite successful, as the two photographers shared commercial space and offices, as well as workers, while technically maintaining their separate businesses, operating under the same roof as Jackson & Rinehart. This was the beginning of Jackson combining with other partners. A few years later Jackson arranged a deal with one of Denver's leading booksellers, Chain & Hardy, with the bookstore owners putting up money to finance several photographic projects that were beyond Jackson's financial means. Then, in 1892, Jackson enticed a silent partner, Walter F. Crosby, himself an amateur photographer, to invest $10,000 in a new photographic company headed by Jackson: W. H. Jackson Photograph and Publishing Company.

Before 1881 ended, Gould's support of Jackson bore fruit, as he received a railroad contract with the D & RG. Once again, just as he had for the UP twelve years earlier, the photographer agreed to take pictures of the landscape and scenery located along the tracks of the D & RG to encourage settlement, tourism, and economic growth. It was a grand opportunity for Jackson that allowed him to relive some of the experiences of his Hayden Survey days. He was able to bring along two of his old survey pals, journalist Ernest Ingersoll and his painter friend, Thomas Moran. All three set out on the railroad-sponsored venture that year with a deal of their own. Ingersoll was to write articles for *Harper's New Monthly*, which Moran was to illustrate with a dozen woodcuts.[11] In addition, the D & RG contracted with Moran to create a set of railroad illustrations to appear in the *Colorado Tourist*, a publication promoting the railroad (as well as other Gould-held rail lines) that was to be published in Denver by the *Rocky Mountain News*.

By the early 1880s four standard-gauge railroads had reached Denver, most during the 1870s. These railroads fanned out in various directions, but they largely operated along Colorado's Front Range, the lands east of the Rocky Mountains. Yet some of the more remote parts of Colorado were still, well, remote, giving Coloradoans pause to determine just how to extend railroads to distant mining camps that might exist one day and be gone the next. A full-fledged railroad was prohibitively expensive. Narrow gauge became the answer. The parallel rails of a standard-gauge track are laid at a distance of four feet, eight and one-half inches. Narrow gauge reduces the distance between parallel rails to three feet and was the type laid initially by the D & RG. Construction costs for three-foot rights of way, including trestles, tunnels, and other modifications, came in at about half the cost of standard-gauge lines.

The D & RG was initially chartered as the state's first narrow-gauge line on October 27, 1870, and its first tracks ran from Denver southward to Colorado Springs, a distance of around seventy-five miles. The line opened in 1871, and by 1884 the line was a spider's web of sixteen hundred miles of narrow-gauge track that snaked through the Rockies and even stretched out to Utah's Ogden and Salt Lake City and across the Colorado–New Mexico border to Santa Fe.

This 1880s photograph of the Mexican Central Railway's Encarnacion Bridge is reminiscent of earlier photographs Jackson had taken of trains parked on bridges in Wyoming and Colorado. Library of Congress. LC-DIG-det-4a27121.

When Jackson, Ingersoll, and Moran hit the road that summer, they went in style. The D & RG provided the trio with a private train car. This was the beginning of several years of Jackson taking such excursions at the expense of the railroad. The arrangement was beneficial for both sides, and Jackson found it rewarding, both professionally and personally: "Thereafter I spent part of every summer on the rails, for one road or another, and usually with a private car, all beautifully equipped. . . . Not infrequently I found it possible to take my family with me."[12]

Traveling with the family was not often ideal for everyone involved. While Jackson thrived on this newer version of his summer treks out West to photograph the landscape, his wife, Emilie, was often left to fend for herself, with the children cooped up in a railcar with no place to play. Circumstances were cramped, privacy was difficult to maintain, and Emilie struggled with such simple chores as washing clothes, since there were no such facilities onboard. The children might enjoy the scenery as their father did, but this did not always compensate for the difficulties of trying to maintain a family life on a moving train. Jackson minimized Emilie's sacrifice in his autobiography: "If it wasn't always as satisfactory for my wife as it was for me, Emilie fully understood and agreed that it was, under the circumstances, the best one possible for all of us."[13]

One of the goals of the 1881 venture was to again photograph the boomtown of Leadville. The mining community had reinvented itself since

Jackson's first arrival. In 1878 this mining town, sitting atop Carbonate Hill, had found new life through additional discoveries of tons of silver—"that damned blue stuff" that miners had earlier cursed when looking for gold as '59ers. New strikes included mines variously named the Little Chief, the Little Pittsburgh, New Discovery, and Crysolite. Miners flooded into the region by the thousands. With so much silver being prospected and mined, inflation hit the town like a ton of bricks, causing in-town rents to soar. One shop on Chestnut Street or Harrison Avenue might rent for $500 a month. "Rents are higher than in New York City," wrote one frustrated observer.[14] City lots sold for as much as $10,000.

When Jackson arrived in 1881, Leadville was luxuriating in riches that financed two luxury hotels—the Grand and the Clarendon—plus 120 bars and saloons and an abundance of dance halls, including the Silver Thread, the Red Light, the Tudor, and the Odeon. Paying for all this and more, Leadville mines produced three hundred tons of pure silver annually, typically cast in forty-pound ingots.

The 1881 venture involving Jackson, Moran, and Ingersoll followed the rails all over Colorado and beyond to Salt Lake City. While Jackson's photographs were intended to advertise the D & RG and thus entice tourists to leave their humdrum worlds for the tonic that was nineteenth-century Colorado, Ingersoll did his bit as well. Four years following the excursion, he published a travelogue-memoir titled *Crest of the Continent*, in which he described his travels with his companions. In the book's preface he promotes the benefits of travel in the Rockies: "The zest with which one goes about an expedition of any kind in the Rocky Mountains is phenomenal in itself."[15]

The trio traveled from the remote corners of Colorado to the urban oases, including Colorado Springs, passing through the mountains, across great valleys, and wherever the trains of the D & RG could deliver them. For Jackson, the trip included returning to the San Juans, the Sangre de Cristos, and the La Platas. He also returned to the pueblos of the Southwest.

It was a successful tour on a grand scale, one that achieved its goals and then some. Along with Ingersoll's book, which appeared in 1885—its popularity led to four editions—Jackson's photographs drew interested tourists to purchase D & RG tickets to tour Colorado's great landscapes. But it was more than that. Many of Jackson's pictures that summer emphasized the railroad itself and the ways in which it had conquered, even tamed the land. Jackson had entered Colorado in the early 1870s when the territory was still wild and somewhat unknown. Now the land had lost much of its primeval mystery. His pictures drew the curious out to the Rockies to see the mining camps for themselves. Men and women now climbed Colorado's mountains, forded its rivers, mined its riches, bought tickets to ride its railroads, and nailed down its

Jackson shot several photographs over a number of years of Colorado's Rio Las Animas, often with a D & RG train sitting on the edge of a cliffside portion of track. The date for this photo is between 1898 and 1905. Library of Congress. LC-DIG-ppmsca-17816.

landscapes with cabins and storefronts and opera houses and train depots. Jackson had served his purpose as a pioneering photographer who had entered the land with his mule and canvas darkroom; helped banish its dark corners; and managed to open any number of Colorado vistas to railroad stops, restorative spas, and tourist destinations.

Jackson, despite all his previous wanderings across the American West, still managed to find subjects for his camera that were new and even challenging. One of those was southwest Colorado's Animas River and the precarious canyon pass D & RG engineers and workers had carved out of the sheer cliff wall. (When Jackson first visited the Animas, the railroad had not yet been constructed.) Jackson shot several amazing photographs of the "Canyon of the Rio de Las Animas," during the 1880s, some of which became iconic. For several shots, he carefully hauled his equipment down rocky canyon walls—something he had done many times before, especially in the Grand Canyon of the Yellowstone—to gain the best aesthetic shots. In one picture, taken on a sunny day in the summer of 1886, Jackson positioned himself just above the raging river and pointed his camera skyward. On an unseen ledge sits a chuffing D & RG steam engine with four or five cars attached. All along the cliff base lie piles of hard rock chips and boulders railroad workers had blasted from the mountainside—using tons of black powder—to create a high-mountain, level shelf for a train track. Jackson, as was his practice, posed five rail men at the train's edge. The picture combines all the usual Jackson elements, including a wild river against an imposing wall of ancient granite, as the train represents the successful taming of the landscape. Once again, Jackson juxtaposes the rawness of nature with man's capacity to wrench out a place for civilization.

To an extent, Jackson's photography now emphasized this human element as much as the landscape itself. His pictures sought to reveal the vast demographic shifts of more towns and cities, a determined urbanization encouraged by discoverable riches underground and real estate in search of development. He utilized his camera to document the expansion of the urban landscape of Denver as he photographed, often from any high place in the city he could access, the Brown Palace Hotel, the Tabor Opera House, and other locales. His photographs became promotional propaganda, extolling the city's growth as an outpost of the conquering of the American West. In 1891 the booster album *The City of Denver* was published, replete with Jackson's images.

But Jackson's time in the undeveloped West was not yet finished. Over a dozen years he rode western railcars, sponsored by western railroads, taking photographs of places he had not yet visited and some he had. In 1883 he traveled to the Grand Canyon, where he had to climb into difficult spaces— just as he had so often done during his years with the Hayden Surveys—to gain the vantage points he wanted. The 1880s included trips for Jackson into Mexico, where he found yet another tall mountain, Popocatepetl—at nearly eighteen thousand feet, it was taller than any he had ascended in Colorado. On this occasion his rail sponsor was the Mexican Central Railway. (Jackson made at least three trips along the Mexican Central, in 1882, 1883, and 1891.) Jackson returned from this first excursion with a gift for his eight-year-old son Clarence—a tiny Chihuahua—which the boy did not appreciate. Clarence soon traded the hairless pup for a donkey.

Jackson felt he had reached his stride as a photographer during this portion of his career, noting, "As time went on, I found my pictures for the Denver & Rio Grande paying big dividends. . . . And since I enjoyed traveling even more, if possible, as I grew older, it was a thoroughly satisfactory life."[16]

These years of taking photographs for the D & RG were commercially successful for Jackson. Denver proved a good move for both his business and his family. They started out in a rented house on Champa, then moved to nearby 406 Stout, followed by a move to live above Jackson's studio at 18th and Wazee. In late 1882 or perhaps early 1883, the Jacksons took up residence in their own house, a solidly middle-class brick abode on 23rd Street. At last the family gained a maid to help with the housework. That year, 1883, was a productive one for Jackson, socially and professionally. He and Emilie entertained regularly, hosting those belonging to the highest ranks of Denver society. Three years later Jackson was successful enough to build a new house at 1430 Clarkson, up on Capitol Hill, in a neighborhood inhabited by some of Denver's elite. Jackson took several photographs of the house's interior, revealing the home of a well-to-do professional photographer. The furnishings are well appointed, replete with crowded bookshelves, plush carpets, and crystal gas lamps suspended from the ceilings. It is an enviable Victorian pile.

During the summer of 1892 Jackson and Thomas Moran teamed up again on the last of Jackson's great western treks as a photographer. It was very reminiscent of earlier ventures, but this time they were working not for Hayden but for themselves, or rather for sponsors, including the Santa Fe Railroad, to produce yet more works of photographic and artistic skill to sell yet additional corners of the West. The Santa Fe wanted pictures from both men to include in a tourist booster book and for the railroad's planned exhibit at the Columbian Exposition, yet another world's fair celebrating another American milestone, the arrival of Columbus in the New World. The artist and the painter went on their trip in the company of Moran's son, Paul. Their first destination was the Grand Canyon. The railroad did not extend into Arizona until the late 1880s and did not reach the Grand Canyon until 1901, so Jackson and the Morans had to take a stagecoach to reach the canyon. Moran had set out in mid-May from Chicago by train and arrived in Flagstaff, Arizona, by May 22. He arrived at the Grand Canyon on Thursday, May 25, and began scouting out vantage points for his artistic works. In a letter he wrote to his wife, Mary, dated that same day, he informed her, "We are very well provided for here and we shall probably stay one week. You see the Wyoming party cannot start until Jackson gets to them and that is likely to be June 10th."[17] Jackson soon arrived, and the two middle-aged friends were soon venturing along the canyon's rims as if they were still young men exploring Yellowstone more than twenty years earlier. (In 1892 Jackson was forty-nine and Moran fifty-five.) They were still spry enough, taking Hance's Trail down two thousand feet into the canyon. They lived out of tents and cooked on the trail. The following day, Moran wrote in the same letter, "We took it easy as possible but mounting the steep trail to the upper edge was hard and slow work."[18]

Both men worked fast at the canyon, since they had set for themselves a whirlwind schedule. Moran noted later that Jackson produced one hundred negatives of the great chasm in just four days. Moran observed that the weather cooperated with the two artists, aiding them in their efforts to produce photographs and sketches: "On Monday the day before we left we had heavy rain during the night and morning and when it cleared we were treated to the most magnificent sight of all. Clouds and sunshine in the Canyon.

Following the Hayden Surveys, Jackson was sometimes hired by various railroads to photograph their routes. In this photo of Cerro Estrella, taken during the early 1880s, the photographer has gone south of the border, employed by the Mexican Central Railway. Library of Congress. LC-DIG-det-4a26892.

[Jackson] made many photographs of it and will have some splendid effects. I have made some sketches that will serve my purposes well."[19] After only a few days at the canyon, the friends packed up and took the train to Denver, where Moran and his son spent some pleasant time with Jackson's family before heading north to Wyoming. During his time in Colorado, Moran noticed how much Denver and its environs had changed in his absence. "It is wonderful how Denver and Colorado Springs have grown since I was here late. The Casino at Colorado Springs up on the side of Cheyenne Mountain is a beautiful place of resort with a Hungarian band there every evening."[20] Colorado, at least along the Front Range, appeared quite settled and urbanized to the great American painter. The days of the frontier had certainly receded.

From the trip, Moran produced a large painting, *The Grand Canyon of the Colorado*, measuring approximately 53 by 94 inches. It was not the first work Moran had produced of the sweeping view of the great chasm. He had accompanied explorer and survey leader John Wesley Powell into the region in the early 1870s and had already painted a much larger oil work (85 by 144 inches) of the canyon.

Moran and Jackson had an additional sponsor that year, the state of Wyoming, which was also interested in pictures to utilize in the state's display at the Exposition. While the primary destination for both men was Yellowstone

National Park, their first destination in the young state—Wyoming had only gained statehood two years earlier—involved a difficult side trip to Devil's Tower. Though seasoned veterans of basic western travel, both men failed to plan adequately. They hurriedly rented a wagon and a pair of older, mismatched horses and set out across eastern Wyoming with little more than Jackson's photographic equipment in tow, plus Moran's art supplies and some bedding, including a pair of Navajo blankets Moran had purchased in Flagstaff and "a rubber air pillow" Moran had purchased in Denver at Jackson's suggestion.[21] They intended to purchase food along the trail from local ranches.

Local ranchers, however, did not cooperate. In several instances, the ranches they reached were owned by various eastern corporations and run by superintendents who were unsympathetic to the plight of the two strangers. They passed several abandoned homesteads, the earlier sodbusters having gone bust. A few days on a reasonably good trail led them to a fork with no clear means of determining the right path. After choosing one, they watched with concern as the sky turned dark. Moran described what happened next: "We were entirely unprepared for the suddenness and severity with which there broke upon us a storm of hail. . . . Light summer clothing and thin felt hats were our only protection against this awful fusillade of ice-balls that struck us with a force as if coming from a sling."[22]

The storm shifted from hail to a driving, cold rain that left the road sticky with a gooey mud Moran referred to as "gumbo." Prior to the storm, the hired horses had struggled to keep a decent pace on the trail. Now they were trapped in a deep morass. Jackson and Moran had to stop the wagon repeatedly to remove the troubling mud. Wearily the artists continued on, fearing they had missed the Wyoming landmark along the way. Within a couple of days, though, they spotted the tower in the distance. Moran wrote, "The scenery along the river to the tower was fine: a very wide canon in sandstone worn into castellated forms, inclosing a fertile valley studded with the houses and fields of prosperous farmers and ranchers." When they finally arrived at the massive formation, Moran described it with a clear-eyed directness: "This wonderful mass of columnar basalt rises about 2000 feet above the Belle Fourche [River]. It is somewhat of a geological puzzle, standing alone as it does, and rising directly out of a country entirely made up of sedimentary rock. . . . Be that as it may, it is a grand and imposing sight, and one of the remarkable physical features of this country. We sketched and photographed it during the remainder of the day."[23]

On their return trip, Jackson and Moran were chagrined to discover they had chosen the wrong path, which led them along a much longer trail than they needed to follow. Overall, the trip ended in success, but the two friends realized they had not planned well. Still, the excursion to Devil's Tower came as close as any experience Moran and Jackson had that summer to replicating those earlier, exploratory days spent with the Hayden Surveys of the 1870s.

Over the next three weeks, they traveled westward across Wyoming toward Yellowstone. They did not follow a straight path, for Jackson wanted to return to several of his old mountain haunts and photograph them once again. Thus, their route became circuitous. It proved a good decision for the photographer, for it allowed him to once again replicate some of the highlights of expeditions dating back twenty years. After taking pictures of Denver buildings and other late nineteenth-century towns and cities, he was back in his previous element, photographing the timeless landscape and its most outstanding mountains, lakes, and sweeping valleys. He utilized his giant 18-by-22-inch format camera, taking care to avoid any man-made interruptions in the landscape, whether abandoned ranch houses, fences, cast-off mining equipment, or telegraph poles. At one location Jackson's assistant, Walter Crosby, took a photograph of Lake de Amalia, amid the Wind River Mountains. The lake is placid, with a scattering of boulders peaking above its surface. Toward the picture's center are the distant figures of Will Jackson, alongside his large-format camera precariously placed on the rocks, and a seated Thomas Moran, fishing contentedly. At that moment, Jackson was preparing to take a photograph himself of the lake, a two-part panorama measuring 17 by 40 inches.

Jackson, Moran, and their party enjoyed their frontier interlude during these weeks between Devil's Tower and their arrival at Yellowstone National Park. The park presented itself as an urban outpost presiding over a vast natural wilderness. They arrived at Mammoth Hot Springs on July 20 "after a most wearying journey."[24] The Yellowstone the two artists visited in the summer of 1892 had grown up since they had first tromped through its earlier primeval state. It seemed, in some sense, like the Yellowstone they had first encountered, but with some of its luster faded, a bit of its soul gone. Moran observed in a letter to his wife, "I have not yet gone up to look at the Springs but from the Hotel it looks as if they had lost the color they had originally."[25] The frontier edginess was less apparent. Once in the park, the men had the opportunity to stay in one of its hotels, and they did, as Moran wrote to Molly: "I stayed at the Hotel in preference to camp as did Jackson and a couple of others. We have all had enough of camp life."[26] They returned to their old ways in the park, taking photographs, sketching the wonders from the best artistic vantage points, and fishing. Moran returned to Yellowstone as a celebrity of sorts: "I have been made much of at all the places in the park as the great and only 'Moran' the painter of the Yellowstone and I am looked at curiously by all the people at the Hotels."[27] By comparison, Jackson was less hailed. Folks knew who he was, but his days of photographing Yellowstone had receded into the past, and other photographers had picked up the mantle in his place. One was F. Jay Haynes, then the official photographer of Yellowstone National Park.

Ten years younger than Jackson, Haynes was a professional photographer and publisher who played a key role in documenting the settlement of the northwestern United States. Like Jackson, he had learned the photographic trade as a young apprentice, and he had opened his own photographic studio in Moorhead, Minnesota, at the age of twenty-three. In Moorhead he began a long-term business relationship with the NPRR—similar in its own way to Jackson's ties to the D & RG—to create photographic scenes advertising the NPRR's lines to attract settlers and tourists. He bolstered his own business by selling stereoscopes of his photographs to the public, just as Jackson did. In 1885 Haynes purchased an NPRR Pullman car and turned it into a photographic studio on wheels. In exchange for providing photos to the railroad, he was allowed to use the NPRR to deliver his car from place to place for a nominal fee. Haynes operated his mobile studio for twenty years.

In 1877 Haynes met Philetus Norris, then the superintendent of Yellowstone National Park. Norris invited Haynes to visit the park to take photographs, but the photographer, due to his busy NPRR schedule, did not do so until 1881. That same year, in a savvy business move, Haynes applied to the secretary of the interior for appointment as the official photographer of Yellowstone National Park. Although the appointment was not made official until 1884, Norris, with the secretary's approval, leased a small photographic studio to Haynes within park boundaries. During Haynes's 1881 visit to the park, he took two hundred photographs in two months. Afterward, Haynes returned to Yellowstone annually to take and sell photographs, until his death in 1921.

During their 1892 visit to Yellowstone, Jackson likely met Haynes. Moran certainly did, writing in a letter to Mary: "While at Norris [Geyser Basin] I read a dispatch from Haynes asking the price of watercolors and saying he had a customer. I told him they were the same price as oils, but nothing for less than $100.00. Have not heard from him since but I shall see him at the Mammoth Hot Springs on my return."[28]

As for Jackson, he found little new to photograph at Yellowstone. He wound up taking the same pictures from largely the same angles he had done on earlier visits of such spots as Tower Falls, Yellowstone Falls and the Grand Canyon of the Yellowstone, and various geysers, including Old Faithful. Some of his earlier angles had become the standard photographic spots utilized by tourists who visited the park, pointed their Kodaks, and clicked the shutters. As for Haynes, he had replaced Jackson. Yes, he knew of the famed photographer, admired his work, and sometimes emulated it. But he represented the latest photographer to capture the scenery Yellowstone had to offer.

Despite all that, Jackson's pictures included their own elements of new-ness. His work that summer brought his photographic legacy up to date. Yellowstone is an extremely organic place, where nature twists and turns and erupts and redefines itself constantly. Geothermal changes had reinvented mud pots and hot spring basins, sometimes dramatically. Some earlier hot springs had since dried up. New mud pots had been formed. Moran noted that "the Great Blue Geyser that I drew . . . [in 1876] is about 10 times as large as when I saw it last and has become the greatest Geyser in the Basin."[29]

One additional difficulty Jackson faced was taking photographs that did not include some civilizing, human element. His trips in the 1870s had been to a place almost untouched by human hands. Now, with national park status going back twenty years, the sites were no longer wild and natural. Tour-ists may have taken note of the famous photographer—if they knew who he was—but it did not keep them from pressing forward to take their own pictures. In addition, park rangers had installed wooden sidewalks and other modern conveniences within the frame of some of Jackson's favorite picture angles. Still, Jackson pressed on, taking panoramic compilations—something he had not done during earlier visits—that could not be replicated by an amateur with a Kodak. He reshot the Mammoth Hot Springs (this time with a hotel in the background) and the Yellowstone River and its falls. During his two-week stay in the park he shot a great number of photographs, many large formats and several smaller shots, with some likely taken by his assistant, Walter F. Crosby. Many of these photographs were utilized in the Wyoming exhibit at the Columbian Exposition.

The 1892 trip with Moran was Jackson's last great foray into the Ameri-can West for purposes of documentation, capping a generation of trips that had helped form his ultimate legacy as a photographer, and had opened up the West for further settlement, exploitation, and despoilment that may well have sped up the close of the frontier. Jackson and Moran had come out West in the 1870s and found a wilderness waiting to be discovered. Now, much of the West was no longer a mystery. The wild had been tamed. Even their misbegotten jaunt to Devil's Tower took them along roads and trails dotted with farms, ranches, or abandoned versions of the same. To an extent, it was impossible for the wilderness of the West to be completely removed. Even today, much of the West Jackson explored and photographed is underdevel-oped, somewhat raw, even dangerous for the incautious. But it had become, in the words of historian Peter Hales, "a constructed wilderness," one rede-signed for human appreciation. Whereas Jackson and Hayden and Moran and Stephenson and their colleagues had come to Yellowstone in the early 1870s to find scattered camps of invalids and curious would-be exploiters, the park, by becoming a park, had become a place of hotels and organized encampments and dining halls and wagons packed like sardines, wheel to wheel, delivering new batches of tourists daily in season.[30]

Jackson and Moran parted ways on July 30, with Jackson leaving his old friend to finish his photographic work. Moran did spend a couple more days elsewhere in the park, completing sketches at the Grand Canyon of the Yellowstone, but his time that summer with Jackson was over. The Denver photographer soon returned home with new plans for his business. Farther out in the West he had discussed a business proposition with Walter Crosby, which had actually begun the previous year. The two photographers agreed to go into business together, which meant a change of venue for the studio to larger spaces located in the Industrial Building at 433 Colfax in Denver. Jackson made the change and the move because he believed his reputational star would continue to rise, bringing him greater fame and greater prosperity. What Jackson did not foresee was a general downturn in the American economy the following year.

The Panic of 1893 hit the city of Denver hard in general as it did Jackson's business specifically. Jackson pedaled a nonessential commodity. Would-be customers could always postpone photographic orders for another day. He had proven himself a savvy businessman in previous years, marketing and selling his photographs through any number of popular mediums, including mammoth plates to frame and display in one's drawing room; tourist photographs; fold-out visitor booklets; and the perennial favorite, the stereoscopic photographs. But those markets tightened dramatically. In addition, while Jackson had relied on contracts and deals with western railroads to take publicity photographs along their various routes, such contracts dried up as railroads now ran on shaky ground.

But there was another factor that challenged Jackson's business at this time, separate from the nation's economic downturn. Some of Jackson's bread and butter had been the reproduction of photographs directly from his wet plate negatives at actual size. If a newspaper or magazine or journal or tourist book producer wanted to mass produce a photograph, it required the production of a woodcut or wood engraving fashioned from hand-carved blocks, which might resemble a photograph but looked more like a hand-drawn sketch. (Moran had produced any number of woodblock engravings for various publications for years.) This process was always limited. Commercial printers using common mechanically based printing processes could not produce works representing a full range of tones. Such works printed black ink (sometimes colored ink), and that was it.

Enter the half-tone process. In the late nineteenth century, newspaper printers began experimenting with photographic screens to reproduce photographs directly in their newspapers without the step of first creating a woodcut.

The technique took a while to perfect, but they eventually got it down. In a sense, it was a pretty simple process. With black-and-white photographs, the only ink required for duplication is black. Such photographs are based on only two colors: black and white. But in between these two color extremes, photographs include a variety of gray tones, which the half-tone process could begin to replicate by producing these variations in shade through the application of half-tone dots, small specks of ink that, when changed in size, altered the saturation of black ink, resulting in a range of grays. Such dots were named half-tone dots. (Modern-day printers utilize the same basic concept of dots when printing photographs in color by relying on four colors: cyan, yellow, magenta, and key [black].) The application of this technology allowed for the mass production of photographs, which redefined the photographic industry. It became the gold standard for book, newspaper, and other periodical materials during the 1890s. Now publishers could produce a photograph in mass quantities, taking business away from photographers.

Also, Jackson's old reliable, wet plate, collodion photography was passing from the scene, replaced by dry film—which Jackson had experimented with during his fateful 1877 trip across the Southwest, to his great disappointment—and the introduction of simple, hand-held Kodak cameras, which helped to democratize photography and challenge the need for professional photographers. Photographers all across the country were facing the same sea change to their profession. Charles Roscoe Savage, the Mormon photographer whom Jackson had met in 1869 during his first pre-Hayden photographic foray into the West, saw the change come and wrote in his diary in 1894: "Not doing much viewing lately. . . . Nearly everybody is becoming a photographer. . . . Business is changing to developing and finishing views for amateurs. Most of the magazines now published are illustrated by photoengravings—the demand for views is gradually falling off."[31] Jackson's professional career would soon experience a dramatic redirection.

These changes came as no surprise to Jackson, who had always worked to stay ahead of the technological curve, adopting new techniques, new materials, and new cameras in an effort to remain relevant. Now he was up against a difficult tide. He was being replaced by mass production of photographs on a corporate scale, as well as by the Kodak snaps of the amateur photographer. All these changes—economic, professional, technological, and personal— placed Jackson at odds with himself early in 1893. He was uncertain what to expect next in his professional life. Photography was no longer the same field of practice he had entered nearly twenty years earlier. What the future held for him was unclear.

16

Beyond the West, 1893–1896

$\mathcal{I}$n 1893 William Henry Jackson turned fifty. For most of his life he had explored the West for the federal government, various railroads, and his own profit; in doing all this, he had made himself one of the most famous of American photographers. No other cameraman had accumulated a greater reputation or a greater collection of negatives and photographic prints. That same year, several business changes and offers came Jackson's way, starting with a former newspaperman and representative of yet another American railroad, the Baltimore & Ohio (B & O), who approached Jackson with a business proposition. Joseph Gladding Pangborn was the eastern railroad's front man, responsible for publicity and advertising. He asked the famous photographer to produce a number of pictures of scenery along the B & O's rail line, large prints of 18 by 22 inches at the rate of $10 per picture. Jackson was already known for photographing such large prints; in fact, it was his calling card. The purpose for the prints was the World's Columbian Exposition, scheduled to open in Chicago. But Jackson was intrigued by a second proposal:

> Pangborn said: "Jack, I've decided to take you around the world with me." Then he lighted a large cigar and watched me from behind his smoke screen. . . . "I think it sounds very interesting indeed," I responded, rather insincerely, I suspect. Pangborn had so many gaudy notions that I found myself answering most of them with packaged phrases.
>
> "Well, you'll be sure of it in just about five minutes," he retorted. Then Major Pangborn sketched a world tour of fabulous proportions. He had conceived the idea of a transportation commission (with himself as head, of course) to visit foreign countries and study their railroad systems. Everything was to be conducted on a vast scale of gold braid and plumes, and it would require not less than three years of travel.[1]

When Jackson pressed Pangborn for details regarding his multiyear, worldwide photographic tour, the B & O publicist was vague, leading Jackson to believe the railroad advance man was blowing more than just cigar smoke. For the moment, Jackson did not believe Pangborn's offer was a serious one. He would eventually discover he was wrong.

Then the W. H. Jackson Photograph and Publishing Company, with the support of its silent partner, Walter F. Crosby, moved its headquarters into expanded digs on the top two floors of Denver's Industrial Building. The move proved ill timed. In the following year the US economy took a deep downturn, leading to a serious depression, which put the company on shaky ground. Fortunately Jackson had already agreed to take large format photographs for the B & O. He signed on to produce one hundred large format negatives for $10 each. In addition, he agreed to supply a second set of negatives to Harry Tammen, who ran a curio shop in Denver. Tammen was also the publisher of *The Great Divide*, a popular journal touting the West as a surefire destination for American tourists. The deal with Tammen meant an additional $1,000 for Jackson and Company.

Jackson produced the contracted number of photographs for the B & O, which were utilized in the railroad's exhibit at the Columbian Exposition. The display included a thirty-foot panorama, something Jackson had been experimenting with for years. The fair featured many additional sights and wonders: the US Naval Exhibit, a huge Krupp gun, and giant steam turbines. Peoples from around the world were also on display in mock villages. There were a giant Ferris wheel, electric lights, a moveable sidewalk, and new foods, including Cream of Wheat and glasses of diet carbonated soda. The fair hosted a meeting of the Boone and Crockett Club that included a presentation by a young historian named Frederick Jackson Turner, whose paper, "The Significance of the Frontier in American History," cast the frontier experience as crucial to the development of the early United States and the unique American spirit that went along with it. Turner's paper reflected on how the frontier was now closed, a reality William Henry Jackson had helped to facilitate.

At least two sites at the Exposition included Jackson photographs: the vast Transportation Exhibit, sponsored by the B & O, and the Wyoming state exhibit. His old acquaintance from Utah, fellow photographer Charles Roscoe Savage, whose photos were on display at the fair, wrote in his diary regarding his fellow photographer's pictures that they were "larger and better printed than mine, showing his superior facilities."[2] While Jackson made his contributions to a pair of exhibits at the fair, the Exposition itself, with its grand, white, plaster neoclassical buildings, needed its own photographer. A New York architectural photographer had been hired, Charles Dudley Arnold, along with a partner, Harlow N. Higinbotham Jr., who gained his role through

Jackson took photographs of the World's Columbian Exposition in Chicago during the fall of 1893, including this shot of MacMonnies' Fountain located in the Grand Plaza. Photo provided courtesy of Ball State University. Andrew Seager Archive of the Built Environment. DOC-2010.001.

nepotism, as he was the son of the exposition's president. Higinbotham was little more than an amateur, while Arnold did produce mammoth plate photos that interpreted the Exposition as a grand urban event on a scale only large format pictures could begin to capture.

But Arnold and Higinbotham proved disappointing to the fair's organizers. Arnold had fallen behind schedule, having become distracted by peripheral issues over the quality of souvenir photographs and other problems. By August officials were ready to hire a replacement, and they turned to Jackson. One supporter, J. F. Ryder, a well-known photographer in Cleveland, wrote to a popular magazine and made the case for Jackson: "In justice to the wonderful enterprise which gave to the world this magnificent showing, the best possible photographic record should be made and preserved." Regarding the most capable of photographers, "such a man as W. H. Jackson, of Denver . . . should be permitted to face the White City with his largest camera, and give us some photography such as he alone can do. . . . What a regret and what a shame it would be to close the Exposition without having its memory marked by the best possible efforts of photography from the best skilled hands."[3] By mid-fall, Daniel Burnham, the chief architect of the Columbian Exposition, had commissioned Jackson to produce one hundred 11-by-14-inch negatives of the fair's buildings and grounds at the rate of $10 per negative. Like the B & O commission, the exposition contract helped Jackson's bottom line for 1893. He was able to complete the commission within ten days and later doubled his money by selling a second set of negatives to Tammen in Denver for an additional $1,000.

Jackson approached his Exposition photographs with the same sense of space he had typically applied to his western pictures, as he attempted to capture the scale of his subject. Many of the buildings at the fair were oversized and massive, difficult to fit into even his 11-by-14-inch format. He chose not to photograph buildings from a straightforward vantage point, as if the pavilion's front door was intended as the photograph's center of focus. Instead, he took shots of the fair's large buildings at forty-five-degree angles, ignoring (and abandoning) the straight-line symmetry of the neoclassical for more spontaneous views. Just as he sometimes framed a shot of a given mountain by including a lake or other topographical feature in the foreground, so he did with his Exposition pictures.

Thus his photo of the fair's grand, multi-arched Transportation Building features a large lagoon with the building consuming the background. He did the same with his picture of the Exposition's South Colonnade, a three-sided promenade of white columns, arched openings, domes, steeples, and a distant obelisk. (Perhaps in an effort to connect the artificial, sterile world of the Exposition to nature, Jackson's photograph of the South Colonnade includes a foreground promenade marred by scattered pieces of manure, dropped by horses that carried fairgoers around the grounds in fancy carriages.) Again, the lagoon is included at front and center. His photograph of the fair's grand Administration Building is captured at the same forty-five-degree angle as the building gleams in the brilliant light of a warm sun. In many of his photographs of the fair, Jackson was careful to include people to provide scale, a human element dwarfed by the vastness of the fair's architecture. This was a technique he utilized in his western photos as well. Perhaps Jackson's best advantage in taking his photographs was the timing. He shot his pictures just days after the closing of the fair, thus eliminating the problem of large crowds complicating his photographic themes.

One day while attending the Exposition, Pangborn approached Jackson again and announced that all plans were in place for the world tour of railroads he had previously promoted to the famous photographer.

"Well, Jack," said Pangborn. "I hope you have no important engagements for the next three years. And if you have, you'd better find a pinch-hitter, because I want you to be ready to join my World's Transportation Commission. We shall visit every continent and every nation on the globe!"[4]

Pangborn claimed that he had already raised $100,000 to finance the project, including donations from George Mortimer Pullman, George Westinghouse, Andrew Carnegie, and young Cornelius Vanderbilt. The B & O publicist enticed Jackson by assuring him $5,000 for each year he participated in the project, to provide an income for his family in his absence. "You are indispensable," Pangborn assured Jackson. "Think no more about it."[5] As for the Jackson company, its business was no longer based on clients walking in and asking for their portraits to be made. Rather, the money was coming through nationwide sales of Jackson's large collection of negatives and prints. It seemed to Jackson that everything was falling into place to accommodate his leaving Denver for points around the globe. He agreed to join Pangborn and his international plans.

Jackson returned to Denver that fall to arrange for his long-term departure. He would leave his photographic business in the hands of W. H. Rhoads, a Philadelphia photographer who would work closely with Crosby to keep the studio busy and solvent.

But repeated delays kept pushing back the starting date for the world tour as 1893 turned into 1894. In the fall, Pangborn informed Jackson that the photographer's salary had been eliminated by budget cuts—Pangborn had already cut several personnel to save costs—and that he would only be able to reimburse Will for his expenses. All this put Jackson in a difficult position. He had reformed his business to operate in his absence, but the money he had been promised had evaporated. In his later autobiography, he lamented, "I was greatly disturbed. It would be impossible for me to go without a salary. Business in Denver was still far from good, and I could never expect to draw an income from my studio sufficient for my family's needs during my absence. But by this time, with my departure so long advertised, I couldn't afford not to go."[6]

Jackson had to create an alternative means of income for himself. He contacted the editors of *Harper's Weekly*, then one of the nation's most popular journals, and soon an arrangement was made between the journal's editors, Jackson, Pangborn, and the World's Transportation Commission's graphic artist, Edward Winchell. Jackson was to provide photographs and background; Pangborn, a series of articles; and Winchell, pen-and-ink drawings. For all their efforts, the WTC men were to receive $100 per page. Jackson would receive $250 monthly, which was sent directly to Emilie in Denver for the family's support, plus a $1,000 advance to her. Other monies were paid to the WTC. The arrangement proved a boon to the Jacksons. But Jackson knew *Harper's* had signed on as much because of WTC's reputation as his, as he wrote to Emilie in 1895: "I don't imagine for one moment that the *Harper's* would advance me 500 per month on my own account apart from the éclat which surrounds the Commission . . . or even that they would take pictures from me to this extent. . . . I am standing alone and dependent, with hands and feet tied, powerless to do more than drift along with the party."[7] Even before he left for foreign points unknown, Jackson was regretting his involvement in the planned trip. But he remained committed to the project. On October 3, 1894, Jackson was on his way to Europe onboard the ocean liner *Bremen*.

As everything played out, he was gone for seventeen months. Jackson, who had already spanned the nation from coast to coast in his travels, was now taking a trip around the world. He did not pack hundreds of pounds of equipment intended for wet plate production; instead, he took rolls of dry film, which had been improved upon since his fateful film failure in 1877. He was traveling light by comparison with his Hayden expedition days. The worldwide excursion began relatively well, with commission members following a regular routine and planned itinerary. The US government and others were cooperative. The secretary of state, Walter Q. Gresham, sent advance instructions to American consulates and embassies to host the party along their route, so the commission members could enjoy the usual American comforts. They typically traveled by ship and rail—after all, an examination of the world's railroads was ostensibly the point of the trip—and otherwise by more exotic means, including Indian elephants and Siberian sleighs. After weeks in London, the party traveled to the continent and passed through Paris in a matter of hours, then south to Marseilles and across the Mediterranean to Tunis. Jackson eagerly took photos of Carthage, where "in my mind I reconstructed the departure of Hannibal's soldiers and elephants to begin their incredible journey across the water to Spain."[8]

They crossed northern Africa to Algiers by rail, then took a steamship westward to Morocco, circling the Mediterranean with stops at Gibraltar, Malaga, Naples, and Port Said, the Egyptian gateway to the Suez Canal. After spending time in Cairo, Jackson visited the Pyramids of Giza, man-made mountains for Jackson's camera to capture both from a scenic distance and from high above—he had approached the mountains of the West in the same ways—as he scaled the Great Pyramid. From its lofty heights he created an intimate scene featuring not the pyramid, but a trio of Egyptians, two men and a woman, in native dress scanning the ancient horizon below. Jackson managed to reduce the grand scale of the Great Pyramid into a family portrait of sorts, reminding those who viewed his work through their stereoscopes of the human element that had created the pyramids. These were mountains unlike any he had ever captured in Wyoming or Colorado.

Jackson scaled yet another "mountain," this time Egypt's Great Pyramid, in 1894 to capture this intimate shot near the ancient pyramid's summit. The photographer was traveling with the World's Transportation Commission. Library of Congress. LC-D4271-115.

The travel itinerary kept Jackson constantly busy, and the number of places the commission visited seemed endless. After a few weeks of travel, Jackson wrote a letter to Emilie noting this: "I have seen so much and been around so many places. . . . All impressions are somewhat confused from the great multiplicity of them that have been crowded upon me, and I have not had the leisure or the quiet necessary to collect my thoughts in proper shape."[9]

At several destinations along their way, the British government hosted the American visitors. The party passed through the Suez Canal—they celebrated Christmas at sea—and reached the island of Ceylon (modern-day Sri Lanka, then a royal colony). Jackson thoroughly enjoyed the commission's ten-day stay in the colony. "I found myself on the go eighteen hours a day. And I loved every hour."[10] Throughout these weeks, Pangborn wrote his articles and Jackson took his photographs.

The commission reached Tuticorin, India (the modern-day port of Thoothukudi) on January 9, 1895. Ten days later they entered Bombay by train at Victoria Station, "then rated as the world's finest rail terminal,"[11] and were delivered by carriage to the palace of the British governor, Lord

George Harris, who hosted them with a state dinner. The Americans experienced scenes from a Rudyard Kipling novel, seeing "brilliantly uniformed Sepoy lancers lined up on either side, and within, half a dozen turbaned footmen silently relieved us of our hats."[12] The dinner was splendid, and Jackson was thrilled to be seated next to Lord Roberts, a heroic veteran of the Raj.

From Bombay the party took a steamship to Karachi, which was still part of India. (Pakistan would not separate as a nation until the late 1940s.) Retracing the footsteps of Alexander the Great's army, the commission members took a train along the Indus River, still with the assistance of the British. "I was getting to feel like a character in an English novel," wrote Jackson later, "what with dressing for dinner every night and conversing exclusively (so it seemed) with Lord This and Lady That."[13]

Despite all the wining and dining offered by the British, Jackson was assessing the empire through his own lens. He understood he was seeing colonialism up close and personal, with all its flaws and tensions. He was capable of taking a photograph extolling the civilizing virtues of a grand British rail station on foreign soil or a great, crowded European marketplace set in an Algerian port, but he was also aware of the cost of colonialism, a form of occupation with an uncertain shelf life. As he passed out of northwest India, he saw things with clarity, as the scenes around him "brought close to me the realization that Anglo-India was still a thin cover on top of a volcano."[14]

In Kashmir, Jackson received an elephant to carry him from place to place. He saw the royal and the rare and was reminded later as he wrote his second autobiography that he had passed through a real-world Hollywood, a technicolor dreamscape of rich cultures: "Troops on foot, all splashed with gold and green and white and crimson—bearded lancers on black horses—red jacketed and white turbaned artillerymen firing salvo after salvo—charging elephants—the spires of the temples beyond—and, in the far northeast, against a cloudless sky, the snow-tipped Himalayas. I have never seen a sight to match it."[15]

Not all was well at this point in the trip, however. Pangborn had already disappointed Jackson before they left for Europe, especially by the cut in his promised salary. The commission president had proven to be a man of more talk than action. As early as their time in India, Pangborn began cutting the commission's budget, including daily expense allotments from three dollars down to seventy-five cents.

The commission members—the party included twenty or so Americans—reached Afghanistan and soon entered the famed Khyber Pass, which led them beyond the Hindu Kush Mountains. In many places, Jackson saw old worlds he could only have imagined or read about in novels and travelogues.

Despite the railroads and modern technologies transplanted into colonial environs, many of the people he saw were likely reminiscent of the Native Americans he had photographed for more than twenty years. They filled his pictures, dressed in native costumes, washing themselves in sacred rivers, plying their primitive wagons along roads ground out by the Europeans, poling their small boats along the Ganges, and pulling rickshaws along winding Chinese streets.

The party soon reached Singapore, where once again the British served as hosts. But when Jackson took photographs of one of the local military posts, Fort Palmer, overlooking Singapore harbor, security forces arrested the American interloper. That night he "celebrated" his fifty-second birthday under arrest in the fort until the arrival of the American consul, who took the photographer into his custody. The commission then sailed off to Australia and New Zealand. In the latter, Jackson saw the Whakarewarewa Geysers, which reminded him of his previous visits to Yellowstone: "At times I could hardly imagine that instead of the Yellowstone I was at almost exactly its antipodes . . . [though] none of it can begin to compare with the Yellowstone."[16]

Overall, Jackson was disappointed in the natives he encountered in New Zealand, referring to the Maori as "shiftless, good-for-nothing but very amiable and good-natured people."[17] Despite Jackson's private expressions of disappointment regarding the Maori, he seems to have been differently affected by a young Maori girl he identifies as Bella. She was a guide at one point for the commission, and Jackson photographed her in a pensive pose in the midst of a steaming geyser basin. The photographer clearly intended to reflect the young girl's beauty and not the exotic wonder itself. Will wrote to Emilie, in a disappointed tone, that the Maori made a practice of "always delegating the youngest and best looking women of the village" as guides. But his attitude toward Bella seems reflective of his relative infatuation with the Hopi maiden Num-Pa-Yu (Nampeyo).[18]

After New Zealand, the commission sailed to Indonesia, known at that time as the Dutch East Indies. Then the party reached China, whose people had suffered a series of international mishaps, including the near-collapse of the Manchu dynasty at the hands of the British, as well as a significant conflict with Japan. By late September 1895 the commission reached Korea from China onboard a Japanese ship, the *Ghazee*, which operated under an English captain. Given Korea's dramatic tides, the ship docked three miles from the Chemulpo harbor and Japanese sampans delivered the handful of remaining commission members ashore. Many of the men who had started the commission trip had left, some with other business to attend to and others having been disappointed, leaving fewer than half a dozen, including Jackson. Here the photographer repeated a practice he had honed in the Southwest both during and after the Hayden Surveys. He headed off with his camera and limited equipment with only two native guides and a pair of small ponies. It was perhaps an incautious decision on Jackson's part, which he later admitted in his 1940 autobiography. Geopolitical relations between the Chinese, the Japanese, and the Koreans were tense at that time. A westerner traveling across Korea could easily find himself in the midst of violence at any moment. But Jackson saw a unique beauty and opportunity in Korea for his photographic skills. He checked in at the local American legation, but the American minister was away, leaving the charge, Dr. Horace Newton Allen, to welcome Jackson. Allen arranged for Jackson to meet the Korean king, an impromptu afternoon reception that included the two Americans showing up virtually unannounced. As Jackson later described the scene, "We simply rode over to the palace in sedan chairs, waited for fifteen minutes, and were ushered in—and, while we waited, two sedate gentlemen wearing long black robes and fly-trap hats had opened a bottle of champagne for us." The king proved cordial and even informal.[19] Although Jackson only spent a few days in Korea, he took several fantastic pictures, finding "so many wonderful subjects to photograph all along the way that if my guide had not continually urged me along I could never have kept to schedule."[20]

While traveling in New Zealand in 1895, Jackson shot this photograph of a local Maori guide, Bella, in a pensive pose on the edge of a geyser basin. Library of Congress. LC-D426-726.

By this time the greater work of the WTC had been completed. Jackson rendezvoused with Pangborn and the other remaining members of the party in Seoul. In early October the men were in the Russian town of Vladivostok, ready to cross the frozen reaches of Siberia as they headed into the final leg of their adventure. During the following five months, the commission reached its low point. The support money ran out, nearly leaving the party stranded in a remote corner of Russia. Pangborn was forced to borrow money from a local Russian governor. The Russian winter also held them up as the men waited two months for unbridged Siberian rivers to thaw and allow passage. For three thousand miles, the Americans traveled primarily by sleigh, which required nearly six weeks of travel. Jackson, dressed in an elk skin greatcoat that covered him from head to toe, made the most of his time crossing Russia. From his seat in a sleigh, he "rode with the wind in my face and loved it."[21] As the party passed through forty peasant villages, Jackson photographed the Siberian natives just as he had Omaha Indians nearly thirty years earlier. Near the end of January 1896 the commission arrived in the Russian capital of St. Petersburg, where Jackson began thinking of souvenirs for his family, purchasing brooches for his wife and his two daughters. In his absence of seventeen months total, he reflected "that my little girls would be quite grown up when I saw them again; Louise was now seventeen and Hallie nearly fourteen."[22]

Jackson was anxious now. He was soon on his way to Germany. At the border between Russia and Germany, the men boarded the German State Railway and were soon in Berlin. On February 16 they paid their passage on the North German Lloyd liner *Spree*, which reached New York City on March 3. After checking in at the *Harper's* offices in the city, Jackson bought a ticket for a train and was soon back in Denver in the midst of the family circle he had come to miss so much.

17

Legacy Making, 1896–1942

$\mathcal{J}$ackson returned to Denver after an absence of nearly a year and a half to find his photographic business in disarray. The man he had left in charge, W. H. Rhoads, had proven a poor businessman as well as a second-rate photographer, one whose works were so inferior to Jackson's that they cost the business Jackson's old standby customers without recruiting new ones in their places. To an extent, Jackson himself was partially to blame. He had hoped against hope that his participation in the WTC junket would not negatively impact his studio, but it did. In addition, Jackson returned to a perfect storm of additional circumstances, some of which were affecting photographic studios across the country.

Eastman's Kodak cameras and the ease with which the amateur photographer could have negatives reproduced were killing the photographic studio industry as Jackson had always known it. Additionally, large—and small—publishing houses were increasingly making a practice of appropriating photos, without regard for legal copyright, without paying royalties or even providing credit to the original photographer-producer. This was already happening to Jackson on a grand scale. He was, after all, a popular photographer with many pictures in circulation in a variety of forms, making his pictures easy targets for misappropriation. Jackson was furious when he soon discovered that Rand MacNally was publishing guide and tour books that featured his photographs, without payment and even without byline credit. There was little Jackson could do but double down on filing copyrights for future photographs. Previous shots simply remained in the wind.

Jackson was at another crossroads. He knew he could not continue operating his studio and reproducing business in the old way. He needed to rebrand himself. When approached by a promoter to develop a lecture tour—titled "One Hundred Minutes in Strange Lands"—to include himself and 125 of his transportation photographs, he agreed. Although the lecture circuit proved a popular venue for Will, he did not make much money, given the cost of transportation, lodging, and other expenses. The tour did, though, make him even more popular.

Fortunately Jackson was presented with a new business opportunity that seemed to represent the answer to his dilemma. When Jackson returned to New York from his WTC tour, he crossed the path of an old friend:

> During my few hours in New York I had run into an old acquaintance of mine, E. H. Husher, a well-known photographer of California scenes, who had recently returned from Switzerland, where he had been sent . . . to study a new photo-lithographic process for reproducing pictures in color. He told me that American rights to the process had been bought by his associates and that the Photochrom Company had been organized to exploit it. . . . Husher . . . recommended to his superior, William A. Livingstone, that the new company absorb the W. H. Jackson Company in order to acquire a stock of negatives. Furthermore, Husher had urged Mr. Livingstone to offer me a suitable position with the new company.[1]

A viable solution had arrived on Jackson's doorstep. He soon negotiated an arrangement with the Detroit company, bringing two advantages to the table. First, over the years he had produced a vast collection of some of the best photographs ever taken of the American West (and beyond). Second, he brought to the company his years of experience as a photographer and photographic technician. Livingstone agreed to take over the W. H. Jackson Company for $30,000, with $5,000 paid directly in cash to Jackson to cover the debts that had piled up due to his seventeen-month absence abroad. Finally, Jackson was elevated to the role of company director, "at a comfortable salary."[2]

In the following year Jackson left his revitalized business in the hands of his son, Clarence, as he, Emilie, and the other children moved to Detroit. In the move, Jackson carried a portfolio of at least twenty thousand negatives, many on glass plates, pictures he had shot over the years from Wyoming to Colorado to New Mexico, as well as across the broad sweep of the United States. While the financial arrangement proved more than adequate for Will, he had never enjoyed being limited to studio and office work. He soon convinced his Detroit colleagues to let him return to the life of the itinerant picture taker. In 1898, with the Spanish–American War raging through a long Cuban summer, Jackson took pictures at another world's fair, the Trans-Mississippi Exposition, in Omaha, followed by a trip to the Dakotas.

Between photographic trips, Jackson became familiar with the closely guarded Swiss colorization process as he rode herd over the transfer of many of his black-and-white negatives into color conversions. The resulting prints included a wide variety of sizes, from 3-by-5-inch postcards to 17-by-21-inch mammoth plates to the oversized 17-by-40-inch format.

That fall (1898), Jackson left the road and remained busy at the Detroit Photographic Company's publishing house, Detroit Publishing Company, which employed dozens of workers. The plant oversaw production and distribution of color prints in all sizes, including wall pictures, to the tune of approximately seven million prints annually. But Jackson did not want to remain tied down to mass print work for long. The following year, he rode various rail lines and took pictures in California, then went back East to New England.

Throughout the year 1899 he traveled more miles than ever—twenty thousand—usually by train, not pack mule and rickety western wagon as in his earlier years. Jackson retained a lifelong desire to travel, to at least remain constantly in motion, even at the age of fifty-six (his age in 1899) and for the remaining decades of his life. The driving engine of the Detroit Photographic Company lay in the production of popular picture postcards. The company proved a pioneer in this field and "surpassed all others in terms of technical proficiency and scope of issues."[3] Jackson's inventory of western photographs—thousands of them—provided the Detroit Company with even more subjects for its popular cards.

With the coming of the new century, Jackson, now in his late fifties, continued to travel for the company, taking photographs in Canada, along the St. Lawrence River, and in the Thousand Islands. He traveled to the southern United States, where he documented such scenes as cotton plantations and coastal beaches. For so many years he had spent his time in the West, taking first-time photographs of so many places; now he was busy in other regions, giving them their due. He returned to California and took many photographs of life in the Golden State. In Yosemite National Park he took wonderful, breathtaking landscapes, several reminiscent of his earlier work in Yellowstone, including a shot of Yosemite Valley with the Sierras in the distance. Bridalveil Falls, Half Dome, Mount Watkins, the Mariposa Grove of Giant Sequoias—Jackson captured them all. He shot the photo from Glacier Point, perched on a tongue of granite extending from the cliff wall at a height of more than thirty-two hundred feet above the valley floor. A photograph taken by an assistant shows Jackson standing on this precarious rock balcony, his head beneath the black covering of one of his large format cameras, revealing one more of the ultimate lengths to which Jackson would go to capture his photographs.[4]

This 1902 photograph shows a middle-class Jackson traveling in comfort aboard the Detroit Photographic Company's Special. Library of Congress. LC-DIG-det-4a20188.

In 1901 he returned to photograph the Colorado Rockies, a recurring touchstone for Jackson. While in Denver, he was contacted by C. A. Kendrick, who had driven cattle in his earlier days and was then the head of the Kendrick-Bellamy Stationery Company, which owned a large cattle operation in the Texas Panhandle, the Adair Ranch. Kendrick hired Jackson to take pictures at the ranch's annual roundup and branding, and his shots became iconic photos of yet another aspect of life in the American West.

By the early twentieth century, the Detroit Photographic Company served as the parent company of the Photochrom Company, which was producing millions of prints. Jackson worked at the plant under the plant's manager. Business and profits were rolling in, prompting, in 1902, both the Detroit Publishing Company and Photochrom to arrange for a traveling exhibition of photographs all housed in a special rail car, which was to tour the Southwest under the sponsorship of the Santa Fe Railroad. It was all for the sake of publicity, and the "California Special" proved popular with visitors and tourists. Jackson went along as a sort of spokesman, "giving informal talks and answering questions."[5]

In 1903 Jackson's world changed forever. That year, the plant manager at the Photochrom Company left the company and moved to California, which meant Jackson had no choice but to take his place. It was at this point that Jackson's days as a traveling photographer came to an end. The timing seemed right. He was sixty years old that spring, and his long-suffering wife, Emilie, was ready for her husband to hang up his traveling shoes. Jackson seemed resigned and ready: "After so many years of work in the open, I turned gladly, even enthusiastically, to a routine career. For one thing, it was a much easier life, going to an office every day. . . . For another, there was the almost novel pleasure of living with my own family, of sitting at the table with my wife and daughters, of taking them to the theater, and of going with them on little trips to near-by resorts."[6]

Several years earlier, Jackson had seen his first automobile—he was living in Detroit, after all—and he immediately took to this new mode of transportation, although he never gave up on trains. Jackson had gone west ahead of the railroads, which soon caught up with him, and the photographer and trains maintained a love affair for the remainder of his life. Railroads had sponsored him on photographic excursions into the West as early as the completion of the transcontinental railroad in 1869 and his employment with the UP. Other railroads—the D & RG, the B & O, and more recently, the Santa Fe line—had paid his bills while he took photographs touting their routes and encouraging tourists to come out and see the West for themselves.

In 1908, at the age of sixty-five, Jackson took up golf as a pastime, joining the Detroit Golf Club, where he played on a regular schedule. Life was moving forward at a relentless pace. Jackson's father, George, had passed away in 1904 when Will was sixty-one. Will and Emilie's children all got married, and their first grandchild arrived in 1902, the son of Clarence, named William Henry Jackson II, making Will's mother, Harriet, a great-grandmother before she passed ten years later in 1912. "With my mother's death," Jackson wrote years later, "I found myself the oldest member of the Jackson family."[7]

When the last of the Jackson children married, Will and Emilie were finally back to the place where they had started out in life together—just the two of them. They had few obligations tying them down. He continued to travel from time to time, with Emilie at his side. "Those trips," he wrote, "after thirty-five years of married life, were the first really complete holidays we had ever had together."[8] These opportunities became even more precious to Jackson during the final years of their marriage. When Emilie passed away in 1918—just weeks before the end of World War I—he was devastated. He had her buried in the Friends Cemetery in Baltimore next to her mother and father. She and Will had shared nearly forty-five years, although many years were spent apart, due to Jackson's professional wanderlust. "We had lived together in love and harmony," Jackson later wrote.[9]

Jackson's relationships with his two wives, Mollie and Emilie, are rather enigmatic in their details. Jackson, although he wrote hundreds of pages of diaries and published two autobiographies (1929 and 1940), rarely mentioned either of his spouses, other than to indicate that each was long-suffering in her own way. It is worth remembering that Jackson carried a photograph of Caddie Eastman, the fiancée that got away, throughout the years spanning both of his marriages.

But Jackson's life was far from over. He remained active over the next twenty-five years. He continued as an integral member of the Detroit Photographic Company until the firm went into bankruptcy in 1924, due to greater competition and further changes in the field of photographic technology. "My investment of course disappeared," Jackson wrote wistfully, "and, at the age of eighty-one, I found myself without either capital or any certain means of livelihood. It wasn't exactly an encouraging situation."[10] He had some resources, including $6,000 due him in back pay from the Detroit Company, which he subsequently received. Otherwise, he had his Civil War pension of $75 per month. He invested his $6,000 in the stock market, certain he would see big dividends soon.

Once again, Jackson was at odds with his circumstances. But he had never been one to let life situations get the better of him. He packed up his belongings and moved to Washington, D.C., where his married daughter, Hallie, lived with her husband and Jackson's two granddaughters. Over the next five years, Washington was his home. He lived in his daughter's house for the first year, then moved into a room in the Hotel Annapolis, since it was closer to the Library of Congress and the National Museum. He spent many days in the nation's library and the local museums, including the Smithsonian. Officials at the Department of the Interior provided him materials for research and study. Jackson later wrote that he now had the time to "get back to my painting . . . bring my journals up to date and do some writing."[11] One of his old Hayden Survey associates, William Holmes, who by then was the director of the National Gallery, sponsored him for membership into the men's organization the Cosmos Club. This offered him an additional refuge, as the club was "one of the pleasantest places in Washington," observed Jackson. "I spent many hours each week in its comfortable quarters."

During these years, Jackson returned to his painting in earnest. He had spent so many years focusing on his photography, working on the surveys and then compiling the results in Washington for Hayden's reports, that it had been difficult for him to find adequate time to paint. Typically, his paintings, as well as his watercolors, presented themes reminiscent of his younger days spent in the American West. By the 1920s, so many of the nation's earlier pioneers—those who had traveled west in rickety wagons, trapped beaver in icy Rocky Mountain streams, panned for gold in California's American River, or driven Longhorns from southern Texas to a Kansas railhead—had already passed on. Jackson's memories of the West extended back more than sixty years to his days bullwhacking and mustang driving his way across the Great Plains as a recent veteran of the Civil War. Men such as Jackson were quickly fading from the American landscape. With his name firmly established as a pioneer photographer, Jackson's reputation as an artist spread. Technically, many of the paintings he created were from "memory," visions of his past specifically and America's frontier precedents generally. He had watched the development of the western half of the United States in real time. Soon museums were contacting him to create a painting here or a mural there to provide his "founding father" hand to documenting an era that was quickly receding into history.

As early as the summer of 1924, Jackson received a letter from Robert Spurrier Ellison, an oil executive living in Casper, Wyoming, who had read an article Jackson wrote for *Colorado Magazine* in which he referred to Mesa Verde and his days spent with the Hayden Surveys. (Ellison was surprised to discover Jackson was still alive!) The two men struck up a recurring correspondence in which Ellison was supportive of the elderly Jackson and encouraged him to write and publish more, especially stories about the West that might appeal to younger, male readers. He was soon contacted by another interested fan, Howard R. Driggs, a part-time college professor of English at New York University and writer of books for boys, including the Pioneer Life Series published by the World Book Company. Driggs was interested in writing a book about Jackson and his youthful adventures in the West.

The timing of Jackson's first autobiography proved crucial. That same year (1929), the stock market crashed, and Jackson lost his investments. The book provided some additional income. Also, during the months Jackson was working on the book with his collaborator Driggs, which necessitated his traveling by train from Washington to New York, the aging photographer usually stayed at the Hotel Latham. There he met the elderly Ezra Meeker. Born in 1830, Meeker was a true western pioneer, who, like Jackson, had driven an ox team along the Oregon Trail in 1851, followed by settling down on his own frontier homestead. In his later years he spent much of his time working at preserving the legacy of the old Oregon Trail. When Meeker died in late 1928, Driggs succeeded him as the president of the Oregon Trail Memorial Association and then, in turn, offered Jackson the role of research secretary, which came with a "comfortable little salary."[12] With this new role—so much for Jackson's quiet retirement—he moved to New York City to carry out his duties. The aged photographer was eighty-six.

"Nothing could have pleased me so well," Jackson wrote a few years later. "It was work that I was well prepared to do. It enabled me to keep on traveling extensively."[13]

Throughout the next decade, Jackson typically spent his winters in New York and his summers out West. He became a sort of elder statesman of the West. So many of those whom Americans readily identified as the founders of the American frontier had long since passed. Legends such as William Becknell, Davy Crockett, John C. Fremont, and Kit Carson had not lived long enough to see the twentieth century. And others, latter-day contemporaries of Will Jackson's, had already shuffled off, including Frederick Remington (1909), Buffalo Bill Cody (1917), Bat Masterson (1921), Charles Russell (1926), and Wyatt Earp (1929). Jackson had outlived them all.

When he initially reached New York City, Jackson took lodgings at the Explorers Club, located at that time on West 110th Street. By 1932 the Great Depression hit the club hard, forcing the loss of its headquarters, and Jackson moved to the Army and Navy Club, near the Harvard Club, on 44th Street. In time, he moved into a room in the Latham Hotel where he had met Ezra Meeker. This became his permanent residence. Much of his later, hand-written correspondence was penned on hotel stationery.

During these late years, Jackson was seemingly always on the move, speaking somewhere, writing something, or painting something else, most often with the frontier and the West as the overarching subject matter. In 1935 he took a train to Washington, D.C., to participate in a ceremony marking the seventy-fifth anniversary of the Pony Express. If Jackson had not actually been in the West that early—he missed the express by five years—at least he had traveled the route many times during his long life, whether on foot, in a wagon, by rail, or eventually, by automobile. Three hundred Boy Scouts replicated a Pony Express ride, delivering a message for President Franklin Roosevelt. Once the last youth arrived in St. Joseph, Missouri, the message was transferred to an airplane to finish the trip across the eastern portion of the United States. Jackson was honored with a seat on the plane. Upon arrival, he handed FDR the message, along with a gold medallion.

As long as he was in Washington—the date was August 23—he stopped in at the Department of the Interior to look up some old friends, and while there he received from Arno B. Cammerer, the director of the National Park Service, a plum commission from the Department of the Interior to paint four large murals for the department's new headquarters in Washington. The paintings were intended to memorialize the heady and early days of the Geological Surveys and the contributions made by Ferdinand Hayden, Clarence King, George Montague Wheeler, and John Wesley Powell. Jackson was given a year to complete the murals, which were paid for through the New

Deal program Works Progress Administration (WPA); Jackson received $150 per month.

At 30 by 60 feet, these murals dwarfed those Moran had painted of the Grand Canyon, the Mount of the Holy Cross, and even the Grand Canyon of the Yellowstone. The task before Jackson was not an easy one. After all, he was intimately familiar with only one of the four surveys. He wanted to treat all four with the same sense of accuracy and respect each was due. To gain insight on the surveys of Wheeler, Powell, and King, he had to study their published reports and their accompanying photographs. When he completed the project, he depicted the King Survey camping in Carson Valley with the Sierra Nevada framing the background; the Wheeler Survey of 1873 in the Pueblo village at Zuni, with Thunder Mountain in the distance; the Powell party working along the Colorado River deep inside a high canyon; and the Hayden Survey in Yellowstone, as Old Faithful erupts in the background. In the end, the commission was extended to eighteen months, allowing Jackson to produce a half dozen 25-by-30-inch oil paintings and more than one hundred water colors depicting a variety of western scenes, including such highlights as Mesa Verde, Yellowstone, the Rockies, and Grand Canyon. "It was one of the most gratifying tasks of my life," wrote Jackson.[14]

Despite his painting commission with the Interior Department, Jackson still made his annual pilgrimage out West, including a return to Denver, where forty thousand of his glass negatives remained in storage since the bankruptcy of his photographic business. Their future seemed precarious, but Jackson wanted the legacy they represented to be preserved if possible. Fortunately, he found a sponsor in the Ford family, including the father Henry and the son Edsel, who arranged to have the great collection removed to the Ford museum in Dearborn. The preserved negatives became the W. H. Jackson Historical Collection. Later that same summer, Will traveled to Santa Fe and then through Mesa Verde, then returned to Washington to help mark the centennial of the Whitman Mission at Walla Walla. Passing through San Francisco and later Yellowstone, he returned finally to New York.

That winter he completed his four Interior Department paintings. In July 1937, at the age of ninety-four, he took a train out to the University of Colorado, Boulder, and received a gold medal. The Latin inscription included a wrong letter (B) for Jackson's middle name. While still out West, visiting Cheyenne, the aged Jackson experienced "the only severe accident of my life."[15] While window shopping in the Wyoming town, he tripped over an open cellar door, fell, and landed on a concrete floor on his back ten feet below the street. He fractured several vertebrae and was bed-bound for a month. At his age, the fall could easily have killed him. (He never rode a horse again, due to his injury.) Over the following months, he was nearly inactive and overly cautious regarding his recovery, since he was desperate to participate in the commemoration of the seventy-fifth anniversary of the Battle of Gettysburg.

By the spring of 1938 he seemed fully recovered (though he was not) and attended the ceremony in celebration of his four murals being placed on display. As the days of the Gettysburg commemoration approached, Jackson was flown from Arlington Cemetery to Gettysburg. The reunion of the remaining soldiers, both federal and Confederate, was held over six days from June 29 to July 4, 1938. (The actual days of the battle were July 1, 2, and 3.) Surprisingly, nine thousand veterans attended, with many living out of tents during the grand encampment on the Gettysburg battlefield. Jackson enjoyed it all: "I took care not to miss any of the important festivities. The climax was the dedication, by President Roosevelt, of the Eternal Light."[16]

Jackson's time spent at Gettysburg fatigued him a bit, so he postponed his usual trip out West until August, then limited his trek to attending the annual meeting of the Oregon Trail Memorial Association, which was held that summer in Scottsbluff, Nebraska. While there he hiked around and identified a spot where he had camped out seventy years earlier as a bullwhacker and drove a stake into the ground as an informal dedication of his own.

Jackson was enjoying his twilight years immensely. He was recognized by many as the grandfather of photography in the West, and his work had withstood the long haul of scrutiny, including by those who represented a new generation of American photographers. Among them was one of the greatest of twentieth-century photographers of the West, Ansel Adams. When Adams arranged a special photographic exhibition at the Museum of Modern Art in New York, he included several of Jackson's early photographs. Jackson visited the exhibition and, while standing in front of one of the pictures, he turned to Adams and said, "That's a pretty good picture, Mr. Adams. Who took it?"

"You did," answered Adams, smiling.

Jackson looked it over and nodded his head. "Why so I did. But I can do better now and in color with this." From his pocket he removed a small camera and laughed.

"And no need for a string of mules!"[17]

In 1939, two great world's fairs opened their doors, and Jackson visited both of them. At the New York World's Fair, advertised as "The World of Tomorrow," the elderly photographer walked all over the grounds located at Flushing, Queens, until he tired, and then finished his visit in a wheelchair. In his autobiography written the following year, he states that he visited every exhibit and pavilion. He enjoyed the displays of the latest photographic equipment and cameras and was satisfied to watch an elaborate pageant titled "Railroads on Parade." The historical drama was staged in a three-thousand-seat outdoor theater, with a cast of 250 and several full-sized historical train replicas, all to commemorate the history of American railroads beginning in the 1820s. For Jackson, the highlight of the program was a reenactment of the joining of the UP and CP rails at Promontory Summit, Utah, on May 10, 1869. He had missed the original event, as "it had conflicted with my wedding day," wrote Jackson.[18]

Following the old Pony Express route by automobile, Jackson went out to California and enjoyed a second world's fair in San Francisco, where the Oregon Trail Memorial Association held its annual meeting. He then traveled down to Los Angeles and saw, for the first time, two of his great-grandchildren and his grandson, William Henry Jackson II. As he traveled, he kept that camera he had shown Adams in his pocket, loaded with color film, and took pictures. In his autobiography, he observed: "All I need say is this: if I were at the beginning of my career, I should wish to do everything in color."[19]

That fall he visited the towns of his early days, both Plattsburg and Keeseville. After leaving Keeseville, his birthplace, in 1862 as a newly minted Union soldier, he never went back until 1934. Now, five years later, he visited for the second and last time. The old family farmhouse was gone, save for a "vine-covered excavation."[20] He went to the county clerk's office and dug up old deeds dating back to his grandfather, James. Perhaps out of such nostalgia, Jackson soon signed a contract to write a second, more complete autobiography.

In the final pages of this, his second life's story, Jackson mused, not only on his long life, but on himself as he was in 1940, an old man, much older than most ever get to be, and expressed in his words his love of the life he had been given: "There has always been so much to do tomorrow that I haven't ever relaxed to any great extent. I have been too busy doing interesting things and getting ready to do even more interesting things."[21] That year, Jackson was interviewed in Washington for a sound reel recording in which the reporter asked the great photographer how many miles he might have traveled in his lifetime.

"Two million," Jackson answered, "from plodding along behind an ox team to flying in an airplane."[22]

When Jackson completed his autobiography, seventy-five years had passed since the culmination of the Civil War in which he had served. A new war was on the horizon, an expanding threat Jackson found "disheartening."[23] With the manuscript finished, he marched in his last Memorial Day parade, up New York's Riverside Drive, past the reviewing stand and the Soldiers and Sailors Monument, one of only six soldiers of the War Between the States able to endure the march.

A reflective Jackson poses, along with a bust of a young Lincoln, for a photograph. The photo dates from the early 1940s. Photo provided courtesy of Scotts Bluff National Monument. SCBL-2662: "William Henry Jackson in the Lincoln Room."

Jackson's days came to an end on June 30, 1942, at the age of ninety-nine. Four days earlier, on the way to the bathroom in his hotel room, he had slipped and broken a hip in two places. Alone, he lay on the floor for three hours before someone heard him knocking on the bathroom door. The following day, surgeons operated on him, pinning the breaks in place. But Jackson declined almost immediately. When he died, he was surrounded by friends and family.

In a letter dated a week following Jackson's passing, written to his friend Horace Albright, the first superintendent of Yellowstone National Park, Jackson comrade Joseph Robinson described Jackson's final moments:

If I did not tell you, perhaps you have learned by now that Mr. Jackson died at 2:45 AM. He slipped from life as quietly as a child falling asleep releases its toy. A few minutes before, in the presence of his son [Clarence] and daughter-in-law, his last words—"What time is it? Where have you been and what are you up to"—were spoken to me in an almost playful tone, his voice clear and strong.

And now he sleeps in Arlington! There beneath starlit skies he rests, as was his wish, among his comrades of civil war days—sleeps beneath the soil and under the flag of a Union he fought to preserve—carelss [*sic*] alike of sunshine or storm.[24]

Albright soon received a second letter regarding Jackson's death, this one from the great western photographer Ansel Adams: "I was deeply shocked to read today of the passing of Mr. Jackson—what a real shame he could not have rounded out his century. I shall always treasure the memory of quite a few hours with him on numerous occasions, and not the least of these was the hour with you when we went to visit him in the hospital.

"Something very adequate should be done to memorialize his life and work; and I only hope it will be a memorial in terms of photography and not a stupid bust or placque [*sic*]."[25]

Jackson left behind three children, seven grandchildren, and four great-grandchildren. His work lived on, of course, through the continued publication of magazines, travel books, and the like that relied on his photographs as standard depictions of the real West. Today, thousands of his photographs—those cumbersome, wet collodion glass plate negatives—still occupy archives from New York to Denver, Laramie to Washington, D.C. They tell the story of a life spent documenting a nation in constant kinetic movement, as Jackson himself seemingly remained in constant motion, ever aware of places his lens had not captured.

In Laramie, at the University of Wyoming's American Heritage Center, amid the Fritiof M. Fryxell Papers, is a postcard-sized ink sketch. It's a deceptively simple piece, small in size, one of hundreds and hundreds of such sketches William Henry Jackson created during his long life. But this one serves as a visual summation of those days Jackson thought his best, the ones he spent out West in the company of Hayden or Moran or simply as a photographer on his own hook led relentlessly by a deep-seated need to find and photograph.

Jackson's sketch *Memories* depicts an imaginary landscape of the mind, a western mash-up of the important places Jackson had visited and photographed before anyone else took the opportunity. On the left is Two-Story Cliff House (1874), tucked away between sandstone walls. Yellowstone wonders Mammoth Hot Springs, Old Faithful, and the Lower Falls of the Yellowstone

Titled Memories, *this ink sketch represents a mash-up of western locales Jackson photographed during the heyday of his career as a western explorer and photographer. Photo provided courtesy of the University of Wyoming's American Heritage Center, box 29, "William Henry Jackson Material, Photographs," Fritiof Fryxell, Collection #01638.*

(1871) occupy the center foreground. Behind them Jackson has placed the Wind River Mountains (1870), and off in the distance, Devil's Tower (1892). On the right is the snow–etched Mount of the Holy Cross (1873). In the foreground is Jackson sitting astride a horse, his back to the viewer, as he scans this artificial landscape depicting a career that helped open the West. The sketch serves as Jackson's note to himself and to us, the recipients of his life's work, that he had experienced so much, accomplished so much.

Endnotes

INTRODUCTION

1. William Henry Jackson, *Time Exposure: The Autobiography of William Henry Jackson* (New York: G. P. Putnam's Sons, 1940), 38.

2. Jackson, *Time Exposure*, 38, 40.

3. Jackson, *Time Exposure*, 39.

4. O. S. Fowler, "Phrenologist Report on WHJ," MSS 341, box 3a, file folder 23, William Henry Jackson Collection, 1875–1942, The Colorado History Museum, Colorado Historical Society (History Colorado), Denver, CO.

CHAPTER 1

1. Jackson, *Time Exposure*, 3.

2. Jackson, *Time Exposure*, 4.

3. Jackson, *Time Exposure*, 7.

4. Jackson, *Time Exposure*, 8–9.

5. Jackson, *Time Exposure*, 6.

6. Jackson, *Time Exposure*, 11.

7. Jackson, *Time Exposure*, 11–12.

8. Jackson, *Time Exposure*, 13.

9. Jackson, *Time Exposure*, 14.

10. Jackson, *Time Exposure*, 14.

11. Jackson, *Time Exposure*, 15.

12. Jackson, *Time Exposure*, 16.

13. Jackson, *Time Exposure*, 18.

14. Jackson, *Time Exposure*, 18.

15. Jackson, *Time Exposure*, 19.

16. Jackson, *Time Exposure*, 20.

17. William Henry Jackson, with Howard R. Driggs, *The Pioneer Photographer: Rocky Mountain Adventures with a Camera* (Santa Fe: Museum of New Mexico Press, 2005), 5.

18. Jackson, *Time Exposure*, 20–21.

19. J. G. Chapman, *The American Drawing-Book: Manual for the Amateur* (New York: J. S. Redfield, Clinton Hall, 1847), 99–100.

20. Jackson, *Time Exposure*, 21.

21. Jackson, *Time Exposure*, 22.

22. Jackson, *Time Exposure*, 22.

23. Jackson, *Time Exposure*, 22.

24. Jackson, *Time Exposure*, 24.

25. Jackson, *Time Exposure*, 25.

26. Jackson, *Time Exposure*, 26.

27. Jackson, *Time Exposure*, 27.

28. Jackson, *Time Exposure*, 28.

29. Jackson, *Time Exposure*, 24–25.

CHAPTER 2

1. Jackson, *Time Exposure*, 34.

2. Jackson, *Time Exposure*, 36.

3. Jackson, *Time Exposure*, 37.

4. Jackson, *Pioneer Photographer*, 6.

5. Jackson, *Time Exposure*, 33.

6. Jackson, *Time Exposure*, 38.

7. Jackson, *Time Exposure*, 38.

8. Jackson, *Time Exposure*, 39–40; and Fowler, "Phrenologist Report on WHJ."

9. Jackson, *Time Exposure*, 42.

10. Jackson, *Time Exposure*, 47.

11. Jackson, *Time Exposure*, 49.

12. Jackson, *Time Exposure*, 49.

13. Jackson, *Time Exposure*, 49–50.

14. Jackson, *Time Exposure*, 50.

15. Jackson, *Time Exposure*, 51.

16. Jackson, *Time Exposure*, 54.

17. Jackson, *Time Exposure*, 54.

18. William Henry Jackson, Diary: 1862–1863, 1915, "Reconstructed Diary Account," December 28, 1862, William Henry Jackson Papers, Manuscripts and Archives Division, Astor, Lenox and Tilden Foundations, The New York Public Library, New York, NY.

19. Jackson, *Time Exposure*, 56; and Jackson, "Reconstructed Diary Account."

20. In his journal, Jackson refers to Blunt having the rank of colonel. But at that time, Blunt was still a captain. His colonelcy came at a later date.

21. Jackson, *Time Exposure*, 58.

22. Jackson, *Time Exposure*, 61.
23. Jackson, *Time Exposure*, 63.
24. Jackson, *Time Exposure*, 63.
25. Jackson, *Time Exposure*, 63–64.
26. Jackson, *Time Exposure*, 68.
27. Jackson, *Time Exposure*, 68.
28. Jackson, *Time Exposure*, 71.
29. Jackson, *Time Exposure*, 72.
30. Jackson, *Time Exposure*, 73.
31. Jackson, *Time Exposure*, 73–74.
32. Jackson, *Time Exposure*, 77.
33. Jackson, *Time Exposure*, 78.
34. Jackson, *Pioneer Photographer*, 8.
35. Jackson, *Time Exposure*, 81–82.
36. Jackson, *Time Exposure*, 82; and Jackson, *Pioneer Photographer*, 8.

CHAPTER 3

1. Jackson, *Time Exposure*, 83-84.
2. Jackson, *Time Exposure*, 83.
3. Jackson, *Pioneer Photographer*, 11
4. Jackson, *Time Exposure*, 87.
5. Jackson, *Pioneer Photographer*, 11.
6. Jackson, *Time Exposure*, 92.
7. Jackson, "Diary entry," June 6, 1866, MSS 341; and LeRoy R. Hafen, ed., *The Diaries of William Henry Jackson, Frontier Photographer, to California and Return, 1866–67; and with the Hayden Surveys to the Central Rockies, 1873, and to the Utes and Cliff Dwellings, 1874* (Glendale, CA: Arthur H. Clark, 1959), 25.
8. Jackson, "Diary entry," June 3, 1866, The William Henry Jackson Collection, MSS 341; and Hafen, *Diaries of WHJ*, June 6, 1866, 25.
9. In Jackson's first autobiography, he states that the advertisement read: "WANTED: TEAMSTERS FOR THE PLAINS." In a reconstructed version of his 1866 diary, he quotes directly from the advertisement in the *St. Joe Herald*: "One hundred teamsters wanted for Plains. Apply at Intelligence Office on St. Francis St. between 2nd and 3rd. Jackson, *Pioneer Photographer*, 13; and Jackson, *Time Exposure*, 103.
10. Hafen, *Diaries of WHJ*, June 22, 1866, 29.
11. Jackson, *Time Exposure*, 106.
12. Jackson, *Pioneer Photographer*, 16.
13. Jackson, *Time Exposure*, 110–11.
14. Jackson, *Pioneer Photographer*, 18.
15. Hafen, *Diaries of WHJ*, July 2, 1866, 42, 43.
16. Hafen, *Diaries of WHJ*, July 2, 1866, 40.
17. Jackson, *Time Exposure*, 117.
18. Jackson, *Pioneer Photographer*, 19.

19. Jackson, *Pioneer Photographer*, 22.

20. Jackson, *Pioneer Photographer*, 22.

21. Jackson, *Pioneer Photographer*, 23.

22. Jackson, *Time Exposure*, 124.

23. Jackson, *Time Exposure*, 124.

24. Jackson, *Time Exposure*, 125.

25. Jackson, *Time Exposure*, 125.

26. Jackson, *Pioneer Photographer*, 24.

27. Hafen, *Diaries of WHJ*, August 8, 1866, n33, 63.

28. Jackson, *Pioneer Photographer*, 25.

29. Hafen, *Diaries of WHJ*, August 30, 1866, 71.

30. Jackson, *Time Exposure*, 129.

31. Douglas Waitley, *William Henry Jackson: Framing the Frontier* (Missoula, MT: Mountain Press, 1998), 49.

32. Hafen, *Diaries of WHJ*, August 23, 1866, 68–69.

33. Jackson, *Pioneer Photographer*, 25–26.

34. Hafen, *Diaries of WHJ*, August 27, 1866, 70.

35. Hafen, *Diaries of WHJ*, August 29, 1866, 70–71.

36. Hafen, *Diaries of WHJ*, August 30, 1866, 70.

37. Jackson, *Time Exposure*, 131.

38. Jackson, *Time Exposure*, 131.

39. Jackson, *Time Exposure*, 132.

40. Jackson, *Time Exposure*, 132.

41. Jackson, *Time Exposure*, 133.

42. Jackson, *Time Exposure*, 133.

43. Jackson, *Time Exposure*, 133.

44. Jackson, *Time Exposure*, 135.

45. Hafen, *Diaries of WHJ*, October 15, 1866, 78–79.

46. Jackson, *Time Exposure*, 136–37.

47. Jackson, *Time Exposure*, 137.

CHAPTER 4

1. Jackson, *Pioneer Photographer*, 28.

2. Jackson, *Time Exposure*, 138–39.

3. Waitley, *Framing the Frontier*, 55.

4. Hafen, *Diaries of WHJ*, November 11, 1866, 95.

5. Hafen, *Diaries of WHJ*, November 17, 1866, 88.

6. Jackson, *Time Exposure*, 145.

7. Jackson, *Time Exposure*, 149.

8. Waitley, *Framing the Frontier*, 6.

9. Hafen, *Diaries of WHJ*, January 16, 1867, 117.

10. Hafen, *Diaries of WHJ*, January 21, 1867, 119–20.

11. Hafen, *Diaries of WHJ*, January 16, 1867, 117. In this diary entry, Jackson repeatedly spells "desert" as "dessert."

12. Hafen, *Diaries of WHJ*, January 16, 1867, 117.

13. Hafen, *Diaries of WHJ*, January 25, 1867, 121.

14. Hafen, *Diaries of WHJ*, January 28, 1867, 123.

15. Hafen, *Diaries of WHJ*, January 29, 1867, 125.

16. Hafen, *Diaries of WHJ*, January 31, 1867, n44, 125. The original manuscript is located in the Colorado State Historical Society archives under the title "Broncho [*sic*] Drive from the Pacific to the Missouri River in 1867."

17. Jackson, *Time Exposure*, 154.

18. Jackson, *Pioneer Photographer*, 31–32.

19. Jackson, *Time Exposure*, 155.

20. Jackson, *Pioneer Photographer*, 31.

21. Jackson, *Pioneer Photographer*, 32.

22. Jackson, *Pioneer Photographer*, 32.

23. Jackson, *Time Exposure*, 156.

24. Jackson, *Pioneer Photographer*, 33.

25. Jackson, *Time Exposure*, 159.

26. Jackson, *Pioneer Photographer*, 34.

27. Hafen, *Diaries of WHJ*, May 4, 1867, 158.

28. J. Ross Browne, *Adventures in the Apache Country: A Tour through Arizona and Sonora with Notes on the Silver Region of Nevada* (New York: Harper & Brothers, 1871), 48–49. Portions of Browne's book were originally published in *Harper's New Monthly Magazine*, "A Tour through Arizona," 29, no. 173 (1865): 553–74.

29. Hafen, *Diaries of WHJ*, May 4, 1867, 159.

30. Hafen, *Diaries of WHJ*, May 17, 1867, 164.

31. Jackson, *Time Exposure*, 161.

32. Hafen, *Diaries of WHJ*, May 15, 1867, 164.

33. Jackson, *Time Exposure*, 164.

34. Jackson, *Time Exposure*, 164.

35. Jackson, *Time Exposure*, 164; and Hafen, *Diaries of WHJ*, June 28, 1867, 183.

36. Hafen, *Diaries of WHJ*, July 1, 1867, 186.

37. Jackson, *Pioneer Photographer*, 38–39.

38. Jackson, *Time Exposure*, 168.

39. Jackson, *Time Exposure*, 169.

CHAPTER 5

1. Jackson, *Time Exposure*, 169.

2. Jackson, *Time Exposure*, 169.

3. Jackson, *Time Exposure*, 171.

4. Jackson, *Time Exposure*, 171.

5. Jackson, *Time Exposure*, 169.

6. Jackson, *Pioneer Photographer*, 42.

7. Jackson, *Time Exposure*, 173.

8. Jackson, *Pioneer Photographer*, 42.

9. Jackson, *Time Exposure*, 173.

10. Jackson, *Time Exposure*, 173–74.

11. Peter Hales, *William Henry Jackson and the Transformation of the American Land-scape* (Philadelphia: Temple University Press, 1988), 30.

12. Jackson, *Pioneer Photographer*, 44.

13. Jackson, *Time Exposure*, 175.

14. Jackson, *Time Exposure*, 175.

15. Hales, *Transformation of the American Landscape*, 41. Original citation in William Henry Jackson, "Diaries of William Henry Jackson: 1871, the Yellowstone" (photocopy of typewritten diaries; originals in New York Public Library), June 23, 24, 1869, vertical files, National Park Service, Yellowstone National Park Library, Yellowstone Heritage and Research Center, Gardiner, MT.

16. Jackson, *Time Exposure*, 176.

17. Jackson, *Time Exposure*, 177.

18. Jackson, *Time Exposure*, 177.

19. Jackson, *Time Exposure*, 178.

20. Jackson, *Time Exposure*, 179.

21. When Jackson took western photographs in the company of an assistant, the question would sometimes arise of who took which photograph. This is the case with the photograph of Promontory Point (Summit). In *Shutters West* (1962), Arundel Hull's daughter Nina Hull Miller states that the photo was actually taken by her father. Jackson himself could not always remember with certainty if he was the photographer of a given picture. This is to be expected, given that both men took photographs during their 1869 summer excursion along the UP line. Also, it was commonplace in this period for a photographer to claim as his own any photo taken by a hired assistant. See Nina Hull Miller, *Shutters West* (Denver: Sage Books, 1962).

22. Jackson, *Pioneer Photographer*, 48.

23. Jackson, *Time Exposure*, 179.

24. Jackson, *Time Exposure*, 179.

25. Jackson, *Pioneer Photographer*, 49.

26. Hales, *Transformation of the American Landscape*, 51.

27. Jackson, *Pioneer Photographer*, 50.

28. Jackson, *Pioneer Photographer*, 50.

29. Jackson, *Time Exposure*, 185.

30. Waitley, *Framing the Frontier*, 90.

CHAPTER 6

1. Jackson, *Pioneer Photographer*, 51.

2. Jackson, *Pioneer Photographer*, 52.

3. Jackson, *Pioneer Photographer*, 52; and George Black, *Empire of Shadows: The Epic Story of Yellowstone* (New York: St. Martin's Press, 2012), 344.

4. Jackson, *Time Exposure*, 187.

5. For details regarding his early excursion into the West as a geologist, see Richard C. Anderson, Phil Salstrom, and Paul Salstrom, eds., *Ferdinand Hayden: A Young Scientist in the Great West, 1853–1855* (Rock Island, IL: Augustana Historical Society, 2010).

6. Ferdinand Vandeveer Hayden, "On the Geology and Natural History of the Upper Missouri," in *Transactions of the American Philosophical Society Held at Philadelphia for Promoting Useful Knowledge*, vol. 12, pt. 1 (Philadelphia: C. Sherman, Son & Co., Printers, 1863), 60.

7. Richard A. Bartlett, *Great Surveys of the American West* (Norman: University of Oklahoma Press, 1962), 10.

8. Mike Foster, *Strange Genius: The Life of Ferdinand Vandeveer Hayden* (Niwot, CO: Roberts Rinehart, 1994), 171.

9. Jackson, *Pioneer Photographer*, 53.

10. Jackson, *Pioneer Photographer*, 54.

11. Foster, *Strange Genius*, 174.

12. Jackson, *Time Exposure*, 187–88.

13. Jackson, *Pioneer Photographer*, 53.

14. Hales, *Transformation of the American Landscape*, 71.

15. Jackson, *Pioneer Photographer*, 53.

16. Jackson, *Pioneer Photographer*, 55.

17. Jackson, *Pioneer Photographer*, 54.

18. Jackson, *Pioneer Photographer*, 57.

19. Jackson, *Pioneer Photographer*, 58.

20. Jackson, *Pioneer Photographer*, 59.

21. Jackson, *Pioneer Photographer*, 59.

22. Jackson, *Pioneer Photographer*, 60.

23. Jackson, *Pioneer Photographer*, 60.

24. Jackson, *Pioneer Photographer*, 60.

25. Jackson, *Pioneer Photographer*, 61.

26. Jackson, *Pioneer Photographer*, 61.

27. Jackson, *Pioneer Photographer*, 62.

28. Jackson, *Pioneer Photographer*, 63.

29. Tim McNeese, *The Colorado River* (Philadelphia: Chelsea House, 2004), 37.

30. T. H. Watkins, *The Grand Colorado: The Story of a River and Its Canyons* (Palo Alto, CA: American West Publishing, 1969), 95.

31. William Henry Jackson, *Descriptive Catalogue of the Photographs of the United States Geological Survey of the Territories, for the Years 1869 to 1875 Inclusive, Second edition,* Miscellaneous Publications no. 5 (Milwaukee, WI: The Q Press, 1978), 18.

32. Jackson, *Pioneer Photographer*, 64.

33. Jackson, *Pioneer Photographer*, 65.

34. Jackson, *Pioneer Photographer*, 65.

35. Jackson, *Time Exposure*, 192.

36. Jackson, *Pioneer Photographer*, 65.

37. Jackson, *Time Exposure*, 192.

38. John E. Foster, Dick Harrison, and I. S. MacLaren, eds. *Buffalo* (Edmonton: University of Alberta Press, 1992), 5.

CHAPTER 7

1. Jackson, "Diaries of William Henry Jackson," 1–14.
2. Jackson, *Pioneer Photographer*, 66.
3. Jackson, *Time Exposure*, 194.
4. Hiram M. Chittenden, *The Yellowstone National Park* (Norman: University of Oklahoma Press, 1964), 28.
5. Ronald M. Anglin and Larry E. Morris, *Gloomy Terrors and Hidden Fires: The Mystery of John Colter and Yellowstone* (Lanham, MD: Rowman & Littlefield, 2014), 85.
6. Frances Fuller Victor, *The River of the West: Life and Adventure in the Rocky Mountains and Oregon; Embracing Events in the Life-Time of a Mountain-Man and Pioneer* (Hartford, CT: Colombian Book, 1870), 75–76.
7. Chittenden, *Yellowstone National Park*, 31.
8. Dyan Zaslowsky and T. H. Watkins, *These American Lands: Parks, Wilderness, and the Public Lands* (Washington, DC: Island Press, 1994).
9. Black, *Empire of Shadows*, 81. Original citation: The Executive Documents of the Senate of the United States, "Extract from Instructions to Captain W. F. Raynolds, Topographical Engineers," 1024 Cong. Rec. 550 (1860).
10. National Park Service, "Expeditions Explore Yellowstone," accessed September 30, 2021, https://www.nps.gov/yell/learn/ historyculture/expeditions.htm. .
11. Kim Heacox, *An American Idea: The Making of the National Parks* (Washington, DC: National Geographic, 2009), 93.
12. John W. Simpson, "A Tale of Two Parks," *Landscape Architecture Magazine* 77, no. 3 (May/June, 1987): 61.
13. Merrill D. Beal, *The Story of Man in Yellowstone* (Yellowstone National Park, WY: Yellowstone Library and Museum Association, 1960), 118.
14. C. W. Cook, "Remarks of C. W. Cook, Last Survivor of the Original Explorers of the Yellowstone Park Region, during the Celebration of the Park's Golden Anniversary, 1922," National Park Service, Yellowstone National Park Library, Mammoth Springs, WY.
15. In addition to Folsom's article, the expedition's geologist, F. V. Hayden, wrote up an extensive report based on the geological studies he made. But few outside the government read the report. See Ferdinand Vandeveer Hayden, *Geological Report of the Exploration of the Yellowstone and Missouri Rivers* (Washington, DC: Government Printing Office, 1869).
16. Roderick Nash, *Wilderness and the American Mind* (New Haven, CT: Yale University Press, 1967), 109.
17. Aubrey L. Haines, *The Yellowstone Story: A History of Our First National Park* (Yellowstone National Park, WY: Yellowstone Library and Museum Association, 1977), 1:14.

18. Nathaniel P. Langford, "The Wonders of the Yellowstone," *Scribner's Monthly* 2, no. 1 (May 1871): 1.

19. Langford, "Wonders of the Yellowstone," *Scribner's* 2, no. 1, 3.

20. Langford, "Wonders of the Yellowstone," *Scribner's* 2, no. 1, 2.

21. Langford, "Wonders of the Yellowstone," *Scribner's* 2, no. 1, 4.

22. Langford, "Wonders of the Yellowstone," *Scribner's* 2, no. 1, 5.

23. Langford, "Wonders of the Yellowstone," *Scribner's* 2, no. 1, 7.

24. Langford, "Wonders of the Yellowstone," *Scribner's* 2, no. 1, 8.

25. Langford, "Wonders of the Yellowstone," *Scribner's* 2, no. 1, 10.

26. Langford, "Wonders of the Yellowstone," *Scribner's* 2, no. 1, 10.

27. Langford, "Wonders of the Yellowstone," *Scribner's* 2, no. 1, 12.

28. Langford, "Wonders of the Yellowstone," *Scribner's* 2, no. 2, 121.

29. Langford, "Wonders of the Yellowstone," *Scribner's* 2, no. 2, 123.

30. Nash, *Wilderness and the American Mind*, 110; Haines, *Yellowstone Story*, 130; and Chittenden, *Yellowstone National Park*, ch. 10.

31. Nathaniel P. Langford, *The Discovery of Yellowstone* (self-published, 1905), 117–18.

32. Langford, *Discovery of Yellowstone*, 118;

33. Simpson, "Tale of Two Parks," 61.

34. Aubrey L. Haines, *Yellowstone National Park: Its Exploration and Establishment* (Washington, DC: U.S. Department of the Interior, National Park Service, 1974), 85.

35. David Michael Delo, *The Yellowstone, Forever!* (New York: Kingfisher Books, 1998), 207; and Bradly J. Boner, *Yellowstone National Park: Through the Lens of Time* (Boulder: University Press of Colorado, 2017), 10.

36. Lewis W. Selmeier, "First Camera on the Yellowstone," *Montana: The Magazine of Western History* 22, no. 3 (Summer 1972): 45.

37. Jackson, *Pioneer Photographer*, 68.

38. Jackson, *Pioneer Photographer*, 68.

39. J. W. Barlow and David P. Heap, *Report of a Reconnaissance of the Upper Yellowstone in 1871*, 42d Cong., 2d Sess., S. Exec. Doc. 66, SN-1479, vol. E (Washington, DC: Government Printing Office, 1872), 3.

40. William Henry Jackson, *Descriptive Catalogue of the Photographs of the United States Geological Survey of the Territories for the Years 1869 to 1873* (Washington, DC: Government Printing Office, 1874), 32.

41. Weldon F. Heald, "Thomas Moran: Depicter of Western Grandeur," *Montana: The Magazine of Western History* 15, no. 4 (Autumn 1965): 44.

42. William H. Truettner, "'Scenes of Majesty and Enduring Interest': Thomas Moran Goes West," *Art Bulletin* 58, no. 2 (June 1976): 241–59.

43. Jackson, *Time Exposure*, 194.

44. Jackson, *Time Exposure*, 196.

45. Jackson, *Time Exposure*, 196.

46. Jackson, *Pioneer Photographer*, 68.

CHAPTER 8

1. Kirby Lambert, "The Lure of the Parks," *Montana: The Magazine of Western History* 46, no. 1 (Spring 1996): 54.

2. Jackson, *Pioneer Photographer*, 70.

3. Jackson, *Pioneer Photographer*, 70.

4. Jackson, *Time Exposure*, 197.

5. Baird to Hayden, June 2, 1871, microfilm 623, reel 2, National Archives and Records Administration, Washington, DC.

6. Ferdinand Vandeveer Hayden, *Preliminary Report of the United States Geological Survey of Montana and Portions of Adjacent Territories* (Washington, DC: Government Printing Office, 1872), 65.

7. Ferdinand Vandeveer Hayden and A. R. C. Selwyn, eds., *Stanford's Compendium of Geography and Travel: North America* (London: Edward Stanford, SS, Charing Cross, S.W., 1883), 63.

8. Bartlett, *Great Surveys of the American West*, 47.

9. Hayden and Selwyn, *Stanford's Compendium*, 63.

10. Ferdinand Vandeveer Hayden, "The Wonders of the West—II: More About the Yellowstone," *Scribner's Monthly* 3, no. 4 (February 1872): 390; and James Richardson, ed., *Wonders of the Yellowstone* (New York: Scribner, Armstrong, 1974), 30.

11. Jackson, *Time Exposure*, 198.

12. Jackson, *Time Exposure*, 198.

13. Hayden, *Preliminary Report*, 76.

14. Jackson, "Diaries of William Henry Jackson," 8.

15. Bartlett, *Great Surveys*, 49.

16. Jackson, *Time Exposure*, 199.

17. Selmeier, "First Camera on the Yellowstone," 49.

18. Jackson, "Diaries of William Henry Jackson," 9.

19. Jackson, *Pioneer Photographer*, 75.

20. Jackson, *Pioneer Photographer*, 74; and Hiram Martin Chittenden, *The Yellowstone National Park: Historical and Descriptive* (Cincinnati: Robert Clarke Co., 1904), 83.

21. Bartlett, *Great Surveys*, 51.

22. Bartlett, *Great Surveys*, 51.

23. Bartlett, *Great Surveys*, 51; and Hayden, *Preliminary Report*, 96.

24. Bartlett, *Great Surveys*, 54.

25. Report No. 7, Ferdinand Hayden to Spencer Baird, Yellowstone Lake, WY, August 8, 1871, in *Yellowstone and the Great West: Journals, Letters, and Images from the 1871 Hayden Expedition*, ed. Marlene Deahl Merrill (Lincoln: University of Nebraska Press, 1999), 154.

26. Jackson, *Pioneer Photographer*, 77.

27. R.G. 57, Hayden Survey, General Letters Received, vol. 3, 1871, National Archives.

28. Ferdinand Vandeveer Hayden, "The Hot Springs and Geysers of the Yellowstone and Firehole Rivers," *American Journal of Science and Arts*, 3rd ser., 3, no. 15 (March 1872): 176.

29. *New York Times*, Monday, October 23, 1871, 4.

30. *New York Times*, Monday, October 23, 1871, 4.

31. Jackson, *Time Exposure*, 202.

CHAPTER 9

1. Jackson, *Time Exposure*, 204–5.

2. Hayden's Report to the Committee on Public Lands, appendix 4, in Merrill, *Yellowstone and the Great West*, 208.

3. Cong. Globe, 42d Cong., 2d Sess. (December 18, 1871), 159.

4. Hayden, *Preliminary Report*, 163.

5. Hayden, "Wonders of the West—II," 396.

6. Thurman Wilkins, *Thomas Moran: Artist of the Mountains* (Norman: University of Oklahoma Press, 1998), 91.

7. Merrill, *Yellowstone and the Great West*, 269.

8. William Henry Jackson, "With Moran in Yellowstone," *Appalachia* 21, no. 2 (December 1936): 154.

9. George Sheldon, *American Painters* (New York: D. Appleton, 1881), 125–26.

10. Joni Louise Kinsey, *Thomas Moran and the Surveying of the American West* (Washington, DC: Smithsonian Institution Press, 1992), 52.

11. John Moran, "Reflections on Art," *Philadelphia Photographer* 12 (October 1875): 294.

12. Mary Panzer, "Great Pictures from the 1871 Expedition: Thomas Moran, William Henry Jackson, and the Grand Canyon of the Yellowstone," in Birmingham Museum of Art, *Splendors of the American West: Thomas Moran's Art of the Grand Canyon and Yellowstone* (Birmingham, AL: Birmingham Museum of Art, 1990), 51.

13. Moran to Hayden, March 3, 1872, microfilm 623, reel 2, National Archives.

14. Wilkins, *Thomas Moran*, 101.

15. Clarence Cook, "Fine Arts," *New York Tribune*, May 4, 1872, cited in *Appleton's Journal of Literature, Science and Art* 7, no. 166 (June 1, 1872), American Periodicals Series Online.

16. United States Department of the Interior Geological Survey, *Ferdinand Vandeveer Hayden and the Founding of the Yellowstone National Park* (Washington, DC: Government Printing Office, 1973), 11.

17. Diana Seave Greenwald, "The Big Picture: Thomas Moran's The Grand Canyon of the Yellowstone and the Development of the American West," *Winterthur Portfolio* 49, no. 4 (Winter 2015): 207.

18. Carol Clark, *Thomas Moran: Watercolors of the American West: Text and Catalogue Raisonne* (Fort Worth, TX: Amon Carter Museum of Western Art, 1980), 40.

19. Ferdinand Vandeveer Hayden, *Sixth Annual Report of the United States Geological Survey of the Territories* (Washington, DC: Government Printing Office, 1873), 8.

20. "An Explosion in the Studio Building," *New York Times*, February 8, 1871, 8.

21. Jackson, *Pioneer Photographer*, 80.

22. Jackson, *Pioneer Photographer*, 80.

23. Jackson, *Pioneer Photographer*, 81.

24. Jackson, *Pioneer Photographer*, 81.

25. Nathaniel P. Langford, "The Ascent of Mount Hayden: A New Chapter in Western Discovery," *Scribner's Monthly* 6, no. 2 (June 1873): 129–37.

26. Jackson, *Pioneer Photographer*, 83.

27. Bartlett, *Great Surveys*, 69.

28. Jackson, *Pioneer Photographer*, 88–89.

29. Jackson, *Pioneer Photographer*, 91.

CHAPTER 10

1. Ferdinand Vandeveer Hayden, "Letter to the Secretary," [*Sixth*] *Annual Report of the United States Geological and Geographical Survey of the Territories, Embracing Colorado, Being a Report of Progress of the Exploration for the Year 1873* (Washington, DC: Government Printing Office, 1873), 1.

2. Jackson, *Time Exposure*, 210.

3. Jackson, *Time Exposure*, 210.

4. Waitley, *Framing the Frontier*, 122.

5. Waitley, *Framing the Frontier*, 123.

6. Jackson, *Time Exposure*, 210.

7. Waitley, *Framing the Frontier*, 125.

8. Jackson, *Time Exposure*, 211.

9. Jackson, *Time Exposure*, 212.

10. Jackson, *Time Exposure*, 212.

11. Waitley, *Framing the Frontier*, 133.

12. Jackson, *Pioneer Photographer*, 101.

13. Hales, *Transformation of the American Landscape*, 113.

14. Hafen, *Diaries of WHJ*, July 12, 1873, 232. While Hafen's published version of Jackson's 1873 diary entries was utilized for this book, I also accessed a typed copy of these entries: "W. H. Jackson's Diary for 1873," MSS 341, box 3A, William Henry Jackson Collection, The Colorado History Museum, Colorado Historical Society.

15. Jackson, *Pioneer Photographer*, 103.

16. Jackson, *Pioneer Photographer*, 102.

17. Jackson, *Time Exposure*, 214.

18. Jackson, *Time Exposure*, 214.

19. Jackson, *Time Exposure*, 215.

20. Jackson, *Time Exposure*, 215.

21. Jackson, *Time Exposure*, 215.

22. Jackson, *Pioneer Photographer*, 111.

23. Jackson, *Pioneer Photographer*, 112.

24. Jackson, *Pioneer Photographer*, 113.

25. Jackson, *Pioneer Photographer*, 111.

26. Jackson, *Pioneer Photographer*, 113.

27. Jackson, *Pioneer Photographer*, 113.

28. Jackson, *Time Exposure*, 216, 217.

29. Jackson, *Pioneer Photographer*, 113.

30. William Henry Jackson, "The Mountain of the Holy Cross," William Henry Jackson Collection, MSS 341, box 3A, The Colorado History Museum, Colorado Historical Society. The archival manuscript consists of a typed copy, double-spaced, running seven pages in length, dated April 20, 1922, Detroit, Michigan, and signed W. H. Jackson.

31. Jackson, *Time Exposure*, 217.

32. Jackson, *Pioneer Photographer*, 115.

33. Hafen, *Diaries of WHJ*, August 24, 1873, 252.

34. Hafen, *Diaries of WHJ*, August 24, 1873, 252.

35. Jackson, *Pioneer Photographer*, 116.

36. Jackson, *Time Exposure*, 218.

37. Jackson to Fryxell, April 30, 1933, Fritiof M. Fryxell Papers, 1853–1973, MSS 1638, box 29, correspondence file, American Heritage Center, University of Wyoming, Laramie, WY.

38. William Henry Jackson to Thomas Dawson, January 30, 1922, William Henry Jackson Collection, MSS 341, Mini-Manuscript Collection, The Colorado History Museum, Colorado Historical Society.

CHAPTER 11

1. Jackson, *Pioneer Photographer*, 118.

2. Jackson, *Time Exposure*, 224.

3. Chittenden, *Yellowstone National Park: Historical and Descriptive*, 88; and Ingersoll, "Mountain Harry, a Character Sketch," *Appleton's Journal* 3, no. 18 (December 1877): 524–27.

4. Waitley, *Framing the Frontier*, 144.

5. Waitley, *Framing the Frontier*, 145.

6. Hafen, *Diaries of WHJ*, August 17, 1874, 284.

7. Hafen, *Diaries of WHJ*, August 18, 1874, 286.

8. William Henry Jackson, "A Visit to the Los Pinos Indian Agency in 1874," *Colorado Magazine* 15, no. 6 (November 1938): 206.

9. George Ingersoll, *Knocking 'Round the Rockies* (New York: Harper & Brothers, 1883), 90.

10. Hafen, *Diaries of WHJ*, August 21, 1874, 290.

11. Jackson, *Time Exposure*, 227.

12. Waitley, *Framing the Frontier*, 149.

13. Hafen, *Diaries of WHJ*, August 28, 1874, 297.

14. Hafen, *Diaries of WHJ*, August 31, 1874, 302.

15. Thomas Moran to Mary Nimmo Moran, August 10, 1874, in *Home-Thoughts, from Afar: Letters of Thomas Moran to Mary Nimmo Moran*, ed. Amy O. Bassford and Fritiof Fryxell (East Hampton, NY: East Hampton Free Library, 1967), 45.

16. Thomas Moran to Mary Nimmo Moran, August 24, 1874, in Bassford and Fryxell, *Home-Thoughts*, 55.

17. Jackson, *Pioneer Photographer*, 140.

18. Jackson, *Pioneer Photographer*, 140.

19. Waitley, *Framing the Frontier*, 154.

20. Jackson, *Descriptive Catalogue*, Miscellaneous Publications no. 5, 71.

21. Hafen, *Diaries of WHJ*, September 12, 1874, 319.

22. Hafen, *Diaries of WHJ*, September 1, 1874, 320.

CHAPTER 12

1. Jackson, *Pioneer Photographer*, 148.

2. Jackson, *Pioneer Photographer*, 133.

3. Jackson, *Pioneer Photographer*, 133.

4. Jackson, *Pioneer Photographer*, 134.

5. Jackson, *Descriptive Catalogue*, Miscellaneous Publications no. 5, 69.

6. Jackson, *Descriptive Catalogue*, Miscellaneous Publications no. 5, 77.

7. Jackson, *Descriptive Catalogue*, Miscellaneous Publications no. 5, July 13, 1874.

8. Jackson, *Pioneer Photographer*, 137.

9. Jackson, *Pioneer Photographer*, 151.

10. Jackson, *Pioneer Photographer*, 151.

11. Jackson, *Pioneer Photographer*, 152.

12. Jackson, *Pioneer Photographer*, 153.

13. Jackson, *Pioneer Photographer*, 153.

14. Jackson, *Pioneer Photographer*, 153.

15. Jackson, *Pioneer Photographer*, 153.

16. Jackson refers to this as Canyon Bonito Chiquito.

17. Jackson, *Pioneer Photographer*, 154.

18. Jackson, *Pioneer Photographer*, 154; and Robert S. McPherson and Susan Rhoades Neel, *Mapping the Four Corners: Narrating the Hayden Survey of 1875* (Norman: University of Oklahoma Press, 2016), 137.

19. Jackson, *Pioneer Photographer*, 155.

20. E. A. Barber, *New York Times*, October 1, 1875, cited in Harry Clebourne James, *Pages from Hopi History* (Tucson: University of Arizona Press, 1974), 198. The quote is included in Jackson, *Pioneer Photographer*, 156.

21. Jackson, *Pioneer Photographer*, 158.

22. Jackson, *Pioneer Photographer*, 160.

23. Jackson, *Pioneer Photographer*, 162.

24. Jackson, *Pioneer Photographer*, 163.

25. Jackson, *Pioneer Photographer*, 163.

26. Jackson, *Pioneer Photographer*, 164.

27. Jackson, *Pioneer Photographer*, 165.

28. Jackson, *Pioneer Photographer*, 166.

29. Jackson, *Pioneer Photographer*, 167.
30. Jackson, *Pioneer Photographer*, 168.

CHAPTER 13

1. Jackson, *Time Exposure*, 242.
2. Jackson, *Time Exposure*, 242–43.
3. Jackson, *Time Exposure*, 243.
4. Jackson, *Time Exposure*, 243.
5. Jackson, *Time Exposure*, 243.
6. Jackson, *Pioneer Photographer*, 170.
7. Jackson, *Time Exposure*, 244.
8. Jackson, *Pioneer Photographer*, 170.
9. Jackson, *Time Exposure*, 244.
10. Jackson, *Time Exposure*, 245.
11. Jackson to Holmes, April 27, 1877, Fritiof M. Fryxell Papers, MSS 1638, box 29, correspondence file, American Heritage Center, University of Wyoming.
12. Waitley, *Framing the Frontier*, 166.
13. Waitley, *Framing the Frontier*, 169.
14. Ferdinand Vandeveer Hayden, *Tenth Annual Report of the United States Geological and Geographical Survey of the Territories, Embracing Colorado and parts of adjacent territories, being a report of progress of the exploration for the year 1876* (Washington, DC: Government Printing Office, 1878), 446–47.
15. Jackson, *Pioneer Photographer*, 180.
16. Jackson, *Pioneer Photographer*, 171.
17. Jackson, *Time Exposure*, 246.
18. Jackson, *Time Exposure*, 246.

CHAPTER 14

1. Jackson, *Pioneer Photographer*, 183.
2. Jackson, *Pioneer Photographer*, 184.
3. Jackson, *Pioneer Photographer*, 185.
4. Jackson, *Time Exposure*, 248.
5. Jackson, *Pioneer Photographer*, 187.
6. Jackson, *Pioneer Photographer*, 188.
7. Jackson, *Time Exposure*, 249–50.
8. Jackson, *Pioneer Photographer*, 190.
9. Jackson, *Pioneer Photographer*, 191.
10. Jackson, *Pioneer Photographer*, 192.

CHAPTER 15

1. Hales, *Transformation of the American Landscape*, 135.

2. Columbus Delano, "Letter from the Secretary of the Interior and Report of the Superintendent of the Yellowstone National Park for the Year 1872," 42d Cong., Long 3d Sess., S. Exec. Doc. 35, S. Rep. 1545 (1873).

3. Jackson, *Time Exposure*, 251.

4. Jackson, *Time Exposure*, 251.

5. Jackson, *Time Exposure*, 251.

6. Jackson, *Time Exposure*, 251.

7. Jackson, *Time Exposure*, 252.

8. Jackson, *Time Exposure*, 253.

9. Jackson, *Time Exposure*, 254.

10. Jackson, *Time Exposure*, 254.

11. Ernest Ingersoll, "Silver San Juan," *Harper's New Monthly Magazine* 64, no. 383 (April 1882): 689–704.

12. Jackson, *Time Exposure*, 259.

13. Jackson, *Time Exposure*, 260.

14. Lucius Beebe and Charles Clegg, *Narrow Gauge in the Rockies* (Berkeley, CA: Howell-North Press, 1958), 19. For a full history of the Denver & Rio Grande, see Lucius Beebe and Charles Clegg, *Rio Grande: Mainline of the Rockies*. (Berkeley, CA: Howell-North, 1962).

15. Ernest Ingersoll, *The Crest of the Continent: A Record of a Summer's Ramble in the Rocky Mountains and Beyond* (Chicago: R. R. Donnelley & Sons, 1885), 3.

16. Jackson, *Time Exposure*, 259.

17. Thomas Moran to Mary Nimmo Moran, May 25, 1892, in Bassford and Fryxell, *Home-Thoughts*, 87.

18. Thomas Moran to Mary Nimmo Moran, June 5, 1892, in Bassford and Fryxell, *Home-Thoughts*, 91.

19. Thomas Moran to Mary Nimmo Moran, June 5, 1892, in Bassford and Fryxell, *Home-Thoughts*, 92.

20. Thomas Moran to Mary Nimmo Moran, June 7, 1892, in Bassford and Fryxell, *Home-Thoughts*, 95.

21. Thomas Moran to Mary Nimmo Moran, June 16, 1892, in Bassford and Fryxell, *Home-Thoughts*, 101.

22. Thomas Moran, "A Journey to the Devil's Tower in Wyoming," *Century Illustrated Monthly Magazine* 47, no. 3 (January 1894): 452. Moran did not write articles often describing his artistic travels. This article in *Century Magazine* was one of a few.

23. Moran, "Journey to the Devil's Tower," 454–55.

24. Thomas Moran to Mary Nimmo Moran, July 20, 1892, in Bassford and Fryxell, *Home-Thoughts*, 117.

25. Thomas Moran to Mary Nimmo Moran, July 20, 1892. in Bassford and Fryxell, *Home-Thoughts*, 117.

26. Thomas Moran to Mary Nimmo Moran, July 26, 1892, in Bassford and Fryxell, *Home-Thoughts*, 119.

27. Thomas Moran to Mary Nimmo Moran, July 26, 1892, in Bassford and Fryxell, *Home-Thoughts*, 121.

28. Thomas Moran to Mary Nimmo Moran, July 26, 1892, in Bassford and Fryxell, *Home-Thoughts*, 121.

29. Thomas Moran to Mary Nimmo Moran, July 29, 1892, in Bassford and Fryxell, *Home-Thoughts*, 123.

30. Hales, *Transformation of the American Landscape*, 194.

31. Charles Roscoe Savage, "Diaries" (1894), Harry B. Lee Library, Brigham Young University, Provo, UT.

CHAPTER 16

1. Jackson, *Time Exposure*, 261.

2. Hales, *Transformation of the American Landscape*, 202.

3. J. F. Ryder, "Photography at the World's Fair," *American Amateur Photographer* 5, no. 9 (September 1893): 421. In 1893, famed American photographer Alfred Stieglitz was the journal's editor.

4. Jackson, *Time Exposure*, 263.

5. Jackson, *Time Exposure*, 265.

6. Jackson, *Time Exposure*, 265.

7. William Henry Jackson to Emilie Jackson, May 14, 1895, William Henry Jackson Papers, MSS col. 1541, series I, Letters to his wife Emilie, 1894–1896, Manuscript and Archives Division, Rare Books and Manuscripts Collection. Astor, Lenox and Tilden Foundations, New York Public Library.

8. Jackson, *Time Exposure*, 267.

9. William Henry Jackson to Emilie Jackson, October 12, 1894, William Henry Jackson Papers, New York Public Library. This letter is included in a collection of eighty-five handwritten letters between Will and Emilie. They have not been digitized. Reading these missives can be difficult, as Jackson's handwriting is not always that legible. The New York Public Library provided the author with copies of Jackson's letters, some of which are quite lengthy.

10. Jackson, *Time Exposure*, 268.

11. Jackson, *Time Exposure*, 269.

12. Jackson, *Time Exposure*, 270.

13. Jackson, *Time Exposure*, 271–72.

14. Jackson, *Time Exposure*, 272.

15. Jackson, *Time Exposure*, 278.

16. William Henry Jackson to Emilie Jackson, June 23, 1895, William Henry Jackson Papers, New York Public Library.

17. William Henry Jackson to Emilie Jackson, June 23, 1895, William Henry Jackson Papers, New York Public Library.

18. William Henry Jackson to Emilie Jackson, June 23, 1895, William Henry Jackson Papers, New York Public Library.

19. Jackson, *Time Exposure*, 285.

20. Jackson, *Time Exposure*, 286.
21. Jackson, *Time Exposure*, 304.
22. Jackson, *Time Exposure*, 318.

CHAPTER 17

1. Jim Hughes, *The Birth of a Century: Early Color Photographs of America* (New York: Tauris Parke Books, 1994), 36.
2. Jackson, *Time Exposure*, 323.
3. Waitley, *Framing the Frontier*, 192.
4. Keith Wheeler, *The Chroniclers* (New York: Time-Life Books, 1976), 208–9.
5. Jackson, *Time Exposure*, 325.
6. Jackson, *Time Exposure*, 327.
7. Jackson, *Time Exposure*, 329.
8. Jackson, *Time Exposure*, 328.
9. Jackson, *Time Exposure*, 329.
10. Jackson, *Time Exposure*, 330.
11. Jackson, *Time Exposure*, 330.
12. Jackson, *Time Exposure*, 332.
13. Jackson, *Time Exposure*, 332.
14. Jackson, *Time Exposure*, 335. Several of these paintings are held by the Scotts Bluff National Monument's Oregon Trail Museum Association in western Nebraska. The small museum, which lies in the shadow of the great bluff, displays copies of these paintings. The originals are maintained in an off-site vault. One of the best sources regarding this collection is Dean Knudsen, *An Eye for History: The Paintings of William Henry Jackson, from the Collection at the Oregon Trail Museum* (Washington, DC: Government Printing Office, 1997).
15. Jackson, *Time Exposure*, 336.
16. Jackson, *Time Exposure*, 337.
17. Beaumont Newhall and Diana E. Edkins, *William H. Jackson* (Fort Worth, TX: Morgan & Morgan, 1974), 17.
18. Jackson, *Time Exposure*, 338.
19. Jackson, *Time Exposure*, 338.
20. Jackson, *Time Exposure*, 338.
21. Jackson, *Time Exposure*, 340.
22. Helen Markley Miller, *Lens on the West: The Story of William Henry Jackson* (Garden City, NY: Doubleday, 1966), 182.
23. Jackson, *Time Exposure*, 341.
24. Joseph Robinson to Horace Albright, June 27, 1942, William Henry Jackson Collection, MSS 341, file folder 37, Marian Albright Schenck File, The Colorado History Museum, Colorado Historical Society.
25. Ansel Adams to Horace Albright, July 4, 1942, William Henry Jackson Collection, MSS 341, file folder 37, Marian Albright Schenck File, The Colorado History Museum, Colorado Historical Society. In this same letter, Adams informs Albright:

"I have just returned from wonderful trip to Grand Canyon, Rocky Mountain, Yellowstone, Teton and Glacier National Parks. Got some of the best pictures of my life." Adams was walking in the footsteps of William Jackson.

Bibliography

ARCHIVAL SOURCES

Fritiof M. Fryxell Papers, 1853–1973. American Heritage Center, University of Wyoming, Laramie, WY.

Harry B. Lee Library, Brigham Young University, Provo, UT.

National Archives and Records Administration, Washington, DC.

National Park Service, Yellowstone National Park Library, Yellowstone Heritage and Research Center, Gardiner, MT.

National Park Service, Yellowstone National Park Library, Mammoth Springs, WY.

Robert Spurrier Ellison Papers. The Western History Collection, Denver Public Library, Denver, CO.

William Henry Jackson Collection. The Colorado History Museum, Colorado Historical Society (History Colorado), Denver, CO.

William Henry Jackson Collection, L. Tom Perry Special Collections, Harold B. Lee Library, Brigham Young University, Provo, UT.

William Henry Jackson Papers, 1862–1942. Manuscripts and Archives Division. Rare Books and Manuscripts Collection. Astor, Lenox and Tilden Foundations. The New York Public Library, New York, NY.

GOVERNMENT DOCUMENTS/REPORTS

Barlow, J. W., and David P. Heap. *Report of a Reconnaissance of the Upper Yellowstone in 1871*. 42d Cong., 2d Sess., S. Exec. Doc. 66, SN-1479, Vol. E. Washington, DC: Government Printing Office, 1872.

Cong. Globe. 42d Cong., 2d Sess. (December 18, 1871).

Delano, Columbus. "Letter from the Secretary of the Interior and Report of the Superintendent of the Yellowstone National Park for the Year 1872." 42d Cong., Long 3d Sess., S. Exec. Doc. 35, S. Rep. 1545 (1873).

The Executive Documents of the Senate of the United States. "Extract from Instructions to Captain W. F. Raynolds, Topographical Engineers." 1024 Cong. Rec. (1860).

Hayden, Ferdinand Vandeveer. *Annual Report of the United States Geological and Geographic Survey of the Territories, Embracing Colorado, Being a Report of Progress of the Exploration for the Year 1873.* Washington, DC: Government Printing Office, 1874.

———. *Geographical and Geological Surveys West of the Mississippi River.* 43 Cong., 1st Sess., H.R. Rep. No. 612 (1874).

———. *Geological Report of the Exploration of the Yellowstone and Missouri Rivers.* Washington, DC: Government Printing Office, 1869.

———. *Preliminary Report of the United States Geological Survey of Montana and Portions of Adjacent Territories.* Washington, DC: Government Printing Office, 1872.

———. *Sixth Annual Report of the United States Geological Survey of the Territories.* Washington, DC: Government Printing Office, 1873.

———. *Tenth Annual Report of the United States Geological and Geographical Survey of the Territories, Embracing Colorado and Parts of Adjacent Territories, Being a Report of Progress of the Exploration for the Year 1876.* Washington, DC: Government Printing Office, 1878.

Jackson, William Henry. *Descriptive Catalogue of the Photographs of the United States Geological Survey of the Territories for the Years 1869 to 1873.* Washington, DC: Government Printing Office, 1874.

———. *Descriptive Catalogue of the Photographs of the United States Geological Survey of the Territories, for the Years 1869 to 1875 Inclusive, Second edition.* Miscellaneous Publications No. 5. Reprinted by Raymond Dworczyk/ Milwaukee, WI: The Q Press, 1978.

"List of Congressional and Departmental Publications." In *Checklist of the United States Public Documents*, vol. I, 3rd ed. Washington, DC: Government Printing Office, 1911.

Rhoda, Franklin. "Report on the Topography of the San Juan Country." In *[Eighth] Annual Report of the United States Geological and Geographical Survey of the Territories Embracing Colorado and Parts of Adjacent Territories; Being a Report of Progress of the Exploration for the Year 1874.* Washington, DC: Government Printing Office, 1875.

ARTICLES/CHAPTERS/LECTURES

Browne, J. Ross. "A Tour Through Arizona." *Harper's New Monthly Magazine* 29, no. 173: 553–74.

Bueler, William M. "Langford's Grand Teton Diary." *American Alpine Journal* 21 (1978): 471–76.

Cook, Charles W. "Remarks of C. W. Cook, Last Survivor of the Original Explorers of the Yellowstone Park Region, during the Celebration of the Park's Golden Anniversary, 1922." Unpublished manuscript, Yellowstone Park Library, Mammoth Springs, Wyoming.

Cook, Clarence. "Fine Arts." *New York Tribune*, May 4, 1872. Cited in *Appleton's Journal of Literature, Science and Art* 7, no. 166 (June 1, 1872). American Periodicals Series Online.

Greenwald, Diana Seave. "The Big Picture: Thomas Moran's *The Grand Canyon of the Yellowstone* and the Development of the American West." *Winterthur Portfolio* 49, no. 4 (Winter 2015): 175–210.

Harper's New Monthly Magazine. "Editor's Drawer." 39, no. 232 (September 1869): 623.

Hayden, Ferdinand Vandeveer. "The Hot Springs and Geysers of the Yellowstone and Firehole Rivers." *American Journal of Science and Arts*, 3rd ser., 3, no. 15 (March 1872): 161–76.

———. "On the Geology and Natural History of the Upper Missouri." In *Transactions of the American Philosophical Society Held at Philadelphia for Promoting Useful Knowledge*, vol. 12, pt. 1. Philadelphia: C. Sherman, Son & Co., Printers, 1863.

———. "The Wonders of the West—II: More about the Yellowstone." *Scribner's Monthly* 3, no. 4 (February 1872): 388–396.

Heald, Weldon F. "Thomas Moran: Depicter of Western Grandeur." *Montana: The Magazine of Western History* 15, no. 4 (Autumn 1965): 42–53.

Hermes, Matthew E. "Lost and Found: William Henry Jackson's Albertype Prints." *Points West*, Summer 2016, 4–9.

History Nebraska. "Herndon House (Omaha, Neb.)." https://history.nebraska.gov/collections/herndon-house-omaha-neb-rg3034am.

Ingersoll, Ernest. "A Colorado Cavern." *Century Magazine* 24, no. 3 (July 1882): 347–48.

———. "Mountain Harry: A Character Sketch." *Appleton's Journal* 3, no. 18 (December 1877): 524–27.

———. "Silver San Juan." *Harper's New Monthly Magazine* 64, no. 383 (April 1882): 689–704.

Jackson, William Henry. "A Visit to the Los Pinos Indian Agency in 1874." *Colorado Magazine* 15, no. 6 (November 1938): 201–8.

———. "With Moran in Yellowstone." *Appalachia* 21, no. 2 (December 1936): 149–58.

Lambert, Kirby. "The Lure of the Parks." *Montana: The Magazine of Western History* 46, no. 1 (Spring 1996): 42–55.

Langford, Nathaniel P. "The Ascent of Mount Hayden: A New Chapter in Western Discovery." *Scribner's Monthly* 6, no. 2 (June 1873): 129–37.

———. "The Ascent of Mount Hayden, Grand Teton, 1872." *Scribner's Monthly* 6, no. 2 (June 1873): 129–57.

———. "The Wonders of the Yellowstone." *Scribner's Monthly* 2, no. 1 (May 1871): 1–17.

———. "The Wonders of the Yellowstone." *Scribner's Monthly* 2, no. 2, (June 1871): 113–28.

Messa, Cole. "Jim Bridger: Yellowstone's Spinner of Tall Tales." Accessed September 30, 2021. usgs.gov/center-news/jim-bridger-yellowstone-s-spinner-tall-tales.

Moran, John. "Reflections on Art." *Philadelphia Photographer* 12 (October 1875): 294–95.

Moran, Thomas. "A Journey to the Devil's Tower in Wyoming." *Century Illustrated Monthly Magazine* 47, no. 3 (January 1894): 450–55.

National Park Service. Accessed September 30, 2021. "Expeditions Explore Yellowstone." nps.gov/yell/learn/historyculture/expeditions.htm.

Noel, Thomas J. "All Hail the Denver Pacific: Denver's First Railroad." *Colorado Magazine* 50, no. 2 (Spring 1973): 91–116.

Panzer, Mary. "Great Pictures from the 1871 Expedition: Thomas Moran, William Henry Jackson, and the Grand Canyon of the Yellowstone." In Birmingham Museum of Art, *Splendors of the American West: Thomas Moran's Art of the Grand Canyon and Yellowstone*. Birmingham, AL: Birmingham Museum of Art, 1990.

Philadelphia Photographer. "Fire." February 1875, 54.

Ryder, J. F. "Photography at the World's Fair." *American Amateur Photographer* 5, no. 9 (September 1893): 421.

Selmeier, Lewis W. "First Camera on the Yellowstone." *Montana: The Magazine of Western History* 22, no. 3 (Summer 1972): 42–53.

Simpson, John W. "A Tale of Two Parks." *Landscape Architecture Magazine* 77, no. 3 (May/June 1987): 60–67.

Toll, Roger W. "The Hayden Survey in Colorado in 1873–1874." *Colorado Magazine* 6, no. 4 (July 1929): 146–57.

Truettner, William H. "'Scenes of Majesty and Enduring Interest': Thomas Moran Goes West." *Art Bulletin* 58, no. 2 (June 1976): 241–59.

Wilson, Robert. "The Great Diamond Hoax of 1872." *Smithsonian Magazine* 35, no. 3 (June 2004): 70–79.

NEWSPAPERS

New York Times, February 8, 1871.

New York Times, September 18, 1871.

New York Times, October 23, 1871.

New York Times, October 1, 1875.

BOOKS

Anderson, Richard C., Phil Salstrom, and Paul Salstrom, eds. *Ferdinand Hayden: A Young Scientist in the Great West, 1853–1855*. Rock Island, IL: Augustana Historical Society, 2010.

Anglin, Ronald M., and Larry E. Morris. *Gloomy Terrors and Hidden Fires: The Mystery of John Colter and Yellowstone*. Lanham, MD: Rowman & Littlefield, 2014.

Bartlett, Richard A. *Great Surveys of the American West*. Norman: University of Oklahoma Press, 1962.

Bassford, Amy O., and Fritiof Fryxell, eds. *Home-Thoughts, from Afar: Letters of Thomas Moran to Mary Nimmo Moran*. East Hampton, NY: East Hampton Free Library, 1967.

Beal, Merrill D. *The Story of Man in Yellowstone*. Yellowstone National Park, WY: Yellowstone Library and Museum Association, 1960.

Beebe, Lucius, and Charles Clegg, *Narrow Gauge in the Rockies*. Berkeley, CA: Howell-North Press, 1958.

———. *Rio Grande: Mainline of the Rockies*. Berkeley, CA: Howell-North, 1962.

Black, George. *Empire of Shadows: The Epic Story of Yellowstone*. New York: St. Martin's Press, 2012.

Boner, Bradly J. *Yellowstone National Park: Through the Lens of Time*. Boulder: University Press of Colorado, 2017.

Browne, J. Ross. *Adventures in the Apache Country: A Tour through Arizona and Sonora with Notes on the Silver Region of Nevada*. New York: Harper & Brothers, 1871.

Chapman, J. G. *The American Drawing-Book: Manual for the Amateur*. New York: J. S. Redfield, Clinton Hall, 1847.

Chittenden, Hiram M. *The Yellowstone National Park*. Norman: University of Oklahoma Press, 1964.

Chittenden, Hiram Martin. *Yellowstone National Park: Historical and Descriptive*. Cincinnati: The Robert Clarke Company, 1904.

Clark, Carol. *Thomas Moran: Watercolors of the American West; Text and Catalogue Raisonne*. Fort Worth, TX: Amon Carter Museum of Western Art, 1980.

Darrah, William Culp. *Stereo Views: A History of Stereographs in America and Their Collection*. Facsimile edition. Gettysburg, PA: Times and News Publishing, 1964.

Delo, David Michael. *The Yellowstone, Forever!* New York: Kingfisher Books, 1998.

Diebert, Jack E., and Brent H. Breithaupt. *Tracks, Trails & Thieves: The Adventures, Discoveries, and Historical Significance of Ferdinand V. Hayden's 1868 Geological Survey of Wyoming and Adjacent Territories*. Boulder, CO: The Geological Society of America, 2016.

Driggs, Howard R. *The Old West Speaks*. New York: Bonanza Books, 1956.

———. *Westward America*. New York: Somerset Books, 1942.

Ford, Colin, and Karl Steinorth, eds. *"You Press the Button, We Do the Rest": The Birth of Snapshot Photography*. London: Dirk Nishen, Publishing, 1988.

Forsee, Aylesa. *William Henry Jackson: Pioneer Photographer of the West*. New York: Viking Press, 1964.

Foster, John E., Dick Harrison, and I. S. MacLaren, eds. *Buffalo*. Edmonton: University of Alberta Press, 1992.

Foster, Mike. *Strange Genius: The Life of Ferdinand Vandeveer Hayden*. Niwot, CO: Roberts Rinehart, 1994.

Fritiof, M. Fryxell. *William H. Jackson: Photographer, Artist, Explorer*. Catalog for Special Exhibit No. 4, April 4 to May 4, 1940. Department of Interior, Museum of the United States Department of the Interior, 1939.

Hafen, LeRoy R., ed. *The Diaries of William Henry Jackson, Frontier Photographer, to California and Return, 1866–67; and with the Hayden Surveys to the Central Rockies, 1873, and to the Utes and Cliff Dwellings, 1874*. Glendale, CA: Arthur H. Clark, 1959.

Haines, Aubrey L. *Yellowstone National Park: Its Exploration and Establishment*. Washington, DC: US Department of the Interior, National Park Service, 1974.

———. *The Yellowstone Story: A History of Our First National Park*. Vol. 1. Yellowstone National Park, WY: Yellowstone Library and Museum Association, 1977.

Hales, Peter. *William Henry Jackson and the Transformation of the American Landscape*. Philadelphia: Temple University Press, 1988.

Harrell, Thomas H. *William Henry Jackson, An Annotated Bibliography [1862–1995]*. Nevada City, CA: Carl Mautz Publishing, 1995.

Hayden, Ferdinand Vandeveer, and A. R. C. Selwyn, eds. *Stanford's Compendium of Geography and Travel: North America*. London: Edward Stanford, SS, Charing Cross, S.W., 1883.

Heacox, Kim. *An American Idea: The Making of the National Parks*. Washington, DC: National Geographic, 2009.

Hughes, Jim. *The Birth of a Century: Early Color Photographs of America*. New York: Tauris Parke Books, 1994.

Ingersoll, George. *Crest of the Continent: A Record of a Summer's Ramble in the Rocky Mountains and Beyond*. Chicago: R. R. Donnelley & Sons, 1885. Reprint, Frankfurt, Germany: Outlook, 2018.

———. *Knocking 'Round the Rockies*. New York: Harper & Brothers, 1883.

Jackson, Clarence S. *The Veritable Art of William Henry Jackson, Picture Maker of the Old West*. Minden, NE: Harold Warp Pioneer Village, 1958.

Jackson, Clarence S., and Lawrence W. Marshall. *Quest of the Snowy Cross*. Denver: University of Denver Press, 1952.

Jackson, William Henry, with Howard R. Driggs. *The Pioneer Photographer: Rocky Mountain Adventures with a Camera*. With original text from the 1929 edition. Santa Fe: Museum of New Mexico Press, 2005. Originally published Yonkers-on-Hudson, NY: World Book Company, 1929.

———. *Time Exposure: The Autobiography of William Henry Jackson*. New York: Putnam, 1940.

James, Harry Clebourne. *Pages from Hopi History*. Tucson: University of Arizona Press, 1974.

Jones, William C., and Elizabeth B. Jones. *William Henry Jackson's Colorado*. Golden: Colorado Railroad Museum, 1975.

Kinsey, Joni Louise. *Thomas Moran and the Surveying of the American West*. Washington, DC: Smithsonian Institution Press, 1992.

Knudsen, Dean. *An Eye for History: The Paintings of William Henry Jackson, from the Collection at the Oregon Trail Museum*. Washington, DC: US Government Printing Office, 1997.

Kornhauser, Elizabeth Mankin, and Tim Barringer. *Thomas Cole's Journey: Atlantic Crossings*. New York: Metropolitan Museum of Art, 2018.

Lamar, Howard. *The Readers Encyclopedia of the American West*. New York City: Crowell Publishing, 1977.

Langford, Nathaniel P. *The Discovery of Yellowstone*. Self-published, 1905.

Lee, W. Storrs. *The Great California Deserts*. New York: Putnam, 1963.

McNeese, Tim. *The Colorado River*. Philadelphia: Chelsea House, 2004.

———. *Conestogas and Stagecoaches*. New York: Crestwood House, 1993.

McPherson, Robert S., and Susan Rhoades Neel. *Mapping the Four Corners: Narrating the Hayden Survey of 1875*. Norman: University of Oklahoma Press, 2016.

Meagher, Mary, and Douglas B. Houston. *Yellowstone and the Biology of Time: Photographs across a Century*. Norman: University of Oklahoma Press, 1998.

Merrill, Marlene Deahl, ed. *Yellowstone and the Great West: Journals, Letters, and Images from the 1871 Hayden Expedition*. Lincoln: University of Nebraska Press, 1999.

Miller, Helen Markley. *Lens on the West: The Story of William Henry Jackson*. Garden City, NY: Doubleday, 1966.

Miller, Nina Hull. *Shutters West*. Denver: Sage Books, 1962.

Nash, Roderick. *Wilderness and the American Mind*. New Haven, CT: Yale University Press, 1967.

Newhall, Beaumont, and Diana E. Edkins. *William H. Jackson*. Fort Worth, TX: Morgan & Morgan, 1974.

Olson, James, and Ronald C. Naugle. *History of Nebraska*. Lincoln: University of Nebraska Press, 1997.

Richardson, James, ed. *Wonders of the Yellowstone*. New York: Scribner, Armstrong, 1974.

Schullery, Paul, and Lee Whittlesey. *Myth and History in the Creation of Yellowstone National Park*. Lincoln: University of Nebraska Press, 2003.

Sheldon, George. *American Painters*. New York: D. Appleton, 1881.

Thompson, Edith M. Schultz, and William Leigh. *Beaver Dick: The Honor and the Heartbreak*. Laramie, WY: Jelm Mountain Press, 1982.

Towler, John. *The Silver Sunbeam: A Practical and Theoretical Textbook of Photography*. New York: Joseph H. Ladd, 1864. Facsimile edition published by Beaumont Newhall. Hastings-on-Hudson, NY: Morgan & Morgan, 1969.

United States Department of the Interior Geological Survey. *Ferdinand Vandeveer Hayden and the Founding of the Yellowstone National Park*. Washington, DC: Government Printing Office, 1973.

Victor, Frances Fuller. *The River of the West: Life and Adventure in the Rocky Mountains and Oregon; Embracing Events in the Life-Time of a Mountain-Man and Pioneer*. Hartford, CT: Colombian Book, 1870.

Waitley, Douglas. *William Henry Jackson: Framing the Frontier*. Missoula, MT: Mountain Press, 1998.

Watkins, T. H. *The Grand Colorado: The Story of a River and Its Canyon*. Palo Alto, CA: American West Publishing, 1969.

Wheeler, Keith. *The Chroniclers*. New York: Time-Life Books, 1976.

Wilkins, Thurman. *Thomas Moran: Artist of the Mountains*. Norman: University of Oklahoma Press, 1998.

Wood, Nancy. *When Buffalo Free the Mountains: The Survival of America's Ute Indians*. New York: Doubleday, 1980.

Zaslowsky, Dyan, and T. H. Watkins. *These American Lands: Parks, Wilderness, and the Public Lands*. Washington, DC: Island Press, 1994.